**Evaluative Research in Correctional
Drug Abuse Treatment**

Evaluative Research in Correctional Drug Abuse Treatment

A Guide for Professionals in Criminal Justice and the Behavioral Sciences

Edited by

Jerome J. Platt
The Hahnemann Medical College
and Hospital of Philadelphia

Christina Labate
University of Chicago

Robert J. Wicks
The Hahnemann Medical College
and Hospital of Philadelphia

Lexington Books
D.C. Heath and Company
Lexington, Massachusetts
Toronto

Sincere appreciation is expressed by the authors to the following for permission to use copyrighted material in this book: Saul Feldman "Editorial Comments," *Administration in Mental Health* p. 41, (1973); Jerome Platt, A.R. Hoffman, R.K. Ebert, "Recent Trends in the Demography of Heroin Addiction Among Youthful Offenders," *International Journal of the Addictions,* Vol 11, pp. 221-236, Marcel Dekker, Inc., N.Y. 1975; Scarpitti/Stephenson, "A Study of Probation Effectiveness," reprinted by special permission of the *Journal of Criminal Law, Criminology and Police Science,* Copyright © 1968 by Northwestern University School of Law, Vol. 59, No. 3, pp. 361-369; England, "Some Dangers in Parole Prediction," *Crime & Delinquency,* pp. 266-269, July 1962, reprinted with permission of the National Council on Crime and Delinquency.

Library of Congress Cataloging in Publication Data

Main entry under title:

Evaluative research in correctional drug abuse treatment.

    Includes indexes.
    1. Drug abuse—Treatment—Evaluation. 2. Corrections—Evaluation.
3. Evaluation research (Social action program) I. Platt, Jerome J.
II. Labate, Christina. III. Wicks, Robert J.
HV5801.E89   365'.66   76-12687
ISBN 0-669-00724-2

Published simultaneously in Canada.

Printed in the United States of America.

International Standard Book Number: 0-669-00724-2

Library of Congress Catalog Card Number: 76-12687

Contents

List of Figures and Tables

Figure

Foreword

There is general agreement among professionals and informed members of the general public that difficult and important policy issues confront the American Criminal Justice System, in general, and the field of corrections in particular. This system and its major components are being closely scrutinized and even severely criticized by many groups in the community including the courts, penal reform groups, the media, legislatures, the offenders themselves, and employees of the agencies involved. This situation is related to the lack of confidence in the capability of governmental agencies to deal effectively and honestly with social problems and particularly with the problems of offenders. Administrators and policymakers in this field seem to be unwilling or unable to use social scientific knowledge and techniques in developing new programs or in modifying existing ones. And what is more crucial is a general reluctance to subject their programs to the critical analysis of evaluative research.

Unfortunately, in the past, correctional administrators viewed evaluative research as an unwarranted attempt to investigate their efforts and even as a ruse to identify incompetence, negligence and corruption. More recently, the claims of some professionals and academicians that rehabilitation programs are ineffective has generated considerable anxiety among administrators which has served to reinforce their reluctance to permit their programs to be assessed. Moreover, even in situations where programs have been researched, too many of the evaluations have been undertaken in very special or temporary projects. The net effect has been that in corrections, evaluative research has generally been sporadic and rarely incorporated as an integral component of agency operations.

However, there are indications of a growing realization for the need to routinize evaluative research in corrections. Jerome Platt and his collaborators have made a significant contribution to this effort. Their work represents one of the few attempts to provide a practical and extremely useful guide in this field. It is a clear, step-by-step exposition of the evaluative process that has applicability not only in criminal justice organizations, but in the broader realm of human service agencies. The authors have addressed the central issues and the methodological problems involved in a straightforward manner, and have illustrated the usefulness of the principles developed in their presentation of the evaluation of a correctional-treatment program for young-adult narcotic addicts.

Professor Platt and the other authors of this book are uniquely qualified to address practical issues involved in conducting evaluative research in correctional settings as they have personally experienced the problems they describe in this book. By focusing attention on the importance of learning to cope with the interpersonal issues that confront the researchers and the organizational pressures that face the administrators, they have clearly pinpointed a fundamental reason why it has been so difficult to conduct program evaluations. Their recognition of this problem and their willingness to develop techniques for coping with it should be encouraging to both researchers and correctional administrators.

The authors have produced a remarkable product, one that I believe will contribute immeasurably in assisting researchers to establish a secure foothold in corrections. By exposing the underlying problems facing evaluative researchers in the criminal justice system to the critical light of analysis and demonstrating how they coped successfully with them, these authors have set the stage for others to follow.

Many professional and lay critics of correctional programming have characterized the field as having nothing to look back to with pride or to look forward to with hope. The authors of this study have shown that careful and intelligently planned and executed research efforts can improve agency practice and contrbute to the body of knowledge in the field of corrections at a critical time in its history. And, at the same time, it can reflect the potential for generating both pride and hope for the practitioners.

Albert Elias

Preface

Evaluative research is a topic which has unfortunately long elicited negative responses from many criminal justice and drug abuse professionals. The reasons for this have been varied. Primary among them was a belief on the part of some program and institutional administrators that research was either too difficult or too expensive to set up. In addition, there was considerable question as to the merit of expending the effort to conduct it.

Today this situation has changed considerably in the criminal justice field in general, and in the drug abuse treatment area in particular. Funds are now being withheld from numerous existing programs pending their evaluation. Pressure is also being exerted now to prevent major innovative experiments (i.e., juvenile corrections) from being attempted if there is no provision for a research element in the overall project design.

Accordingly, correctional administrators and drug program directors are being encouraged to become familiar with basic concepts in evaluative research. Also, in a similar vein, consultants and professors in criminal justice and the behavioral sciences are being asked to examine and teach ways in which research can be applied that are least expensive and most suitable, considering the needs of criminal justice and drug abuse personnel.

This book addresses this very recent increased interest in applied evaluative research in the criminal justice and drug abuse treatment fields. It is set up to provide the correctional or other criminal justice/drug abuse treatment program director/consultant with a guide to initiating and understanding the research and assessment process.

This is accomplished by providing an overview and broad introduction to research and evaluation as it is applied (1) in general, (2) in the correctional setting in particular, and (3) with a drug abuse treatment project as a specific illustration. Both theory and application are emphasized. Optimally, the authors hope that if the research consultant, criminal justice professional, and program administrator can see the potential for low-cost evaluation, realize how the process works, and further understand their roles in its operation, they will be able to accept and utilize research to an advantage.

For the consultant and professional in criminal justice and the behavioral sciences in particular, this book is designed to serve a twofold purpose. It is meant to be a vehicle for this person to use to apply his/her research skills in a setting that needs, and is now demanding, research evaluators. Also, it is set up to provide an illustration of how one program was organized, dealt with operational difficulties, and ultimately showed positive results.

In essence, then, this book is set up to provide an introduction to research evaluation in corrections and in drug abuse treatment by offering basic principles and practical issues, with a well-known project as an illustration of how they can be brought to reality in today's modern criminal justice system.

Acknowledgments

The research conducted on the Wharton Tract Narcotics Treatment Program, and reported in Part III was carried out, in part, while this program was supported by the State Law Enforcement Planning Agency (SLEPA) of New Jersey through Criminal Justice Improvement Grant Number 1493. Grateful acknowledgement is extended for this support. SLEPA is not responsible for the statements and interpretations presented here, which are solely those of the authors.

The research program at the Wharton Tract and at its parent institution, the Youth Reception and Correction Center, would not have been possible had it not been for the high level of interest in evaluation of institutional programs demonstrated by the successive Superintendents of the institution: Albert Elias, Richard A. Seidel, and Thomas Lynch. The Research Coordinator responsible for the Wharton Tract program, Alan R. Hoffman, assumed substantial responsibility in the implementation of the research program. Jerry C. Cavatta, who succeeded him, contributed to the success of the research endeavor. William C. Scura and Donald Zelinsky also greatly facilitated the research reported here, as did the successive program supervisors, Gregory Stosuy, Anthony C. Turner and their staffs.

Much of the data collection and analysis was carried out by James R. Hannon and Kim Zelley while Grace Verna and Joan Bryson did an outstanding job of typing and otherwise preparing the manuscript, and they deserve our special thanks.

Part I

Basic Concepts of Evaluative Research in Correctional Drug Abuse Treatment

Introduction to Part I

Often, the success or failure of an evaluative research effort depends not so much on the planning for the evaluation, the care with which the evaluation is being carried out, or even the competence of the evaluator, but on the interpersonal issues surrounding the implementation and conduct of the evaluation. One purpose of Chapter 1 is to call attention to both the organizational context within which the evaluation is conducted and the need for the evaluator to recogize the pressures on the various persons involved. The second half of Chapter 1 focuses on the unique evaluation problems presented by drug abuse treatment efforts within the correctional setting.

Chapter 2 presents an overview of the basic principles of evaluation methodology, again with emphasis upon the unique evaluation problems presented by the correctional setting. In doing so, this chapter draws upon the recent literature to provide the reader with an introduction to current thinking about evaluation approaches, methodology, and related topics.

Evaluative Research in Correctional Drug Abuse Treatment: Practical Issues, Implications, and Questions

Jerome J. Platt, Robert J. Wicks, and *Christina Labate*

Today a correctional program is expected to develop an evaluation plan as an integral part of the project. Despite the difficulty of evaluation programs (i.e., correctional ones), the process must be undertaken. No longer will funding be released in most cases if evaluation is not an element of program design. Quantitative analysis in lieu of a subjective report is expected, and the program should be in a position to conduct such a procedure. Consequently, the correctional administrator or the assistant/consultant for research and evaluation should be concerned with at least the following questions:

1. What is the overall goal of the program?
2. How can this general objective be broken down and measured quantitatively to determine program effectiveness?
3. Who will conduct the evaluation?
4. Will the data be available that will be needed by the evaluator?
5. Are the data being measured reliable?
6. When will the evaluation be conducted?
7. What are the methods of evaluation?
8. What part will each member of the correctional team play in the evaluative process?

Evaluation Implementation and the Correctional Team

The first seven questions listed above are ones which researchers grapple with in all types of settings. The eighth one, however, is a crucial one for evaluators in the correctional environment, for unless it is properly dealt with early in the program, the research will be difficult or impossible to conduct.

The correctional setting has traditionally been closed to "outsiders." Included in this category were professionals and nonprofessionals who are not part of the direct service staff (i.e., correction officers, correctional psychologists, work supervisors). In some settings there is even suspiciousness among full-time staff groups. For instance, custodial and nonuniformed treatment staffs are often at odds as to how inmates are to be treated. The evaluator must be aware of these traditional rivalries if the research is to be conducted with the compliance of these two groups. Moreover, despite the acceptance of the value of research in corrections at the higher echelons of administration (i.e., at the level

5

of commissioner), unless the evaluator appreciates the position of the institutional community and is prepared for their reactions, the place of research within the correctional environment will be questionable at best.

Correctional Administrator

The correctional administrator is often caught in the middle when it comes to conducting research. On the one hand, he is asked by the commissioner to give all the necessary support to the research staff. This entails providing the researcher(s) with access to prison inmates, staff, and records. Although this seems reasonable on the surface, implementing it is another question. There are the line personnel and inmates to contend with. Often they are not in a position to see the part research plays in the total picture. Also, administrators are usually not trained researchers, and unless the researcher personally interprets his findings, the administrator may feel put off or resistant to research operations.

Correctional Line Personnel

Custodial and treatment line personnel are not always amenable to assisting in conducting research. Research is frequently viewed negatively for a number of reasons:

1. Research, like training, is often viewed as being much less important than those activities related to day-to-day institutional operations.
2. Researchers are viewed as an interference from without that is unnecessarily jeopardizing normal prison operations.
3. There is a suspicion that researchers may find out something that will be detrimental to the program, i.e., will result in closing or curbing program activities.
4. Researchers are seen as being unfamiliar with what inmates and prison life are *really* like; therefore, it is felt that they cannot appreciate what is actually going on in prison.

Inmate Population

The institutional population can also present problems which will hinder research. The type of difficulties which may occur is dependent upon how the inmates view the research process. On the one hand, if they see no benefit for themselves, they may resist any efforts which require their compliance. After all, why help "the system" prove they are being helped or that they are deviant and in fact in need of assistance?

However, if they feel there is something to be exploited, some prisoners may in fact cooperate in a way that is favorable to them. For instance, if by helping prove the program is effective they can gain early release, they might be more than willing to comply. In addition, the researcher must always question the results if the inmates find out and perceive themselves as the experimental group and a placebo effect results.

Researcher Actions

Unless the researcher appreciates the difficult position of the administrator and the daily pressures the staff is under—institutions are often tinder boxes of pressure—and can see that inmates may be resistant or exploitive because of their own position, the evaluative process can run into a good deal of trouble. Then, the next logical question is, How is the researcher to proceed considering these interpersonal difficulties?

The solution (as is the case of most interpersonal problems) unfortunately is not simple. Interviewing skills are a must as is some knowledge about the general attitudes of correctional personnel at different levels. Such information can be gained from reading (Wicks and Josephs 1972), but nothing can substitute for the personal gathering of information from the personnel themselves.

How does the correction officer view the treatment staff? Does the administrator see research as a necessary political end or as a potentially valuable aid to program improvement? Are the treatment workers threatened by evaluation? Can the inmates cooperate with the evaluation? All these questions will have to be answered if the research process is to work.

If one tries to circumvent the staff, the research will not get off the ground. If one doesn't expend enough energy in informal discussions with the staff concerning the need and operations of research, it may begin satisfactorily, but it will shortly run into opposition. In essence, the staff has to be talked to, credited for what they know, and given an introduction to the technical areas they are currently unfamiliar with.

Records

The "people problems" inherent in correctional research are sometimes supplemented by ones arising from haphazard record keeping. Although sometimes all a consultant can do is make the best of a difficult situation, there arise occasions when the researcher is asked—or offers—to assist in the setting up of a viable information system.

Such a system not only would prove useful for research purposes, but also would aid in making day-to-day decisions. To ensure accuracy and uniformity in making initial and reclarification determinations regarding housing, security, and treatment programs, it would be helpful to have information on past and current offenses, health, and other issues directly affecting institutional adjustments. Information systems can also provide data which can assist the administrator to routinely and automatically determine such ordinary information as what prisoners are due for early release, what each prisoner's current sentence is, and the number of inmates put into administrative/disciplinary segregation during any given period of time.

By introducing an information system, a researcher will not only help himself then, but will also assist the administrator in his work. However, as Hill (1972) notes, ". . . information requirements for management have been difficult to identify. This is not so much because of reluctance on the part of management to specify its information needs but rather because management cannot always anticipate what it will need to know" (p. 3). With this in mind, Hill has attempted to provide a generic model for correction information systems which takes into account variances in institutional practices. Through elucidation here of this model and through similar ones applicable to corrections beyond this chapter's scope, the point being emphasized is that the development and use of an information system in the correctional setting can be important in the ultimate determination of a research project's success or failure.

Issues in Correctional Research

Once the researcher has grappled with the interpersonal and record-keeping problems of the correctional institution/community setting, his problems are not over. There are other basic issues that must be dealt with if the work is to proceed to the desired end result—attainment of sound, useful research findings.

These factors are not new. They have been discussed by such investigators as Hood (1967), Glaser (1965), and Ward (1967), as well as being pointed up in the Task Force Report on Corrections released in 1973. These essential readings for correctional researchers raise a number of questions. Included among them are the following which are particularly relevant:

(1) In doing research on offender treatment effectiveness, what criteria does one use—recidivism, improved attitude or work record, severity of subsequent crime, cost effectiveness of the program?

(2) What general approach should be used to determine efficacy of treatment—a single treatment study or a comparison between therapeutic modalities?

(3) How and when are the results to be released? Is it to be done in a report which no administrator without a master's degree in evaluative research can understand? And is this report to be released before a follow-up is done?

(4) Does the evaluator plan, and have a forum, to present (and interpret) the findings and suggest innovations?

These are far from idle questions. They tap right into the heart of the primary question: If one uses good research procedures, can one produce useful studies on correctional treatment?

Issues in Correctional Drug Abuse Treatment Evaluation

Drug abuse treatment programs operating within a correctional institution present several unique problems to the researcher/evaluator. Some of these problems will, of course, affect all efforts to meet the special needs of subgroups of offenders in an overcrowded prison system, including restricted access to limited numbers of treatment personnel and a reduction in the amount of physical space and resources which will become available for those offenders with special problems (particularly the drug-addicted offender). However, there are additional problems arising from the traditional methods and goals of drug abuse treatment that are offered to the offender. The preponderance of correctional treatment programs rely on psychotherapy, individual or group counseling, and vocation rehabilitation counseling. All these approaches depend heavily on the individual's desire for self-analysis and exploration to achieve his or her goals. Such motivations are by no means necessarily characteristic of an offender who is forced into treatment often as a prerequisite for parole.

Treatment efforts . . . are seriously compromised in a prison system, where the client is additionally an "offender," and as an offender, is told to accept treatment, and change behavior by criteria defined and imposed by an authority responsible for determining the length of punishment by confinement (Helms, Scura, and Fisher 1975, p. 362).

The freedom to determine the nature and extent of the therapeutic process, which is absent in the correctional treatment program, may be fundamentally related to a successful outcome. Einstein and Garitano (1972) in particular point out that many drug abuse treatment programs fail because they have homogeneous goals for a heterogeneous population. Abstinence may not be the *only* desirable objective for the drug addict unless medical evidence suggests long-term chronic substance abuse entails substantial harm. Furthermore, in order to effectively alter drug-abusing behavior, a variety of other behaviors will probably also need to undergo modification. For this reason, drug abuse treatment programs, be they correctional or not, *must* provide a range of support services to make such behavioral changes possible. In light of unique strengths and weaknesses, treatment goals need to be appropriate, flexible, realistic, and meaningful to each individual drug-addicted offender.

On the other hand, comparative evaluation of drug abuse treatment programs is seriously hampered by variable outcome criteria. The problems involved in selecting and defining appropriate outcome measures will be repeatedly discussed throughout this book; yet they remain a major issue in evaluation in correctional settings. Such problems are simply confounded when the offender is additionally a drug addict and the correctional process includes drug abuse treatment. Outcome criteria must be selected to reflect this dual status—recidivism with respect to criminal behavior alone is insufficient. Furthermore, Maddux and Bowden (1972) suggest that ". . . the frequency of arrest or conviction does not directly measure criminal behavior but represents interactions between alleged offenders and the law enforcement system" (p. 443). The "interactions" may vary as a function of continued postrelease participation in a community treatment program such as methadone maintenance. Certainly the selective enforcement of parole provisions makes comparative evaluation exceedingly difficult, if not impossible.

The therapeutic community approach has enjoyed substantial popularity within correctional institutions, and again there are problems encountered in such treatment efforts. High attrition rates which are characteristic of many therapeutic community programs often lead to evaluation of outcome on steadily shrinking samples increasingly biased in a favorable direction. In light of selective attrition, it is difficult to determine how much of the success of the therapeutic community is due to its program and how much is actually due to the high levels of motivation which must be present in its continuing members. Such evaluation problems are confounded in the correctional system where motivations for volunteering for treatment may certainly include reasons unrelated to a desire to eliminate drug abuse (for instance, a desire for early release which is believed to result from participation in an institutional treatment program).

There are additional problems in evaluating the therapeutic community programs operating within the correctional system. The creation of dependence on the community which is characteristic of the Synanon-type approach often results in an inability to create a satisfying drug-free life outside. The transition from "drug abuser" to "productive member of society" is doubly difficult in the case of the offender who is handicapped by both a history of drug abuse and a criminal record. Stable employment, which has been repeatedly shown to be empirically related to successful outcome in both drug abusers and offenders, is increasingly difficult for the drug addict offender to obtain. Yet there are dangers in assuming a role of ex-addict paraprofessional, often the most available option, which are related to the restriction of mobility outside the therapeutic community. Many ex-addicts remain in the addiction field because they lack the requisite skills for making it elsewhere. However, in order to avoid relapse to drug use, meaningful alternatives must somehow be provided. The role of aftercare is coming to be increasingly recognized as a critical factor in avoiding relapse or recidivism, but the extensive support services it entails are often beyond the scope of the limited resources of an overcrowded and understaffed prison complex.

The issues involved in correctional drug abuse treatment are certainly not limited to those briefly outlined above. It is clear that the evaluation of correctional drug abuse treatment programs is complex and requires careful planning and coordination of resources if valid indices of effectiveness are to be obtained.

Final Comments

Research is necessary if correctional treatment programs are to become more effective. As J. D. Grant, then Chief of the California Department of Corrections, said as far back as 1962, "Any correctional agency not using a prediction procedure to study the effectiveness of its decisions and operations is perpetrating a crime against the taxpayer" (Grant 1962, p. 259). Today, few—if any—new offender treatment projects are missing an evaluation component.

However, now that research evaluation is becoming a "given" in corrections, professionals involved in this area are realizing how much we don't know about approaching problems in corrections. The questions of what are the criteria and the method of approach are still being debated. Some feel recidivism (i.e., does the offender return to prison for *any* crime?) is a poor criterion for evaluating a program's success. They feel that if a person returns on a lesser crime, this may indicate progress. Naturally there are many who dispute this point of view.

As was previously indicated, staff resistance and/or misunderstandings as well as the absence of an adequate information system on the inmate population which lends itself to producing accurate quantitative data also give the correctional researcher problems. The bottom-line question, then, is, Does correctional research have to continue to be a nightmare? Or, to repeat again, is meaningful research in the penal setting possible?

Simply stated, the answer is, of course! Useful research has been proceeding at a steady pace for years now. (See "The Status of Evaluation in Corrections" in Adams 1975.) So, more pertinent questions here are, What can one expect in conducting research in corrections and how does one proceed considering the unique factors involved?

The answers to these questions are obviously not so simple. This chapter, by way of a brief introduction to the topic, pointed out some of the more basic questions and issues involved. Clearly, the illustrative model and more technical chapters included in this book are meant to provide further elaboration and clarification.

Yet, even with this information, little can be accomplished if the researcher is unwilling to accept two realities about himself and his work. First, research cannot be conducted without the cooperation of the correctional staff, and so time must be set aside to help them appreciate the role of evaluative research. Second, research, of itself, cannot correct the failure of years of haphazard offender treatment; rather, it can only point to what is, so that steps can be taken to attempt to offer alternatives for future improvement.

In relation to both of these points, the underlying theme is the evaluator's personal active involvement. Unless he is willing to present himself and his work to the staff before, during, and after the process to explain its need, operation, and *outcome*, correctional research will continue to remain on poor footing. Research involves both people and procedures; without the cooperation of the people involved, the procedures will eventually lead nowhere—or worse (as in the past), it may lead in the wrong direction altogether.

References

Adams, S. *Evaluative Research in Corrections: A Practical Guide*. Washington: U.S. Government Printing Office, 1975.

Einstein, S., and Garitano, W. "Treating the Drug Abuser: Problems, Factors, and Alternatives." *International Journal of the Addictions* 7 (1972): 321-31.

Glaser, D. "Correctional Research: An Elusive Paradise." *Journal of Research in Crime and Delinquency* 2 (1):3, 5-8, 1965.

Grant, J. D. "It's Time to Start Counting." *Crime and Delinquency* 8 (1962): 259-64.

Helms, D. J.; Scura, W. C.; and Fisher, C. C. "Treatment of the Addict in Correctional Institutions." In *Medical Aspects of Drug Abuse*, edited by R. W. Richter, pp. 360-66, Hagerstown, Md.: Harper & Row, 1975.

Hill, H. *Correctionetics*. Sacramento, Calif.: American Justice Institute, 1972.

Hood, R. G. "Research on the Effectiveness of Punishments and Treatments." In *Collected Studies in Criminological Research*, vol. 1, pp. 74-86, 89-102. Strasbourg: Council of Europe, 1967.

Maddux, J. F., and Bowden, C. L. "Critique of Success with Methadone Maintenance." *American Journal of Psychiatry* 129 (1972): 440-46.

National Advisory Commission on Criminal Justice Standards and Goals, Task Force on Corrections. *Corrections*. Washington: U.S. Government Printing Office, 1973.

Ward, D. "Evaluations of Correctional Treatment: Some Implications of Negative Findings." In *Law Enforcement, Science and Technology*, edited by S. A. Yefsky, pp. 201, 204-208. Washington: Thompson Book Co., 1967.

Wicks, R. J., and Josephs, H., Jr. *Techniques in Interviewing for Law Enforcement and Corrections Personnel*. Springfield, Ill.: C. C. Thomas, 1972.

2

Basic Principles of Evaluation
Methodology in Correctional
Drug Abuse Treatment
Jerome M. Siegel and
Jerome J. Platt

Why Evaluation?

Eighteen months ago, Lockstep Penitentiary, a venerable and conservative institution more known for harsh treatment than for innovative penology, embarked on an ambitious new program whose focus was to "rehabilitate the drug abusing segment of the inmate population." To this end, all inmates with a history of drug abuse were housed together in a separate building. Within this building the custodial staff was reduced, and a whole new department called "treatment" was established. Psychologists, social workers, and one half-time psychiatrist were hired for the new treatment department. A Ph.D. psychologist became head of the new department. New policies were instituted which changed the daily lives of these inmates in numerous ways. The treatment department created changes in the administrative structure of the institution because its psychologist head became a deputy warden with coequal status to the deputy warden who ran the custody department. The institution's budget was increased, and much of this budget was for treatment and attendant innovations in this new program. These latter included the hiring of teachers for an expanded institutional education program for the drug program inmates, a work release program, and weekend passes. Solitary confinement as a punishment for recalcitrant inmates was eliminated, and closer supervision of the disciplinary activities of the custodial staff was instituted.

Eighteen months after inception, an interested state legislator who controlled funds for the program asked the warden, "Is the program working?" This question caused a tremor among the staff of Richter scale proportions because no systematic plan to study the effects of the program had ever been put into effect. Numerous questions now seemed to require answers to deal with the vague and very general question asked by the legislator. These included the following: Has recidivism been affected since the new program began? How is the new treatment staff spending its time? How is the custodial staff spending its time? What effects has the new program had on the administrative structure of the institution? What is the relationship between treatment and custody? How many inmates are in work release programs? What is the cost of the program per inmate? These are some of a long list of questions that suddenly seemed to require urgent answers.

The motivation behind the legislator's question was simply that funding for new prison programs was being cut back, and he was determined that only programs whose efficiency could be demonstrated would be funded in the future. He had to decide whether the program should be continued.

A systematic attempt to answer questions about the efficacy of programs is called *program evaluation*, and the major purpose of program evaluation is to provide information to decisionmakers, as illustrated in the above vignette about the new drug program at Lockstep Penitentiary. As Lockstep Penitentiary's plight after the legislator asked his question also illustrates, it is better to plan the evaluation of the program before the program begins than to have to hastily construct an evaluation after the program has been running for some time.

As well as providing information for decisionmakers, there are a number of reasons for doing program evaluations that are devious inasmuch as their purpose is not to seek the truth about program effectiveness, but rather to accommodate political needs. These include delaying actions and decisions that should be taken by seeking "facts", seeking "facts" to justify decisions which have already been made, selecting only the strongest aspects of weak programs for evaluation, and providing a ritual evaluation to satisfy the conditions of a government grant (Weiss 1972). Suchman (1972) has dubbed such evaluations "pseudoevaluations." Pseudoevaluations aside, however, the major reason for doing program evaluation is to provide information for decisionmaking.

What Is Evaluative Research?

Like many new areas that are outgrowths of previously existing fields of study, evaluative research has resisted precise definition. This section will attempt to define evaluative research and some other frequently used and frequently confused, but very basic, terms in evaluation.

Attempts at definition have almost uniformly begun with the distinction between "pure," or "basic," research and applied research. *Pure research* is generally defined as the attempt to discover knowledge through rigorous adherence to the controlled experiment. The testing of theory generally plays a prominent role in pure research. The social usefulness gained through such research is frequently not evident, although its eventual utility may be enormous. Applied research shares common elements with pure research: the seeking of knowledge and the methodology of the controlled experiment. Applied research, however, has social utility as its primary object; usefulness of the results is not a serendipitous and happy by-product as in pure research; rather it is applied research's raison d'être. Hemphill (1969) and Suchman (1967), with social utility as the main object, place evaluative research firmly under the rubric of applied research. Returning to the case of Lockstep Penitentiary, it seems evident that usefulness for decisionmaking was the prime motivation of the hasty evaluative research that began when the interested legislator asked whether the program was working.

Both theory testing and experimental methodology were mentioned in the above distinction between pure and applied research. Theory-testing experiments or the setting forth of specific hypotheses designed to shed light on the explanatory power of abstractions are largely the stuff of pure research. Applied research, on the other hand, rarely deals with abstractions or the larger questions that theoretical studies raise. Applied research is concerned largely with the here-and-now, with concrete and practical issues such as: Is the program working? Is this program better than that program? Is the cost of the program worth the results obtained?

Experimental methodology is a factor that overlaps pure and applied research. However, in terms of distinguishing between the two, there is the issue of degree of rigor of experimental control. Suchman (1967) notes that as one moves from a pure or theoretical study to an applied or evaluative one, the number of variables which can be controlled in the experimental methodology decreases, while the number of uncontrolled extraneous variables that may affect results increases. This is the case because pure research concerns itself experimentally with the study of observables which, as Suchman (1967) further points out, are derived from theoretical concepts or abstractions and of interest only in the light that they cast upon the concepts. All other factors in the experimental situation that may relate to the theoretical concepts must be neutralized so that observables that form the experimental subject matter can be related unambiguously to the theoretical concepts. This neutralizing or control of other factors in the situation by necessity is the heart of experimental rigor.

Applied or evaluative research, on the other hand, is frequently concerned only with the observables themselves, such as drug abuse, recidivism, staff attitudes, etc. There is little interest in relating these observables to more abstract elements and hence less interest in controlling the numerous factors which may affect the observables in question. A possibly more practical explanation for the lesser degree of rigor in evaluative studies is the fact that such studies are conducted in fluid, ongoing social situations where it is impossible to control extraneous factors which affect the observables in question. The applied research stage is a broad operatic one, which is always filled with the swirl and color of numerous players, some making totally unexpected entrances and exits, and all deviating, either slightly or greatly, from the script. The pure research stage, on the other hand, is a circumscribed and restricted setting, typically a laboratory situation in which the experimental "script" or scenario is carefully adhered to.

Now, to briefly summarize in our search for definitions, evaluative research is a type of applied research in which there is the seeking of knowledge that has clear social utility. This seeking of knowledge is conducted within the structure of the scientific experiment, but the degree of control in the experimental situation is generally considerably less than that found in pure research studies.

This, then, is our definition of evaluative research. What is *evaluation* or *program evaluation*, a term frequently used in place of evaluative research, and does it differ from evaluative research? Suchman (1967) deals with the distinction between evaluation and evaluative research by defining the former as essentially a judgment of worth which can be applied to a single individual or a social organization. The process of evaluation or judging worth does not depend upon a systematic set of procedures for assembling objective evidence for the judgment, in Suchman's view. Such a set of procedures for assembling evidence is evaluation. In Suchman's words (1967, pp. 7-8),

"Evaluative research" on the other hand, will be restricted to the utilization of scientific research methods and techniques for the purpose of making an evaluation. In this sense, "evaluation" becomes an adjective specifying a type of research. The major emphasis is upon the noun "research," and evaluative research refers to those procedures for collecting and analyzing data which increase the possibility for "proving" rather than "asserting" the worth of some social activity.

Suchman's distinction is echoed in the Hargreaves et al. (1974) brief glossary of evaluation terms in the National Institute of Mental Health's five-volume series on program evaluation.

Evaluation: a judgment or decision as to the degree to which a program service, or project has achieved its objectives at any given time, or of the degree to which it is congruent with goals or values from which it ensues.
Evaluative Research: Research conducted in order to provide the data and information upon which an evaluation may be based. Its focus is upon program functioning and outcome, as opposed to clinical research, which focuses upon the discovery or testing of new treatment methodologies (Hargreaves et al. 1974, p. 110).

Returning to our earlier example of Lockstep Penitentiary, if the legislator were to go to the prison, talk to inmates and staff, inspect new physical facilities like classrooms, and then assert that the program seemed good to him, this would be an evaluation. However, if instead he directed that recidivism figures be collected since the new program began operation and that these figures be compared to preprogram recidivism statistics, or to recidivism statistics for the part of the institution outside the drug program, this would be evaluative research.

Types of Evaluative Research

There have been numerous attempts to formulate typologies of evaluative research. It is beyond the scope of this chapter to provide a complete and detailed list of these typologies. What will be presented is a brief description of some of the most prominent and conceptually useful typologies as well as a description of some specialized types of evaluative studies.

Process-Structure-Outcome Evaluation

There is considerable consensus among evaluation specialists that one typology is suggested by focusing on different aspects of the programs one is evaluating. This is the *process-structure-outcome* approach (Zusman and Ross 1969; Fox and Rappaport 1972).

Process Evaluation. This type of evaluation is an attempt to assess an organization's delivery of service. The basic assumption in process evaluation is that some agreement can be reached as to what constitutes good service without actually assessing the outcome of services (Fox and Rappaport 1972).

In community mental health, in which evaluation is much more widely used than in corrections, process evaluation has played a prominent role in evaluative efforts, and the following draws heavily from Fox and Rappaport (1972). Utilization studies are a type of process evaluation. They entail collecting characteristics of patients served by the agency, such as age, sex, race, income, and diagnosis, and comparing these characteristics with overall population characteristics of the area served, as from census data. This type of process evaluation permits judgments to be made about whether particular groups in the agency's service area are being served. For instance, if only 50 percent of the area's population were poor blacks, but only 5 percent of the patient population were black, it would be evident that the agency was not serving the needs of its area population. Extending this example to a correctional setting such as our Lockstep Penitentiary, one of the questions that might be asked is whether the ethnic composition of the staff was similar to that of the inmates.

Another type of process study in mental health service delivery involves examining *continuity of care*. Continuity of care involves the assessment of whether patients referred from one treatment modality (e.g., a mental hospital) to a second (e.g., outpatient clinic) actually arrive at the second modality. In a correctional setting, a continuity-of-care–type study might involve assessing whether parolees are picked up by rehabilitation agencies when they leave the institution.

Cost studies are another type of process evaluation. In mental health they generally involve computing costs per unit of service (hospital day or outpatient session). For Lockstep Penitentiary a cost study might involve the per inmate cost of the new treatment program.

The final kind of process study to be discussed here in mental health is called *analysis of treatment failures*. It focuses on patients who seem to be treatment failures. Characteristics of these patients are studied for commonalities that might suggest ways in which to make treatment more effective. At Lockstep Penitentiary, such a study might involve parole failures who had left the institution since the treatment program began.

Structure Evaluation: This second type of evaluation concerns itself with analysis of the organization (and its resources) that is rendering the service (Zusman and Bissonette 1973). Structure evaluation in the mental health field involves studying different staff-patient ratios, the amount of staff time available for patient treatment, numbers of staff of different disciplines (i.e., how many psychiatrists, how many social workers, etc.), availability of specific services such as those to children, and the state of the physical facilities (Fox and Rappaport 1972). Structure evaluation at Lockstep Penitentiary might involve some of but not all the above. For example, staff-inmate ratios would be an appropriate structure evaluation for correctional settings, as would adequacy of physical facilities and availability of specific services such as education, recreation, and prerelease counseling. In the mental health field this sort of evaluation has been part of the accreditation procedure for hospitals (Zusman and Ross 1969).

Outcome Evaluation: This type of evaluation is the type that most people associate with the term *evaluation*. Outcome studies involve the measurement of the degree to which programs meet their objectives. Of the three types of evaluation mentioned so far, outcome is the most likely to involve the controlled experiment, and outcome studies are the most difficult to perform.

Outcome studies in corrections generally group into two categories, *in-program* and *postprogram* evaluations. In-program evaluation might involve some measure of inmates' adjustment to the institutional environment, such as number of disciplinary infractions or participation in special programs. Postprogram evaluation deals with the ex-inmates' adjustment to a free environment after release. Recidivism is, of course, a postprogram outcome measure. Cavior and Cohen (1975) have pointed out the basic discontinuity between in-program success, noting that success at each level may involve different skills. In-program success frequently involves adapting to prison culture. Successful adaptation to prison culture may not ensure successful adaptation to the larger world after release, which means that in-program success may not predict postprogram success. This indeed was one of the findings of the evaluation of a correctional drug treatment program which is discussed in Chapter 6. Cavior and Cohen recommend that evaluative studies deal with in-program and postprogram phases separately. Outcome measures and the unique problems that they present will be discussed in greater detail below.

Formative-Summative Evaluation

A second typology which makes frequent appearances in evaluation literature is formative and summative evaluation (Scriven 1972; Weiss 1972).

Formative evaluation is the assessment of the operation of a program during the earlier or formative part of the program. Such evaluation may cause modifications in the basic operation of the program through feedback to those managing the program. Wortman (1975) has likened formative evaluation to pilot studies in experimental psychology. Mackler (1974) makes the point that knowledge gained through formative evaluation is not public knowledge but rather private knowledge for the developers of programs.

Summative evaluation is similar if not identical, to outcome evaluation. In Wortman's words (1975, pp. 564-65),

Summative evaluation, on the other hand, assumes that the treatment has been properly implemented and is thus concerned with how effective the program is in attaining its objectives. An essential component of this procedure is an evaluation of the goals of the program.

Goal Attainment Systems Evaluation

Schulberg, Sheldon, and Baker (1969) have called outcome or summative evaluation the *goal attainment model*, and they clearly see the measurement of the success or failure of the program in meeting a priori goals as the essence of the goal attainment model. However, Schulberg, Sheldon, and Baker, in their examples, lump studies that might fall under the above rubrics of process and structure evaluation under the goal attainment model.

For Schulberg, Sheldon, and Baker (1969), a second type of evaluation is called the *systems model*. In the systems model, the emphasis is on the fact that an organization functions at a number of different levels. It must attempt to achieve organizational goals, but it must also maintain itself and recruit new members, to renew itself. The systems model looks at the degree to which an organization achieves an optimal distribution of its resources in pursuing its various organizational needs. Success is not overallocating resources to any one need at the expense of others. Unsuccessful systems evaluation may be successful goal attainment evaluation, since an organization may achieve its prime organizational goal (e.g., reducing recidivism at Lockstep Penitentiary through allocating a disproportionate amount of the budget for the new treatment program) at the expense of other goals or needs (e.g., decreased services to the inmates not in the new drug program, or poor custodial staff morale as the

20

result of a reduction of custodial staff due to the new program). As Schulberg, Sheldon, and Baker (1969, pp. 9-10) put it,

In contrast to the goal-attainment approach which directs evaluation efforts at measuring how well a specific organizational goal was achieved, the systems model contends that such an approach is unproductive and even misleading, since an organization constantly functions at a variety of levels. Even though directing part of its means directly to the goal activities, an organization must simultaneously devote segments of its resources to such other functions as maintenance and recruitment.

The systems model is essentially the same as structure evaluation discussed above.

Adams's Correctional Evaluation Model

Adams (1975) has developed an evaluation model for corrections that incorporates six different types of evaluation. The first is called *methodological models*. There are six of these methodological models, most of which are evaluative research designs (see below).

Subject matter models is Adams's second category. This is very similar to the process-structure-outcome typology in its concern with various aspects of the system. For Adams, under this model, there is an outcome model which involves itself with results, a system model concerned with operation and structure, an input-output model which deals with results as they relate to effort, a process model which involves focusing on procedures to obtain results, and finally the means-ends model which focuses on "the extent to which the processes or structures that make results possible have been provided" (Adams 1975, p. 48).

Actor-oriented models are the third category. In this category the role of the evaluator himself is the major concept. There are *apprentice* and *advocacy models* as well as the traditional model. The apprentice model is the in-house evaluator from the organization's own staff who is not a professional evaluator. He may be trained by an outside professional. The advantage of the apprentice model is that it keeps knowledge gained during a program within the setting. Adams points out that outside evaluations in correctional settings are frequently of limited value because of imperfect communication between outside professionals (*traditional model*) and staff, as well as the fact that much of the knowledge gained in the evaluation is carried off in the heads of the outside evaluators.

The advocacy model has the evaluator not only do an evaluation but also make recommendations based on the results of the evaluation, and even take an active part in implementing the recommendations.

Goal-oriented models is a category somewhat similar to subject-matter models discussed above. The major focus here is on efficiency of programs. The emphasis can be on *managerial efficiency*, on *effectiveness* in terms of *client*

behavior, or on *cost return efficiency.* These three form, for Adams, an evaluation hierarchy with cost return efficiency at the apex, followed by client behavior and managerial efficiency.

Broad strategy models is the fifth category. This refers to three classes of evaluation activity. *Exploration,* the first, is somewhat vaguely stated and confusing. In Adams's words, *"Exploration* is a search for leads or ideas, using non-experimental methods in critical or promising areas, with receptiveness to the possibility that 'something may turn up' " (Adams 1975, p. 51). *Innovation,* the second, ". . . is a firming up and testing of new ideas in the hope that they can be developed into better modes of meeting the objectives of the organization than previous modes" (Adams 1975, p. 51). The third, *adjustment,* means modifying programs in the light of knowledge gained through evaluations.

The final model presented by Adams is called *academic* and *industrial models.* In this category Adams contrasts the academic or social science model with the *industrial* or *policy science model.* The former is concerned with theory, hypothesis testing, and controlled experimentation. The latter is pragmatic, somewhat atheoretical, and its activities are process-oriented. Adams feels that the social science model has dominated correctional evaluation up to the present, but that there is now a switch to the industrial model.

Financial Evaluation

Mention has been made previously of cost analysis, a type of financial evaluation. This section will deal with financial evaluation in more detail, and is indebted to Adams (1975).

Cost Analysis: This type of financial evaluation involves taking the entire cost of a program and dividing the cost by the number of units in the program. These can be the number of days that the program will run, number of contacts, etc. Adams relates two examples of cost analysis.

Cost Comparisons: In this type of financial evaluation, two or more cost analyses for different programs or approaches or methods are compared to determine which has the lowest cost. Adams gives an example of the cost of an expanded probation program versus the cost that would have been spent for the imprisonment, parole, and attendant welfare costs of a group of persons who received probation under the new program but would have been incarcerated prior to the expanded probation program.

Cost Benefit Comparisons: The final type of financial evaluation to be discussed is cost benefit comparison. This is very similar to cost comparison except that in this evaluation the benefits of competing programs or methods are computed as well as their costs. Adams provides an example of a work release program (McArthur, Cantor, and Glendinning 1970) which not only demonstrated lower costs than regular inmate costs because of decreased security needs for the work release prisoners, but also benefits from the work release program in the form of the proportion of earnings of the prisoners in this program that went to the government as taxes or to the community in the form of money to dependents and creditors (for a detailed, excellent treatment of financial evaluation in corrections, see Glaser 1973, chapter 4).

Stages in Evaluative Research

Evaluative research proceeds through a series of stages that has as its first stage the identification of a problem that seems to require an evaluation to solve the problem. Returning to the Lockstep Penitentiary example, the legislator's question posed a problem that the staff felt compelled to answer with an evaluation.

The evaluative research stages are, according to Urban and Ford (1971), in a very general sense very similar to John Dewey's five stages of reflective thinking or problem solving. The five stages are (Urban and Ford 1971, p. 7):

1. The recognition of a difficulty.
2. The definition or specification of the difficulty.
3. Raising suggestions for possible solutions, and a rational exploration of the ideas.
4. Selection of an optimal solution from among many proposals.
5. Carrying out the solution.

Once a problem that seems to require evaluation has been defined, the next step is to determine if an evaluation is feasible, that is, if it can be done (Gibbons, Lebowitz, and Blake 1976). This generally involves the setting of objectives for the evaluation. This is a crucial stage but one that is beset with difficulties. As Twain (1975) points out, some of these difficulties arise from the very real differences which often exist between researchers and practitioners. These differences include (1) incongruent ideologies, (2) the different relationships of the project to the career goals of the researcher and practitioner, and (3) the different orientations of research enterprises and service agencies. The first question that often arises in the setting of objectives is "whose objectives?" The obvious answer is that the objectives would seem to be the goals of the program. However, as Weiss (1972) points out, the program goals may be too general and too vague to be evaluation goals, such as Lockstep's goal of "rehabilitating" drug-abusing inmates. Also, the program may have covert goals that the evaluator may not be aware of (Moursund 1973). An example might be that some members of the administration of Lockstep Penitentiary have the covert goal of keeping their jobs which might be in jeopardy should the program fail (cf. Glaser 1973, on personal versus organizational goals). Finally, there may be confusion between short-term and long-term objectives (Moursund 1973). The long-term objective of Lockstep Penitentiary's new treatment program may be the reduction of recidivism among drug-abusing inmates, and this objective may be endorsed by everyone connected with the program. However, shorter-term objectives to achieve the long-term objective may be the subject of bitter debate among the program staff. An evaluator may perceive the agreement over the long-term goal as extending to the shorter-term goals.

Suchman (1967) has provided a useful list of questions to be asked of various sources to enable the evaluator to define evaluation objectives. These are, as detailed by Moursund (1973, p. 16):

1. What kinds of objectives is the program concerned with? That is, are we primarily interested in behaviors, in knowledge, or in attitudes? Is the program trying to maintain these objectives or to change them?
2. Who is the target of the program—individuals, small groups, the whole community? Does the program deal with the target directly or indirectly through an intermediate target group?
3. What is the time span with which we are concerned? Is the program primarily interested in immediate results, or in long-range change, or in maintenance?
4. Are program objectives unitary or multiple? In either long- or short-range terms, are we talking about a single goal or a cluster of goals?
5. How great must the effect of the program be before we consider it a success? Must it reach all of its potential target or only some proportion of it? Must we be able to observe major changes, or will we be content with small ones?
6. Finally, what are the means to the program goals? Who is to carry out the program, what will they do, and how shall we measure their success? This latter question leads to the problem of setting up criteria, which must be clearly distinguished from setting up the goals themselves.

After objectives are set, the next stage is choosing measurable indicators of the achievement of objectives (American Institutes for Research 1970; Weiss 1972). Such measurable indicators must be logically related to the objectives and clear enough so that it is not difficult to tell if the objective has or hasn't been achieved (Moursund 1973). For some objectives, selecting appropriate measurable indicators may be a simple task. For example, one of Lockstep Penitentiary's objectives under the new treatment program might be to have parolees engaged in gainful employment. An indicator of this might be some operationally defined measure of employment such as "has worked 60 percent of the time since release." Another of the program's objectives might be to have parolees engage in healthy social contact with other persons after release. Finding an appropriate indicator for this commendable, but difficult-to-define, objective might pose many problems.

Following this stage, the next stage is one of collecting data on the measurable indicators for subjects exposed to the program (Weiss 1972). If there is a comparison group or control group of subjects not exposed to the program, then this stage will see data collected on the same measurable indicators on these subjects as were collected on the subjects exposed to the program. In the Lockstep Penitentiary example, the subjects exposed to the program were inmates in the institutional program for drug abusers at that time. A control group of inmates would be a group of inmates who had been drug abusers but who had not been exposed to the program: inmates with a drug abuse problem from a similar prison with no treatment program or from Lockstep Penitentiary before the program began. The next stage is a comparison of the two groups in terms of the amount of change shown on the measurable indicators. If the treatment group's change scores on the indicators are different from the control group's change scores, and these differences logically relate to the objectives, then one may be able to conclude that the treatment did make a difference.

The final stage is drawing general conclusions and making recommendations (American Institutes for Research 1970). This stage is heavily dependent on the personality of the evaluator himself. Some evaluators may play the objective, disinterested scientist's role, presenting the conclusions in terms so cautiously noncommittal that someone else must draw the interpretations that may be an impetus to action. Other evaluators, fitting the advocate role discussed by Adams above, may take the conclusions as rallying cries for a crusade for implementation of the conclusions.

In this final stage of drawing conclusions and making recommendations, the timing of conclusions and recommendations is of considerable importance. If the evaluation drags on and on, critical decisions about the continuation or alteration of the program may have to be made in the absence of the knowledge gained from the evaluation. By the time the study has been completed and conclusions and recommendations drawn up, the findings may be totally useless to people making decisions about the program. Weidman et al. (1975) emphasize the timeliness of reports on evaluation projects. Reports should reach decisionmakers before decisions have to be made, giving them enough time to read and absorb the material. Reports should also not reach decisionmakers so much in advance of the decision that the reports may be forgotten by the time the decision is made or discounted as not recent. Weidman et al. also recommend that reports be readable, and not so lengthy and technical that they will be ignored. Those desiring a thoughtfully written and detailed discussion of the entire process of development and implementation of program research and evaluation should see Twain (1975).

Evaluative Research Designs

The major purpose of evaluative research design is to answer questions about programs unambiguously. However, evaluation in many areas deals with variables that may be impossible to control to the degree that questions about these variables can be answered unambiguously. Designs, therefore, vary in the degree of ambiguity with which questions are answered. In applied settings such as correctional and drug abuse treatment facilities, designs are employed which are less rigorous, with resultant greater ambiguity in answers to evaluation questions than when designs are employed in situations allowing for more clearly delineated and controlled studies.

In this section, a series of evaluative research designs will be briefly presented, with less rigorous designs presented first, followed by more rigorous designs. Much of the following is drawn from Campbell and Stanley (1963) and Suchman (1967).

In the following design X = exposure of a group to the program while O = measurement of the effect of the program. X's and O's on the same line refer to the same persons.

One-Shot Case Study

$X O$

In this design, subjects are exposed to a program and then studied. This very unrigorous design has been dubbed "preexperimental" by Campbell and Stanley. This is perhaps the weakest of all evaluative designs, but it is a very common one. What makes it weak and unrigorous is the fact that there is no preexposure measure to compare to the postexposure measure and no control or comparison group whose postexposure measure can be compared to the program group (Suchman 1967). An example from Lockstep Penitentiary might be looking at the number of disciplinary infractions among inmates after exposure to the program.

One-Group, Pretest, Posttest Design

$O_1 X O_2$

In this design, the group is measured before the program, then exposed to the program, then measured after the program on the same measure as before the program. Measuring before the program or treatment is given is called taking a "baseline." Differences between the before-program measure, or premeasure, and the after-program measure, or postmeasure, might be attributed by some to the effect of the program. However, other uncontrolled factors may have been operating during the temporal span of the program to cause the change in the measure. In some cases, the change in the measure may result from the passage of time alone, and not from the program. An example from Lockstep Penitentiary would be the adding of a premeasure to the above disciplinary infraction example. This design and the next one to be discussed have also been called pre-experimental by Campbell and Stanley.

Static Group Comparison

$$X\ O_1$$
$$O_2$$

In this design, two groups are compared after one of the two groups has been exposed to the program. If the group exposed to the program is different from the other group on the after measure, the difference may be attributed to the program. However, there is no way of knowing if the two groups were similar before the program. Using the Lockstep example once again, two groups of inmates would have been compared after the program on some measure of disciplinary infractions, one exposed to the program and one not exposed. The program group might have had fewer infractions, and the difference might have been attributed to the program. However, if one knew that the nonprogram group was comprised of a large number of disciplinary cases while the program group, even before the program began, had a large number of well-disciplined inmates, then the situation takes on a different light.

Pretest, Posttest, Control Group Design

$$O_1\ X\ O_2$$
$$O_3\ \ \ O_4$$

This is a rigorous, true experimental design. Two equivalent groups are created: one a program or treatment group, the other a control group. (At times, however, one may wish to employ more than one treatment or control group, so as to more precisely determine the relationship between treatment and outcome. For instance, with more than one treatment group, one could determine if the amount of change were related to the *amount* of treatment.) Equivalence is created, ideally, by randomly assigning subjects to the two groups, or, alternatively, where this is not possible, by selecting pairs of individuals matched on as many relevant variables as is possible. It should be recognized that doing the latter will, however, result in a less powerful design. A before measure (O_1 and O_3) is taken to quantitatively determine if the two groups really are equivalent on the relevant measure, and to also provide a baseline against which future change can be measured. (Statistical methods, such as covariance, may also be employed later on to "equate" the two groups if they are not equivalent on the before measure.) The program group is then exposed to the program while the control group is not. Otherwise conditions for both groups during the temporal span of the program are the same. In this way, the equivalent control group controls for the effects of variables that may be operating at the same time as the program which may affect changes from premeasures to postmeasures. After the program is over, the two groups are measured again (O_2 and O_4). Changes between premeasures and postmeasures for each group are analyzed. If the program group has changed more (a significant statistical difference) in the predicted direction than the control group, then one can, with some degree of confidence, conclude that it was the program that did indeed create the postprogram difference between the two groups. In using change scores for the purposes of evaluating program treatments, however, one should be cognizant of the deficiencies such scores possess as true indicators of change. For a discussion of this issue, the reader is referred to Nunnally (1975).

Quasi-Experimental Designs

Besides preexperimental and experimental designs, there are designs which have been labeled by Campbell and Stanley *quasi-experimental* designs. Quasi-experimental designs are generally employed when a rigorous design is needed but the conditions of the setting where the evaluation is to be done do not permit the full control of all relevant variables (Isaac and Michael 1971). In terms of rigor they are roughly intermediate between nonexperimental and true experimental designs (see above).

In the above example of the static group comparison design, two groups of inmates (one exposed to Lockstep's treatment program, one not exposed) are compared on some measure of disciplinary infractions. This would become a quasi-experimental design if the not-exposed group (hereafter labeled the comparison group) were chosen in a way that would make it similar, with respect to relevant characteristics, to the program group. As Adams (1975) notes, this does *not* mean random selection of control group members, but rather their careful selection on an ex post facto basis. In practice, this might mean an intensive records search to find inmates for the comparison group with similar disciplinary records to the program group in a preprogram time period. Inmates from the two groups should have similar experiences in prison except for the program group's exposure to the program. If the comparison group could be chosen on these criteria, then any differences in measurement between the two groups that favored the program group after the program could be interpreted as indicating the beneficial effects of the program on disciplinary infractions.

Many of the designs used in correctional and drug abuse evaluation are quasi-experimental and nonexperimental, since conditions usually do not permit the use of true experimental designs. Prominent among these conditions is the fact that research, even evaluative research, generally takes second place to service delivery, and service delivery patterns often cannot be rearranged (especially in corrections) for the benefit of program evaluation.

Issues in Evaluative Research Design

In designing evaluative research studies, there are a number of issues of which one should be aware. These include internal and external validity, control, and sample size.

Internal and External Validity

Internal validity refers to the procedural and methodological safeguards that make the results of an experiment interpretable. To quote Campbell and Stanley (1963, p. 5), *"Internal validity* is the basic minimum without which any experiment is uninterpretable." *External validity* refers to the generalizability of the experimental findings, "to what populations, settings, treatment variables, and measurement variables can this effect be generalized" (Campbell and Stanley 1963, p. 5).

Frequently these two types of validity are antithetical, with internal validity achieved at the expense of external validity and vice versa. Internal validity has priority, however, in designing evaluative studies since if a design has no internal validity, it follows that there is no external validity. In the one-shot case study detailed above, there is no internal validity, and any results obtained from the postmeasure could not be generalized to any other population. Designs containing both types of validity obviously are a goal (Campbell and Stanley 1963).

Campbell and Stanley mention a number of extraneous variables that pose threats to internal validity unless they are controlled. They are as follows:

1. *History:* What happens in the situation between premeasures and postmeasures in addition to the program or experimental variables.
2. *Maturation:* Changes in the subjects due to passage of time such as growing hungrier, more fatigued, etc.
3. *Testing:* The effect of being tested on a subsequent test.
4. *Instrumentation:* The effect of changes in the calibration of measuring instruments or changes in observers as affecting changes in the measures obtained
5. *Statistical regression:* The effect of groups being selected on the basis of their extreme scores.

6. *Selection:* The effect of differential selection of subjects for the comparison group.
7. *Experimental mortality:* Differential loss of subjects from the comparison group.
8. *Selection-maturation interaction:* Interactions whose effects may appear to be the effects of the experimental variables.

There are also factors which threaten external validity, including:

1. *Reactive or interaction effect of testing:* Experimental situations where a pretest might affect a subject's reaction to the experimental variable in such a way as to make the results ungeneralizable to the untested population from which the subject was drawn.
2. *Interaction:* Effects of the biases for selecting subjects and the experimental variable.
3. *Reactive effects of experimental conditions:* The experimental conditions may be so unique that the results cannot be generalized to a population that hasn't been exposed to the experimental conditions.
4. *Multiple-treatment interference:* This is the effect of subjects undergoing multiple treatments where prior treatments influence subsequent treatments.

Control

A second issue in evaluative research design is *control.* Although it can be defined in terms of attempts to both maximize experimental variance and minimize error variance in statistical treatments of data from experiments, *control* is generally defined as the neutralization of extraneous variables that may affect the results other than the variable(s) being manipulated in the experiment (Isaac and Michael 1971).

Sample Size

A third issue in evaluative research design is the issue of sample size. All things being equal, large samples of subjects are preferable to small samples. This is expecially true in this time of automated data processing in which the data from a program that lasted two years, with hundred of subjects, may be processed in billionths of a second. There are, however, advantages to small samples. The experiment can generally be run more quickly than large-sample experiments, and results and conclusions will go to decisionmakers more quickly. There is also the factor of economy, since small-sample experiments are usually less costly than large-sample experiments. In terms of data processing, the results of small-sample experiments can be computed quickly and accurately with hand calculators. The results of large experiments analyzed by computers may be inaccurate because of the many human operations (e.g., keypunching, programming, etc.) and resultant errors that attend automated data processing (Isaac and Michael 1971).

Measurement Issues

Measurement is, it goes without saying, the great beating heart of evaluative research. Two crucial issues that must be dealt with when one designs a measurement as part of an evaluative study are *reliability* and *validity*.

Reliability

Reliability refers to the trustworthiness of measurement. Is the measurement consistent over time? Do repeated applications of the same measuring instrument yield the same results? A measuring instrument or process is unreliable to the extent that it contains random or chance errors (Kerlinger 1973). Such errors are errors that follow no particular systematic pattern but tend to be self-compensating in that they lean now this way, now that way. These errors may be the result of a number of factors such as fatigue, situational changes, etc., which will be discussed in greater detail below. There is no absolute indication of reliability in a measuring instrument or process (Suchman 1967). An ideal goal in designing a measurement instrument is to reduce error to the barest minimum.

There are different types of reliability. *Test-retest* reliability refers to the same instrument yielding similar results at different points in time. *Interjudge* or *interobserver* reliability is the extent of agreement of different observers of measurable aspects of the event they are observing. *Split-half* reliability is the splitting of a measurement, such as an examination, into two halves to determine if scores on the two halves agree with each other. Test-retest and interobserver reliability are of much more importance in evaluative research than split-half reliability, which is employed mainly in educational settings.

The major sources of unreliability or random errors, in Suchman's (1967) view, are as follows:

1. *Subject reliability:* The mood of the subject, his motivation, and his degree of fatigue, among other transient factors, may produce unsystematic changes in the subject's response to the measuring instrument.
2. *Observer reliability:* All the above "human" factors that affect the subject may also affect the observers who interpret and record the subject's responses.

3. *Situational reliability:* There may be random changes in the measurement environment, such as weather conditions, that may affect the measurement process in unsystematic ways.
4. *Instrument reliability:* Certain aspects of the measuring instrument inself, such as ambiguously worded questions on a questionnaire, may produce random responses.
5. *Processing reliability:* Coding, arithmetic, or mechanical errors may cause random error in the process.

Validity

Validity, the second crucial issue of measurement, may be defined as the degree to which a measurement process or instrument does what it says it is doing. When we speak of errors affecting validity, we generally speak of systematic or constant errors rather than random errors (Suchman 1967). These systematic errors slant the results in one direction rather than randomly. Suchman points out that the precise definition of evaluation goals, as well as the criteria needed for estimating success or failure in reaching the goals, is a sine qua non for any meaningful assessment of validity. Validity is of crucial importance in assessing the efficacy of measurement process or instrument (Suchman 1967). There can be high reliability but little or questionable validity. A case in point is provided by IQ tests which are generally agreed to be reliable but of questionable validity in that there is little agreement as to a common definition of intelligence. If intelligence cannot be defined, then instruments that measure "intelligence" cannot be said to have high validity.

On the other hand, there can be no validity without reliability (Suchman 1967). Validity is a broader problem than reliability. If a primary measure in an evaluation is invalid, then results of the entire evaluation are questionable.

There are several different kinds of validity to be considered in evaluative measurement. These include:

1. *Content or "face" validity:* The measure seems to be valid because in commonsense terms it seems to be obviously related to the thing being measured.
2. *Consensual validity:* A type of face validity in which a panel of experts assert that a measure relates to the thing being measured.
3. *Correlational or criterion validity:* The measure selected is correlated with another measure that is known to accurately measure the things being measured. If the two measures correlate highly, then we say that the experimental measure has criterion validity.
4. *Predictive validity:* If predictions derived from the measure can be demonstrated to accurately predict future events that seem logically related to

constructs underlying the measure, then we say the measure has predictive validity.

5. *Construct validity:* This is generally more important in pure research than in applied. Construct validity deals with attempts to explain the meaning of a measure. In other words, this is an attempt to explain the relationship among the constructs that underlie a measure (Kerlinger 1973).

Factors Affecting Validity

There are a number of factors which may threaten the validity of measurements (Jeffrey 1975). The first Jeffrey has labeled *drift*. Drift occurs when measurement has been taking place for some time and the original observational criteria for recording events begin to be altered in some subtle but systematic way. Drift may be controlled by external monitoring, self-monitoring, and retraining of observers.

The second is *reactivity*, a most important factor in validity. Reactivity refers to the fact that the process of measurement itself causes a change in the thing being measured. People who are subjects in experiments may act differently than they would ordinarily because they are aware of being measured. Subjects may deliberately give false information out of antagonism or give "good" responses from a desire to see the results of the experiment come out a certain way or in the mistaken belief that they will be seen as cooperative. As Isaac and Michael (1971) note, the personal characteristics of the experimenter or observer may also affect the responses of the subject. The powerful effect of reactivity has been demonstrated recently in behavior therapy. Telling patients to self-monitor behavior they wish to change, to provide the therapist with a base line of the behavior from which the effects of the treatment itself may be gauged, frequently results in a change in the behavior even before the treatment begins. The explanation for this is that, as subjects become aware of the behavior through recording its fequency, they begin to exert control over its frequency. Reactivity may be eliminated as a problem by using nonreactive or nonobstrusive measures such as records or unobtrusive observation.

Nunnally (1975) suggests several steps researchers can take to reduce the effects of reactivity. These include (1) use of appropriate research design in order to avoid the problem, (2) employment of nonreactive measures (cf. Webb et. al. 1966), (3) studying the pretest measures one is using to determine if there is interaction with treatment, and (4) disguising items by embedding them in traditional ability and sentiment measures. Nunnally notes that this last approach usually fails.

The third factor is *bias*. This occurs when the observer or experimenter has some expectation of the way responses should appear that deviates from the way that responses actually appear. He records in the direction of his bias. Rosenthal

(1966) has dubbed such a phenomenon the "experimenter bias" effect. Keeping observers or experimenters unaware of the predictions behind a study is one way to control bias. A related problem arises when evaluators with a vested interest in the outcome "stack the cards in their favor" by selecting instruments, raters, or subjects which they more or less know in advance (either consciously or unconsciously) will produce responses in the desired direction. This kind of bias may be avoided by utilizing outside evaluators who have little stake in the outcome of the evaluation (Nunnally 1975).

The final factor is *nongenerality*. This occurs when the behaviors measured in a study are not representative of the total universe of behaviors of interest in the study. For example, if we want to measure violent disturbances at Lockstep Penitentiary, and if we measured only between the hours of midnight and 6 A.M., this 6-hour sample would not be representative of the 24-hour period that might interest us since most inmates are asleep in their cells during this period. One solution would be to monitor violent disturbances continuously. Still another might be to sample different time periods during the 24-hour period.

Measurement Techniques

A large number of measurement techniques are employed in evaluative studies. This section will not attempt to present all these techniques but merely techniques to measure the achievement of goals that play a prominent role in correctional drug abuse programs.

Wilner (1975) classifies "measures of [program] accomplishment" into two categories: (1) *social indicators,* which reflect the impact of the program upon locales, may include crime rates (e.g., DuPont 1972), arrest rates and mortality rates (e.g., DuPont and Greene 1973); (2) *individual measures,* on the other hand, reflect the impact of the program directly upon the participants or other persons touched indirectly by programs, such as families of participants. Individual measures include psychological tests (e.g., MMPI, California Test of Personality), interviews, questionnaires, institutional adjustment, posttreatment adjustment (e.g., number of days before rearrest or resumed drug use; rearrest versus nonrearrest; type and seriousness of offense if parole is revoked or rearrest occurs, etc.), physical condition (including the presence or absence of drug metabolities in urine), and staff judgments of adjustment or improvement.

Often, the measure of accomplishment chosen in evaluating a program may depend as much upon the discipline of the evaulator as upon the objectives of the program to be evaluated. For instance, psychologists are much more likely to choose individual measures of accomplishment, in contrast to other social scientists (i.e., sociologists, economists, criminologists, etc.) who will often use social indicators.

Social Indicators

Wilner (1975) warns that social indicators such as crime and arrest rates are subject to variation through such things as differential reporting (e.g., differential reporting of crimes to police) which limit their value as outcome measures. Wilner does mention some other social indicators which have potential utility as outcome measures. These are performance in school by children of the locale, (achievement, grades, dropouts), aid to dependent children, welfare rates, parole and probation, illegitimacy, suicide, psychiatric hospitalization, psychiatric clinic utilization, rates of cirrhosis of the liver (as a link to alcoholism in the locale) and infectious hepatitis (as an indicator of drug abuse in the community). These also, like crime and arrest data, are subject to a number of flaws (Wilner 1975, p. 41):

. . . the problems include: loose definitions; files not always up to date; record-keeping clerks not always qualified or sufficiently trained; haphazard assembly, subject to "drives" and other pressures; irregular reporting; individual cases subject to status reports only, with reasons for status not given and changes in status not noted; and no geocoding of address, thus making difficult census tract assignment.

Social indicators also do not involve the program participants directly, so any conclusions from measurements about program goals being achieved can be based on inference only. They are, however, in Wilner's phrase, "quality-of-life" indicators, and these may have considerable value in looking at programs aimed at circumscribed and clearly defined geographical areas, a catchment area, a small town, etc. They are also nonreactive measures (see above) with none of the disadvantages of reactive measures.

Individual Measures

Individual measures, as mentioned above, are measures taken of the subjects themselves or of related persons. Of the measures used in correctional drug abuse evaluation, *interviews, questionnaires,* and *psychological tests* play a prominent role.

Isaac and Michael (1971) discuss three types of interviews. The first is *unstructured interviews* which generally follow the broad, nondirective therapy technique of Carl Rogers. In unstructured interviews, the respondent has considerable latitude to tell his own "story." The interviewer may have a general goal for the interview. According to Isaacs and Michael, this interview usually deals with personal and possibly threatening material, and is most subject (of the three types) to subjective bias or errors due to inexperience.

Semistructured interviews have structured questions which may serve as springboards for deeper exploration of the topic of the questions.

The third type is *structured interviews.* In this interview, the format is like that of an objective questionnaire. The questions deal generally with specifics, and there is little attempt to depart from the questions. Skill is an esstential quality in an interviewer (Wilner 1975), and interviewers should be trained prior to the study. Careful consideration should also be given to the language in which the interview is conducted. Both Alksne (1960), in his study of narcotics addicts, and Ward and Kassebaum (1965), who studied a women's prison, found that using the respondents' language style and idioms facilitated interviewing. On the other hand, inappropriate use of the respondents' idiom may lead to discrediting of the interviewer.

Isaac and Michael (1971) discuss the need for some coding of responses so that they can be placed in general categories. They also discuss recording, pointing out that tape recording has advantages over written summaries because writing slows down the interview or causes selectivity of recording. A disadvantage of tape recording is that it may put some subjects on guard. Another is that transcription of responses may be an extremely time-consuming process.

Isaac and Michael (1971, p. 97) also give some useful tips on framing interview questions:

a. Questions must be framed in language that insures effective communication between the interviewer and the respondent. Omit all ambiguous vocabulary.
b. Make certain respondent appreciates the purpose of each question he is asked. Avoid arousing any suspicion or resistance.
c. Ascertain whether the population from which the respondents have been selected actually has the information sought by the interview and that the questions permit the reasonable recovery of this information.
d. Avoid leading questions (questions which suggest a desirable or preferred answer).
e. Insure that the frame of reference surrounding each question is clear so that each respondent hears the question in the same way, avoiding misinterpretations.
f. Pretest the interview in a pilot study to eliminate weaknesses and experiment with alternative items or techniques.

A final issue to be kept in mind when doing interview studies is that the personal characteristics of the interviewer, including such variables as age, sex, race, educational level, and attitude, may affect the data by biasing interviewees' replies. An excellent discussion of the role of these variables in obtaining valid interview data is available in Weiss (1975, pp. 379–87).

Questionnaires are self-administered, structured interviews with help being offered with difficult questions (Wilner 1975). With questionnaires the literacy of the respondent is another important consideration (Wilner 1975). The need to instruct respondents to give truthful responses is frequently quite effective in increasing the validity of self-report, one that is often overlooked (Nunnally 1975).

Psychological tests include intelligence tests, academic achievement tests, personality tests, and vocational tests. Academic achievement tests and personality tests, especially, are more frequently employed in evaluative studies than vocational tests.

Personality tests are divided into two types: *projective* and *nonprojective* (Coleman 1976). Projective tests employ ambiguous stimuli like hazy drawings and inkblots. The subject describes what he sees and in descriptions reveals, according to the theory behind projective tests, "deeper" aspects of his personality such as drives, needs, motives, and conflicts. Two widely employed projectives tests are the Rorschach inkblot test and the Thematic Appreciation Test (TAT). Two other nonprojective tests frequently used in corrections are the House-Tree-Person (H-T-P) technique and the Bender-Gestalt test.

Nonprojective tests are more structured than projectives, and generally use self-inventory or questionnaire-type measurement (Coleman 1976). The most well-known nonprojective personality test is the Minnesota Multiphasic Personality Inventory (MMPI), a self-report inventory containing over 500 true-false questions.

Psychological testing is much too vast an area to discuss in this chapter. For listings of measurement instruments and tests, the reader is referred to Buros' (1972) *Seventh Mental Measurements Yearbook* and for more extensive and detailed treatments of psychological tests to Cronbach (1970), Anastasi (1961), and Robinson and Shaver (1973). The latter is particularly valuable in that it contains many less well-known personality instruments which may be useful in correctional evaluation. These include measures of self-esteem, beliefs about fate control, anomie, authoritarianism, values, sociopolitical attitudes, religious attitudes, and attitudes about people. One principle to keep in mind when using personality measures is that it is almost always more advantageous to use previously developed instruments than to construct one's own. Use of existing measures offers the major advantage of being able to make use of previous research findings to interpret results, as well as great advantages in time and cost savings. With respect to this latter point, it is surprising how often researchers underestimate the difficulties to be encountered in *appropriately* developing new instruments.

Academic achievement tests are essentially used to measure the extent to which educational programs within the institutional setting have achieved their objectives. Widely used is the Stanford Achievement Test (SAT).

Intelligence tests: The most widely used test for measuring the intelligence of adults is the Wechsler Adult Intelligence Scale (WAIS). Both verbal and performance abilities are measured by WAIS (Coleman 1976). Other intelligence tests often used in correctional settings are the Quick Test of Intelligence, The Draw-a-Man test, and the Revised Beta Examination.

Group measures: Data collection on groups should be mentioned. From one perspective, one may use groups of respondents as forums for data collection, particularly when the consensus of the group is of primary interest. In this regard, Weiss (1975) briefly reviews the literature and concludes that "Group interviewing then is effective for collecting information and opinions if the special pressures towards conformity to group norms are recognized (or even desirable in the research)" (p. 362). She notes the particular usefulness of this technique in collecting opinions on responses to programs as well as the postprogram expectations of participants.

From another perspective, the group itself may be the focus of interest, with respect to power, leadership or status structure, decisionmaking process, or communication structure. Measurement techniques exist for measurement of each of these structures and processes, among them Bales's (1950) Interaction Process Analysis, Harary's (1959) formula for determination of social status index, and Glanzer and Glaser's (1959) method for constructing sociometric indices.

Moos (1975) has recently introduced a new methodology for evaluating the social environments of institutionally and community-based correctional programs as well as for other social groups. Initial response to this Correctional Institutions Environment Scale (CIES) seems to be quite positive, and one should soon begin to see its employment in correctional studies by others.

Records

One of the potentially most fruitful sources of information in correctional research is the records system of the institution or system in which the research is being conducted. While the use of records was touched upon in Chapter 1 and the setting up of a records system is also the focus of an entire chapter (Chapter 3), some of the advantages and disadvantages as outlined by Weiss (1975) will be listed here. The obvious advantages include savings in cost, including time, effort, and money. The disadvantages, however, are often so great as to preclude their usefulness. These include the fact that:

They are often incomplete, out-of-date, and painfully inaccurate. Entries are undated. Names are variously spelled. Gaps are unaccounted for. Even where records meet the standards for accuracy of the operating agency (and this is by no means always the case), they may not meet research concerns. Sometimes there are special interpretations or shortcuts, known only to one or two old-time employees that belie the face data (Weiss 1975, p. 357).

Weiss goes on to say that since existing records may also not always contain what the evaluator needs to know, perhaps they should be avoided. Setting up a good record-keeping system has advantages for both the evaluator and the agency, and this is a possibility that should always be considered.

The Problem of Outcome Measurement in Correctional Drug Rehabilitation

Commonly Used Outcome Measures

Adams (1975) has provided a list of over twenty outcome criteria which have been used in correctional evaluation. He notes that several of these have been or are beginning to be used extensively. These include arrests, type or severity of offense, time until arrest, conviction, length of time in lock-up, costs of correctional treatment, and benefits, including those occurring from diversion benefits (averted police, court, and incarceration costs), earnings from employment, and those associated with reduced rearrest and reincarceration. Adams also notes that for narcotics addicts benefits may accrue from reduced health costs after treatment, and that welfare benefits may result from nonincarceration of a family wage-earner. Other measures cited by Adams include observed behaviors and attitudes; personality and attitudinal inventory scores; probation or parole agent ratings; revocations, technical offenses, or new offenses; costs of apprehension and court costs; personal or social adjustment; and job status and earnings improvement.

Besides those variables listed by Adams, the following variables are of particular relevance in evaluating programs for drug-addicted offenders: length of time until drug use is resumed, amount and type of illicit drug(s) used, frequency of illicit drug use, arrests for drug-related offenses, length of participation in residential drug rehabilitation programs, frequency of participation in outpatient drug rehabilitation programs, and presence of drug metabolites in urine. Einstein and Garitano (1972) note that when follow-up of drug abusers is done, the following three variables are most often focused on: "Present use of specific drugs; present vocational and/or school status; and present involvement with the law" (p. 328). They suggest that the use of these criteria reflects a drug use stereotype, and that follow-up, rather than focusing on verifying this stereotype, should focus on present functioning, "given . . . present strengths and weaknesses against a background of available resources" (Einstein and Garitano 1972, p. 329).

In-Program and Postprogram Outcome Measures

Cavior and Cohen (1975) have distinguished between in-program and postprogram outcome measures (see above for a discussion of the discontinuity between the two program phases). For Cavior and Cohen, in-program outcome measurement is primarily a matter of monitoring programs for operational effectiveness. Two subtypes are distinguished: *subprogram evaluation*, which focuses on selected aspects of large programs, and the *keeping of records* on individuals in the program. In-program measurement deals frequently only with program completion or frequency of participation. As Cavior and Cohen warn, participation in a program is not the same as being affected by a program. They also point out that completion of a program is frequently out of the hands of the administrators of a program but may be controlled by external figures such as parole boards.

Postprogram measurement deals with assessing the effects of an institutional program on the postrelease period and is beset with difficulties for Cavior and Cohen. They mention three classes of difficulty: (1) the definition of adequate measures, (2) problems of methodology, and (3) measurement validity. Defining adequate measures is a difficult task because society at large sets criteria for postrelease behavior for released participants in institutional programs. Since these standards focus primarily on self-protection, this means that these criteria for adjustment are most often related to postrelease criminal behavior (Cavior and Cohen 1975).

The postprogram outcome measure that comes to mind immediately when most people think of correctional treatment is *recidivism*. Cavior and Cohen discuss a number of difficulties that arise when recidivism is employed as a measure. They point out that a return to custody for an individual, as an indicator of failure of a program, may mask beneficial effects such as obtaining a job on release as the result of training received as part of the program but losing the job as a result of a drinking problem. They also indicate that there are societal factors such as the state of the economy that are out of the control of the program; e.g., somebody may leave the program with salable employment skills but be unable to find work, and thus may commit a crime.

Cavior and Cohen propose the use of alternative or supplemental measures to recidivism such as "actual new time served, sentence length, severity of new offense, and time elapsed before new offense and/or commitment" (p. 247). They point out, however, that these measures are also confounded by other factors, but that despite this, there are definite advantages of these measures over recidivism. Such advantages are that the measures (Cavior and Cohen 1975, p. 247)

. . . provide indices of severity of new crime and can be compared with severity of the original crime to yield a measure of the effect of program intervention. These data also provide better estimates of cost effectiveness of programs than a conventional recidivism measure. And in principle, these measures are more sensitive and consequently will reflect program differences that are obliterated by a recidivism measure.

Cavior and Cohen further point out that another problem that besets recidivism as a measure is that there is little uniformity in how it should be defined. The definitions range from arrest to reincarceration for some minimal length of time.

Obviously which definition is employed has a good deal to do with the recidivism rate for a given study; i.e., arrest as a definition would probably yield a high recidivism rate while reincarceration for a half-year would yield a low rate. Cavior and Cohen tentatively recommend a definition of reincarceration for at least 2 months.

Duration of a follow-up period provides another difficulty for recidivism as a measure (Cavior and Cohen 1975), since the longer the period, the higher the recidivism (cf. Glaser 1973 for a discussion of the problem of length of follow-up).

Methodological difficulties, for Cavior and Cohen, involve such factors as long-term programs releasing individuals at different points in time, measurement problems, and the problem of the adequate comparison group. The first difficulty is the treatment of individuals released at different points in time as if they were released at the same time. This is a difficulty because there may be numerous changes in the program during a given period as well as changes in the very composition of the inmate population.

Measurement problems include the loss of subjects from a sample for a variety of reasons and inaccuracies in postrelease data. The problem of securing data relating to criminal behavior is addressed by Glaser (1937), who lists a number of procedures for securing such data, including requesting F.B.I. fingerprint arrest reports, state, county, and regional fingerprint arrest reports, contact with agencies holding one's postreleases, and finally tracing postreleases through the files of the myriad of institutions that all of us come into contact with such as medical facilities, selective service, court records, social welfare records, telephone directories, credit bureau files, etc.

In discussing the problem of comparison groups, Cavior and Cohen (1975) note that comparison groups may be one of several types: "(a) previously collected outcome data on comparable populations; (b) outcomes from the same institution but at an earlier point in time; (c) concurrent outcome data from similar institutions, and (d) occasionally, concurrent outcome data from the same institution" (p. 251). They go on to indicate that the first three types of comparison groups suffer from problems mentioned above such as differing definitions of recidivism, differing follow-up periods, and change in programs over time. Even the fourth type would pose difficulties as concurrent outcome data may involve individuals who differ in many ways from the individuals in the program of interest, since randomization is not usually the method of assigning individuals to different programs within an institution.

Measurement validity, the final class of difficulty for Cavior and Cohen, is threatened by the releases' experiences that intervene between release and outcome measurement. Parole is an experience such that individuals on parole are more likely to be returned to prison than those not on parole. Some other experiences of a nonprogrammatic nature that may affect outcome are social service availability, support from family and friends, and economic conditions (Cavior and Cohen 1975).

A fuller treatment of outcome evaluation in drug abuse rehabilitation, from the vantage point of both problems with current approaches and suggestions for improvement, is presented in Chapter 4.

General Issues in Evaluative Research in Drug Abuse Treatment

This final section in the chapter will outline some paramount issues in evaluation that do not fit neatly into the previous sections.

The Role of the Evaluator

The first issue is the question, What is the role of the evaluator? Moursund (1973) describes the personal characteristics that seem to characterize the competent evaluator. These include: a knowledge of and sensitivity to one's own values and those of others, because evaluation is such a value-laden area; a commitment to gradual social change stemming from a social philosophy that is neither radical nor conservative; toleration for ambiguity but at the same time an impatience with ambiguity; attention to small detail but at the same time retention of the "big picture"; and finally, frustration tolerance. The issue of whether the evaluator should be an insider or an outsider has been touched upon briefly above (see the section on Types of Evaluative Research). There are clearly advantages to both perspectives. The outside evaluator may be more objective and, more likely than not, a professional evaluator who will have more time for evaluation than an internal, possibly amateur, evaluator (cf. Adams's apprentice above), who may be distracted with operational problems. His objectivity may be ensured by the fact that, since he is an outsider, he stands to lose little, if anything, should the results of the evaluation look disappointing in terms of program objectives. Arguments against the outside evaluator include his lack of awareness of important nuances that an insider would know, the staff time needed for the outsider to learn the program and the setting, his threat to the staff by the very fact of being an outsider, and the cost (American Institutes for Research 1970).

Regarding the role of the evaluator vis-à-vis administration, Cavior and Cohen (1975) state the importance of educating the administration about the role of evaluation. Such education should include teaching the administration to use evaluation resources (e.g., teaching the administration how to ask researchable questions), dealing with negative findings, and, finally, convincing the administration that evaluation can prevent long-term failure by providing data for ongoing program modification.

42

Resistance to Evaluation

This second issue is as much a continuing problem for correctional drug abuse programs as it is for programs in other fields such as mental health. Zusman and Bissonette (1973) have listed a number of sources of resistance. While Zusman and Bissonette discuss resistance from the mental health frame of reference, most, if not all, of what they say is also relevant to correctional drug abuse treatment. The first is professionalism. Zusman and Bissonette's opinion is that the invocation of professionalism is used as a barrier to evaluation on the grounds that the professional relationships in an organization are so subtle and sensitive that outside evaluation may do considerable disservice to this subtlety and sensitivity. The citation of confidentiality as a means of keeping "prying" researchers out of an area is a tactic also frequently employed by professionals.

Organizational or administrative resistance is a second source. It may evince itself at the stage where evaluation is first proposed or after the results of an evaluation are reported. Suchman (1967) has focused on administrative resistance to evaluation, pointing out that organizations strive to perpetuate themselves, and that as well as negative results, positive results (that show that the organization has solved the problem it was created to solve) will be resisted by finding a new problem for the organization to solve.

The Ethics of Evaluation

A third general issue is *evaluation ethics*. It goes without saying that inmates and parolees in drug abuse correctional and postcorrectional treatment settings are in situations where they are subject to considerable control over their lives. In such situations, the recruiting of subjects for participation in research programs is subject to considerable abuse since inmates and parolees may feel they have little choice in participation. It behooves evaluators in these settings to take necessary safeguards to see to it that there is truly voluntary participation and that the purposes of the research are explained fully and clearly to prospective subjects so that there is informed consent (which should always be obtained in written form in advance of beginning the research).

Keeping confidentiality of records is another ethical (and, in some cases, legal) responsibility of evaluators. The entire issue of confidentiality is a complex and increasingly legalistic one, however, and it is beyond the scope of this chapter to discuss the many ramifications of confidentiality in correctional and postcorrectional drug abuse treatment settings.

Evaluation Realities

Keeping in mind that much of the foregoing in this chapter represents an ideal rather than an actual state of affairs, we shall now list some unpleasant but real truths about evaluation as described by Zusman and Bissonette (1973):

1. The difficulty and expense of complex, large scale evaluation
2. The impossibility of doing good evaluations of some programs
3. The likelihood of many evaluations at present being ". . . poorly designed, underfunded, and forced on people unable or unwilling to implement them" (p. 122)
4. The likelihood of even quality evaluations being misinterpreted or not being attended to
5. The distortion of evaluation findings and the incorporation of these distortions into organizational patterns
6. The influence of values and political bias on the evaluation process
7. Resistance to evaluation as a constant fact-of-life
8. The lag between decisionmaking and evaluation findings

Zusman and Bissonette propose four general guidelines for evaluation that may serve to place the evaluative enterprise within a more realistic framework. Essentially they call for: no evaluation if the evaluation will have no effect on decisionmaking, early evaluation before programs have begun to entrench themselves, no evaluative effort if the evaluation ". . . cannot be done with scientific accuracy " (p. 124), and, finally, the publicizing of results in language understandable to program administrators in such form that results can be translated into program procedures.

References

Adams, S. *Evaluative Research in Corrections: A Practical Guide*. Washington: U.S. Government Printing Office, 1975.

Alksne, H. "Interviewing the Narcotic Addict." Paper presented at the meeting of the American Association for Public Opinion Research, 1960, summarized in *Public Opinion Quarterly* 24 (1960): 473-74.

American Institutes for Research. *Evaluative Research: Strategies and Methods*. Pittsburgh: American Institutes for Research, 1970.

Ammons, R. B., and Ammons, C. H. "The Quick Test (QT): Provisional Manual." *Psychological Reports* 11 (1962): 111-61.

Anastasi, A. *Psychological Testing*. New York: Macmillan, 1961.

Bales, R. F. *Interaction Process Analysis: A Method for the Study of Small Groups*. Reading, Mass.: Addison-Wesley, 1950.

Buros, O. K. *Seventh Mental Measurements Yearbook*. Highland Park, N.J.: Gryphon Press, 1972.

Campbell, D. T., and Stanley, J. C. *Experimental and Quasi-experimental Designs for Research*. Chicago: Rand McNally, 1963.

Cavior, H. E., and Cohen, S. H. "Evaluative Research: Perspectives from a Corrections Setting." *Criminal Justice and Behavior* 2 (1975): 237-57.

Coleman, J. V. *Abnormal Psychology and Modern Life*. San Francisco: Scott, Foresman, 1976.

Cronbach, L. J. *Essentials of Psychological Testing*. 3d ed. New York: Harper & Row, 1970.

DuPont, R. L. "Heroin Addiction Treatment and Crime Reduction." *American Journal of Psychiatry* 128 (1972): 856-60.

DuPont, R. L., and Greene, M. H. "The Dynamics of a Heroin Addiction Epidemic." *Science* 181 (1973): 716-22.

Edwards, W.; Guttentag, M.; and Snapper, K. "A Decision-theoretic Approach to Evaluation Research." In *Handbook of Evaluation Research* (vol. 1), edited by M. Guttentag and E. L. Struening. Beverly Hills, Calif., Sage Publications, 1975.

Einstein S., and Garitano, W. "Treating the Drug Abuser: Problems, Factors and Alternatives." *International Journal of the Addictions* 7 (1972): 321-31.

Fox, P. D., and Rappaport, M. "Some Approaches to Evaluating Community Mental Health Services." *Archives of General Psychiatry* 26(1972): 172-78.

Gibbons, D. C.; Lebowitz, B. D.; and Blake, G. F. "Program Evaluation in Correction." *Crime and Delinquency* 22 (1976): 309-21.

Glanzer, M., and Glaser, R. "Techniques for the Study of Group Structure and Behavior: I. Analysis of Structure." *Psychological Bulletin* 56 (1959): 317-32.

Glaser, D. *Routinizing Evaluation: Getting Feedback on Effectiveness of Crime and Delinquency Programs*. Washington: U.S. Government Printing Office, 1973.

Harary, F. "Status and Contrastatus." *Sociometry* 22 (1959): 23-43.

Hargreaves, W. A., et al., (eds.) *Resource Materials for Community Mental Health Program Evaluation*. San Francisco: NIMH, 1974.

Hemphill, J. K. "The Relationships between Research and Evaluation Studies." In *Educational Evaluation: New Roles, New Means*, edited by R. W. Tyler. 68th yearbook of the National Society for the Study of Education. Chicago: The Society, 1969.

Isaac, S., and Michael, W. B. *Handbook in Research and Evaluation*. San Diego: Robert R. Knapp, 1971.

Jeffrey, D. B. "Treatment Evaluation Issues in Research on Addictive Behaviors." *Addictive Behaviors* 1 (1975): 23-36.

Kerlinger, F. N. *Foundations of Behavioral Research*. New York: Holt, Rinehart and Winston, 1973.

McArthur, V. A.; Cantor, B.; and Glendinning, S. *A Cost Analysis of the District of Columbia Work Release Program*. Washington: D.C. Dept. of Corrections, Research Report No. 24, June 1970.

Mackler, B. "Two Kinds of Research on Evaluation." *Psychological Reports* 34 (1974): 289-90.

Moos, R. H. *Evaluating Correctional and Community Settings*. New York: Wiley, 1975.

Moursund, J. P. *Evaluation: An Introduction to Research Design*. Belmont, Calif.: Brooks/Cole, 1973.

Nunnally, J. C. "The Study of Change in Evaluation Research: Principles Concerning Measurement, Experimental Design, and Analysis." In *Handbook of Evaluation Research* (vol. 1), edited by M. Guttentag and E. L. Struening Beverly Hills, Calif.: Sage Publications, 1975.

Robinson, J. P., and Shaver, P. R. *Measures of Social Psychological Attitudes*. Ann Arbor, Mich.: Institute for Social Research, University of Michigan, 1973.

Rosenthal, R. *Experimental Effects in Behavioral Research*. New York: Appleton-Century-Crofts, 1966.

Schulberg, H.; Sheldon, A.; and Baker, F. "Introduction." In *Program Evaluation in the Health Fields*, edited by H. Schulberg, A. Sheldon and F. Baker. New York: Behavioral Publications, 1969.

Scriven, M. "The Methodology of Evaluation." In *Evaluating Action Programs: Readings in Social Action and Education*, edited by C. H. Weiss. Boston: Allyn and Bacon, 1972.

Suchman, E. A. *Evaluative Research: Principles in Public Service and Social Action Programs*. New York: Russell Sage Foundation, 1967.

_____. "Action for What? A Critique of Evaluative Research." In *Evaluating Action Programs: Readings in Social Action and Education*, edited by C. H. Weiss. Boston: Allyn and Bacon, 1972.

Twain, D. "Developing and Implementing a Research Strategy." In *Handbook of Evaluation Research* (vol. 1), edited by Guttentag and E. L. Struening. Beverly Hills, Calif.: Sage Publications, 1975.

Urban, H. B., and Ford, D. H. "Some Historial and Conceptual Perspectives on Psychotherapy and Behavior Change." In *Handbook of Psychotherapy and*

Behavior Change: An Empirical Analysis, edited by A. E. Bergin and S. L. Garfield. New York: Wiley, 1971.

Ward, D. A., and Kassebaum, G. G. *Women's Prison*. Chicago: Aldine, 1965.

Webb, E., et al. *Unobtrusive Measures: Nonreactive Research in the Social Sciences*. Chicago: Rand McNally, 1966.

Weidman, D. R. et al. *Intensive Evaluation for Criminal·Justice Planning A-gencies*. Washington: U.S. Government Printing Office, 1975.

Weiss, C. H. "Evaluating Educational and Social Action Programs: A 'Treeful of Owls.' " In *Evaluating Action Programs: Readings in Social Action and Education*, edited by C. H. Weiss. Boston: Allyn and Bacon, 1972.

Weiss, C. H. "Interviewing in Evaluation Research." In *Handbook of Evaluation Research*, Vol. 1, eaited by E. L. Struening and M. Guttentag. Beverly Hills: Sage, 1975.

Wilner, D. M. "Evaluation: State of the Technical Art." In *Program Evaluation: Alcohol, Drug Abuse, and Mental Health Services*, edited by J. Zusman and C. R. Wurster. Lexington, Mass.: Heath, 1975.

Wortman, P. M. "Evaluation Research: A Psychological Perspective." *American Psychologist* 30 (1975): 562-75.

Zusman, J., and Bissonette, R. "The Case Against Evaluation." *International Journal of Mental Health* 2 (1973): 111-25.

——— . and Ross, E. "Evaluation of the Quality of Mental Health Services." *Archives of General Psychiatry* 20 (1969): 352.

Part II

Three Basic Evaluative Research Issues

Introduction to Part II

The three basic issues discussed in this section, each by a researcher who has had experience in the respective subject area, are the development of management information systems, approaches to evaluating the outcome of drug abuse treatment, and the prediction of parole outcome.

In Chapter 3, the importance of information systems to the evaluation of drug abuse treatment programs is discussed, with the aim of providing the research evaluator with forewarning of the pitfalls that may occur in the development of such systems.

Chapter 4 presents a critical overview of current evaluation designs used to determine outcome, the kinds and usefulness of the information generated by each, and the relationship of this information to the underlying process of change in program participants. The second half of this chapter offers some suggestions as to how the evaluator can maximize the generation of useful information from evaluations.

Chapter 5 is concerned with the prediction of parole outcome in correctional drug abuse treatment. Recognizing that there has been a dearth of research in this area, attention is focused on the many attempts to predict outcome in corrections, in which a sophisticated methodology has undergone development. The evaluative researcher interested in correctional drug abuse treatment will see here the prototypical methodology which can be applied to his area of interest.

3

**Management Information Systems
for Drug Abuse Programs**
Eugenie W. Flaherty

Introduction

The essential ingredient of evaluation is information. Although, as has been made abundantly clear in previous chapters, information per se is not sufficient for good evaluation, the fact remains that without information there could be no evaluation. This chapter is about information and its collection, management, and use; the common term for this entire process is the *management information system* (MIS). The purpose of the chapter is to expose program administrators, staff, and evaluators to certain critical areas involved in an effective information system, and to provide them with useful principles in each of these areas which should be considered in the development and implementation of a system. The critical areas were selected because they are relevant to any system, from the simplest manual system for use in a single-service agency to a multiagency computerized system. In any management information system, the following areas must always be dealt with: the purpose of the system, staff attitudes and input, the process involved in the development of an information system, procedural details, information utilization, and confidentiality.

At this point what is not included in this chapter should be made clear, lest any readers read on in search of answers specifically applicable to their situations. First, no detailed model of an ideal system is presented, in line with the belief that no system can be "plugged in" to an agency; instead an information system must be developed to suit that agency's unique needs. (Descriptions of various MIS models can be found in Crawford, Morgan, and Gianturco 1974; Laska and Bank 1975; and Taube 1969.) Second, the transformation of raw data (on manually completed forms) into outputs, whether of individuals or on an aggregate basis, is not dealt with here. This transformation is a technical operation developed to satisfy the purposes of the MIS as perceived by the management and staff; the processes of the transformation will be dependent on the particular MIS. Third, the areas discussed and the principles selected as useful are not specific to either a manual or a computerized system; they are relevant to both. Fourth, a budget accounting system is *not* included in this discussion of information systems, because such systems have unique requirements. We are concerned in this chapter with the collection and management of information about an agency's programs, services, staff, and clients.

The Purpose of a Management Information System

The agency administrator most frequently finds himself in one of two situations in regard to information about the agency. On the one hand, the agency may be quite new and as yet have no system developed for the collection and management of information. More frequently, the agency has been in operation for years, although its functions may have changed since its inception, and a somewhat fragmented information system has developed in a piecemeal manner, as different kinds of information were needed to satisfy different demands. Unfortunately, because there is usually no regular review of information needs, these "pieces" often linger on long after the usefulness of the information they generate has expired. In the first situation, the need for an information system is usually made quite apparent when funding or governing bodies demand certain kinds of information from the agency. In the second case, the fragmented information system was probably developed specifically to satisfy such external reporting requirements, as agencies typically have little choice about these requirements. The stimulus for a revision of the system often arises when the lack of adequate information for internal needs is experienced; suddenly there is a realization that the information for internal needs is grossly inadequate.

Whatever the stimulus for change and whatever the current state of the agency's information system, the decision to explore the development of a new or revised system is a serious one—if only because it is such a costly business. It behooves the agency administration and staff to consider very seriously at this point what purposes a new information system should serve *within this particular agency*.

The first step should be a review of all the purposes which an information system of this kind might serve, to ensure that no possibility is overlooked. Cooper (1973) suggests that the elements in an information system should include recipients of service, services provided, staff activities, finance, and the target population (or population at risk). Information about the population at risk is usually obtained from sources other than the agency's information system (such as police statistics, school system data, hospital emergency room statistics, and so on), and thus need not be considered in the information system design. Person (1973) states that the basic question in the design of an information system is: Where does who do what? "Where" translates into the programmed activities or modalities of an agency *and* their location, such as group therapy on an outpatient basis, group therapy on an inpatient basis, individual counseling on the detoxification unit, individual counseling on the maintenance unit, and so on. "What" becomes the staff actions: the information system should provide data on the activities and the clients of individual staff members who have been contacted. "Who" is the patient or the client, and this encompasses all that information it is deemed necessary to know about each patient.

There is little disagreement among these authors about the categories of information which an information system might incorporate. It will ultimately be more useful, however, to explore the issue of an information system by asking another question: What will you want to *do* with this information? That is, how will you want to *use* this information? Once satisfied with answers to these questions, you can then work backward to the data you will need to accomplish these functions. Wilner (1975) suggests that the purposes for collecting program information include at least the following: routine reporting requirements on the volume of program efforts, management guidance, research, and evaluation of outcome. Pollack, Windle, and Wurster (1974) feel that information can satisfy six functions: accountability requirements (of funding and governing agencies), billing, clinical practice, program management, research, and reporting requirements. Weinstein (1975) states that an information system can satisfy four needs: (1) aiding treatment staff in serving individual clients, (2) aiding administration in management of the agency, (3) aiding governmental authorities in developing and monitoring overall programs in a service system, and (4) aiding researchers.

The information system which would satisfy all the above functions would be cumbersome unless it were very carefully designed; at the least a cumbersome system will create staff morale problems and become prohibitively expensive. The agency administrators and staff should consider each potential use extremely carefully, anticipating the feasibility of collecting the necessary information and the actual need to satisfy the given information function. There is by no means agreement in the literature that all information systems can or should satisfy all these functions; we explore some of the more salient issues below.

External Reporting Requirements

Agencies have no choice about the production of information to satisfy the external reporting requirements of funding and governing agencies, and staff usually feel so overburdened by these requirements that any plans to consider information for other functions face a wall of resistance. In the course of a review of the external reporting requirements of almost 30 drug abuse programs, the author found that of the programs 89 percent had at least one federal, state, or local reporting requirement, and 60 percent had two or more. As might be predicted, the burden was greater on methadone programs. The reality is that the program which does not satisfy its external reporting requirements may soon experience a loss of funding and support. Practically speaking, a primary purpose of internally generated information is to satisfy these requirements, and consideration of these requirements should be a first step in design.

One of the first considerations, then, should be to review all the agency's reporting requirements, to compare the separate items required by different sources, and to integrate them when possible. Traditionally, time frames seem to create the greatest barrier to integration; the time frames of certain items—drug use, employment, and arrest histories—frequently differ. Special attention should be paid to this detail in the review of reporting requirements. The review and integration of the separate items will provide those participating in the system development with a core of items, hopefully fairly limited in number, which must be included in the final design.

Program Management

The next function which an information system may assist in serving is program management and the decisions involved therein. Although in the context of immediate survival, satisfaction of external reporting requirements is often the primary determinant of information system design, in the context of program effectiveness, quality information for management decisionmaking should be the primary determinant. It is a sad fact that too often information systems are hastily assembled to satisfy external needs, and thus exist as designed for years, with no thought being given to internal management needs. Management information systems are defined by some as a tool for management decisionmaking (Elpers and Chapman 1973; Person 1973). While many people do not believe it is the sole purpose of a management information system, it is certainly one essential purpose.

What information is necessary for management decisionmaking? This question will not be easy to answer, because most administrators are not accustomed to using information as generated by an information system (Lucas 1975), and they may find it difficult to articulate their information needs. On the other hand, one must avoid the temptation of suggesting to administrators what information they might find useful; they are likely to agree (who can reject an offer of information?), and the end result will be information overload and nonuse (Lucas 1975; Truitt and Binner 1969).

One method of stimulating constructive thought on information needs might be to review administrative decisions made in the past. Those responsible for system design can review memos, minutes, and in-house documents and select a set of significant decisions made within the past year (thus incorporating any decisions specific to a season or time of the year). The decisions selected for study should be representative of all administrative decisions within the particular agency; only administration can be the judge of that. The decisions should then be reviewed, focusing on information the administrator would have found useful in making the particular decision. It cannot be stressed too often that the emphasis must be on information that definitely would have been used and that, in the administrator's view, would have improved the quality of the decision. Information which "it would be nice to know, or nice to have had" clutters up your information system and is apt to be neglected by system users.

The same approach can be used for decisions which administrators anticipate making in the near future. Again, the emphasis is on certainties; avoid the discussion of decisions which *may* come up, and focus instead on those which have a high probability of occurring. The administrator who must decide whether to open a special alcohol unit, for example, will want to know what proportion of the clients in the past had a significant alcohol problem at entry or during treatment (Spitzer and Endicott, 1971). Astrachan (1975) describes another example of information use in decisionmaking. Comparison of program utilization rates by the Puerto Rican population revealed that in several agencies utilization rates for this population were much higher in those agencies employing Spanish-speaking professionals and allied health professionals. The decision was made to establish a special Spanish clinic in an agency with low utilization rates; subsequently the number of Spanish-speaking individuals served increased. Amos, DuPont, and Lau (1973) suggest ways in which an administrator of a multi-modality drug abuse treatment program can use traditionally collected information to assess the effectiveness of the program and plan program modifications.

This process of review will result in a second set of items of information (the first set being those derived to satisfy external reporting requirements). This second set, once collected, requires further review from the standpoint of the frequency with which the information will be required. Smith and Sorensen (1974, chap. 2, pp. 1-2) report an analysis of management information which concludes that three types of data are required to answer three basic managerial questions:

Scorekeeping includes the accumulation of data to help evaluate organizational performance from both an internal and external viewpoint—for example, reports which compare actual results with budgets.

Attention-directing is the reporting and interpretation of data focusing on the day-to-day organizational operations. Red flags are hoisted via performance reports to enable a manager to take prompt action... [1]

Problem-solving involves data used for nonroutine decision-making, long range planning, special program decisions, etc.

Information needed for decisions of the problemsolving type should perhaps not be included in the ongoing information system, but might instead be collected when needed through a special study. Factors to weigh in making this decision are staff time for regular collection of the data, cost of ongoing processing, frequency of the particular problemsolving decision, and cost and inconvenience of the special study. On the other hand, information needed for decisions of the scorekeeping and attention-directing type should be maintained in this second set of items for the MIS.

Treatment Service Delivery

A third potential function of an information system is to assist clinicians in providing services and to improve their service delivery. Taube (1969, p. 7) believes that that is the primary function of an information system:

. . . the single most important requirement for building a successful computer system in a psychiatric facility is that the system must be intended for and tailored to assist the *clinical* staff in their endeavor to do their jobs, that is, to treat patients. . . . The primary objective of the system must be to collect data and produce a tangible product that helps treatment personnel.

Although Taube was concerned with information systems in psychiatric facilities, the option of a primarily clinically oriented system is, in theory, also open to other human service agencies. On the other hand, a clinically oriented system is by no means incompatible with a system satisfying external reporting requirements and management needs as well. A third option, and one used especially in many medical settings, is to have two independent records systems: the first, to satisfy the needs of treatment staff, is usually relatively unstructured and probably not subject to processing; the second, to satisfy other functions, often is of a structured format and is processed regularly. The third option is highly undesirable because it requires duplicated effort by treatment staff, and hence one system, probably the nontreatment-oriented one, would be neglected. While it may always be necessary for treatment staff to keep their own notes on a client, it is desirable to integrate into one system as much as possible the information needs of treatment staff with needs of administration and external agencies.

Ascertaining the information needs of treatment staff is as difficult a process as ascertaining the needs of management for decisionmaking. A prerequisite is the representation of *all levels* of treatment staff in the planning of the system. One procedure might be to select several client cases, which should have represented in their treatment histories the complete variety of courses possible at the given agency (such as movement from one unit to another, canceled appointments, unscheduled appointments, successful and unsuccessful referrals, readmission after both a brief and an extended period of time, counseling of family members, and so on). Each case history can then be tracked, focusing constantly on key decision points in the history and on comparison of the information readily available with the information desired. Elpers and Chapman (1973, p. 13) suggest summarizing all information currently collected and asking the treatment staff "*whether* the data adequately characterized their activities and *what* additional information would be needed to help them in operating their services." [See Lucas (1975) for a similar suggestion, using survey techniques.]

As with management needs, it is essential to focus on information that, if made available, would in reality be used by treatment staff and that treatment staff feel would improve the quality of care (see Seaberg 1965, 1970 for an example of a records system designed to improve quality of care). It may be useful to group information needs by stages of treatment: intake, treatment, periodic review, termination. This will yield a third set of items to be considered for the information system.

Evaluation

A fourth function which an information system can serve is perhaps the most controversial: evaluation. First it is necessary to clarify the term *evaluation*: evaluation is defined in this context as first, the assessment of client change and second, the relationship between client change and certain gross treatment variables (group counseling versus individual counseling, methadone versus nonmethadone, and so on). Evaluation in this context is not defined as research, or even as evaluative research (Suchman 1967). Most people agree that an ongoing information system should not be designed primarily for research purposes (Hornstra and Tritt 1969) and is in any case not a suitable vehicle for research (Bloom 1972), although the information it yields may provide a point of departure for research (Wolford and Keller 1969).

It is the responsibility of any treatment program to be concerned with evaluation, insofar as its objective is to alleviate to some degree the problem with which the client entered treatment. Furthermore, unless the agency wishes to institute occasional special studies (never a desirable option), it should incorporate such evaluation into its ongoing management information system. (A not-trivial by-product of ongoing evaluation is the improvement of service delivery; many espouse the belief that service is improved when treatment staff have goals in mind for the client.)

To simplify the mattter greatly, evaluation of problem alleviation (or of outcome) requires two decisions. First, how will outcome be assessed or measured? Any assessment of outcome must satisfy at least three criteria: it should be appropriate to the initial problem, it should be easily obtained, and it should be relevant to most, if not all, clients. Furthermore, because in reality we know so little about the dimensions of most social and individual problems, several measures should be employed. Traditional measures used in drug abuse treatment programs, for example, are drug and alcohol use, dropout rate, arrest record, work record, and attendance at clinic. Because these measures reflect fundamental changes in an individual's functioning, they often fail to show significant changes. Staff may wish to have the option of setting unique goals for individual cases, perhaps in assistance with the client. This has been used in several ongoing information systems (Bonstedt 1973; Ellis and Wilson 1973; Honigfeld and Klein 1973; Kiresuk 1973; Kiresuk and Sherman 1968). In this case it is essential that outcome be assessed by standard measures (for all clients) as well.

The second decision to be made concerns the timing of the assessment of outcome. Again, assessment should occur for all clients at the same time in the course of treatment. The obvious—and important—time is at termination, but review of outcome should occur at regular intervals prior to termination as well. Periodic reviews can be used as a basis for judging the adequacy of the individual treatment plan, as well as for assessing the relative effectivenesss of gross treatment types. Evaluation after termination—follow-up—should not be done for all clients, as this would require a great deal of staff time. Instead, if the decision is made to do regular follow-up, random samples of clients might be selected on admissions (Kaplan and Smith 1974).

The inclusion of information for purposes of external reporting requirements, management decisionmaking and planning, treatment staff use, and evaluation of outcome has been discussed. Not discussed was information for billing purposes, because such information is fairly straightforward. If at all possible, the information system should be designed to generate billing information; otherwise treatment staff will probably be recording twice information about services delivered.

Consideration of the various purposes of the proposed information system will result in one or more sets of items, or data, each of which has been selected as necessary to satisfy the particular objective. For final review and integration of items, Rosove (1967, p. 107) has proposed a useful set of criteria:

Relevance: The relationship between items and purpose should be explicit.

Nomenclature: all terms used should be "expressed in a language common to the users and designers of the system. There must be no ambiguity in terms."

Grain: The degree of measurement of each item should be clear. For example, if the item is "frequency of use of primary drug," how finely will this be measured?

Sources: The source of each item must be specified, and it should be ascertained that the source in fact has the necessary data.

Destinations: both the intermediate and final destinations of each item should be understood.

Logical relationship: Any causal, covariant or independent relationships among items should be made clear. For example, "date of admissions" must obviously precede "date of discharge." Also, "year of first use" of a given drug cannot occur *after* "year first used once per week or more often."

Alvarez and Moore (1969, p. 129) found that when interviewing professionals in law, medicine, and nursing about the purpose of their recordkeeping systems, "most professionals interviewed were at a loss for an answer." An information system whose objectives are not clear cannot be efficient and useful; articulation of purpose is an essential first step.

Staff Attitudes and Input

Anyone who has worked in a human service delivery system knows that staff have a generally negative attitude toward information systems, and there is a multitude of anecdotal evidence to support this. We do not know the source of this negative attitude, although Lucas (1975) describes evidence suggesting that prior exposure to poorly designed systems is certainly a major source. Morgan and Crawford (1974) suggest that the source of this discontent for computer systems lies in three staff fears: (1) fear that computer technology will change the role of the treatment staff, (2) fear that the technology will interfere with the client-therapist relationship, and (3) fear that management and treatment staff will be replaced by the computer.

Content of Staff Attitudes

Research on the content of staff attitudes toward information systems is primarily limited to studies of attitudes toward computerization. Reznikoff, Holland, and Stroebel (1967) developed a 35-item questionnaire which was completed by all staff in a setting with a sophisticated computer system. Results indicated that men had a more favorable attitude toward computers that women, and that a favorable attitude increased with age and education. Nine factors of the attitude toward computers were found, and these could be grouped into three general categories: (1) "the usefulness and efficiency of computers in dealing with some of the more burdensome aspects of living in an exceedingly complex society"; (2) "the need for constant human control of computer activity and the dangers of dehumanization"; and (3) "the misapplication and exploitation of computers and the unwarranted assumptions that are made about their future potential" (p. 423). Klonoff and Clark (1975) found that when treatment staff were questioned about the potential liabilities of a computer system, the greatest concern was voiced about the negative reactions of clients (41 percent of all respondents), confidentiality (39 percent), assignment of responsibility for errors (36 percent), and loss of interaction between clients and staff (35 percent).

Some Determinants of Staff Attitudes

Given that you are going to institute an information system, and given that you can expect staff to react negatively, can you ameliorate the situation in any way? Klonoff and Clark found that when staff completed a 2½-day course on health information systems, perception of the computer as an efficient tool with potential benefits for society increased, and their fear of the computer's dehumanizing aspects decreased. Interestingly, the staff also expressed more concern after the course about the problems of data handling, the responsibility for errors, and access and corrections of the information. Therefore, knowledge about the information system improves attitudes to some extent, although it also appropriately heightens the staff's sensitivity to potential difficulties.

However, providing staff with a comprehensive description and explanation of the information system is not sufficient to create positive staff attitudes. Staff must be involved in and have input into the development of the system as well. To neglect their involvement invites dissatisfaction, ignores the value of their contribution, and enhances the possibility of designing an imperfect information system for the given situation. Lehman, Struening, and Darling (1969) found that the involvement of the treatment staff in the development of the information system both improved the system and had tangible effects on staff attitudes.

Involvement of all . . . workers in the actual development of the record system they were to use was not merely a strategy to commit them but was essential since we were somewhat dependent upon them for descriptions of their procedures and assessments of forms as they were piloted. Their suggestions and ideas were most viable and frequently became incorporated in the design of the forms. . . . The . . . workers found the forms less time-consuming than they had thought, easy to administer and a valuable frame of reference that helped them evaluate their own case activities (pp. 104–105).

Crawford (1974), on the other hand, provides us with a vivid example of what happens when treatment staff are not involved in the system development. A planning group of psychiatrists, psychologists, and computer scientists developed an objective checklist to replace nursing notes which, despite pilot tests for over a year, never became operational. Why? The checklist did not include some behaviors which the nurses felt were important, the checklist was designed for use on a daily basis and the nurses had not felt the need for daily notes, and the outputs did not provide useful information for the nurses. Crawford (1974, p. 18) concludes that "this nursing application, planned by psychiatrists, psychologists, and computer scientists, failed to meet nursing needs, of which only nurses could have been aware." Clearly nurses, the intended users of the system, should have participated in the planning from the start.

Lucas (1975) studied thirteen small industrial firms and a major university, all of which had management information systems of varying levels of sophistication. Users of the systems, ranging from clerks to vice presidents, completed a questionnaire which included items on the degree of their involvement in the information system, their perception of the quality of the information system, and their perception of the technical competence of the information system staff. Lucas found a positive relationship between user involvement in system design and operation and user perception of system quality, although there was no relationship between user involvement and perception of information system staff.

In light of these findings and experiences, it would indeed be foolhardy to develop an information system without full participation of eventual users in the planning. Rosove (1967) believes that lack of participation will result in a "hypercritical attitude" (p. 287). Symbolic participation is not enough. If, as will usually be the case, the number of users is too great to participate meaningfully in planning meetings, users themselves should select representatives. Whenever possible, the opinion of the total group should be sought.

Methods of Staff Involvement

Methods of effective staff input will vary with the situation. Nelson and Morgan (1973) suggest that a mixed strategy of internal surveying, committee meetings, personal conferences, and demonstrations of proposed systems is best. In the first stages of planning, the authors report interviewing staff representatives from each treatment modality. The study was briefly described to the representatives, and they were asked about their current means of receiving and transmitting information and for any suggestions they might have for improving the existing system. Following the interview, a questionnaire was sent to all staff asking staff by what means (including oral) and with what frequency they were involved with information transmission with each staff group (psychiatrist, psychologist, social worker, and so on). Staff were also asked to comment on the adequacy of the current information system. These strategies were designed with the objectives in mind of gaining "an insight into the existing information system and [providing] a stimulus for staff thought on the inadequacies of their existing information system" (Nelson and Morgan 1973, p. 30). In addition, the staff's contribution to the information system design should not end with the interviews and the questionnaires; having provided valuable information on the current system, they should now assist in the design of the new system. Ulett et al. (1973) suggest a team approach, in which those who will use the instruments work with the system specialists in the design.

A different approach was used by the author for the development of an information system for the monitoring and evaluation of staff consultation activities. Because no system was currently in use, and because the literature had almost no information on such systems, the first step was to ask staff representatives, by means of personal interview, what they felt should be included. Prior to the interview, a series of questions about the content and timing of the system had been made up, based upon a review of the consultation literature and the author's experience with consultation in this setting. Then staff responses to these questions were used to design a set of forms which essentially included all suggestions. The original staff representatives, plus a new group, were then asked to review these drafts with a critical eye toward the utility of each item. Staff were again interviewed personally, after several weeks for review, and their reactions to the drafts were elicited. No new items were suggested in the second interviews; staff (both treatment and management) found that, critically examining the full range of suggested items, they could select those which they would really use.

The final version, consisting of far fewer items, was then submitted to a 7-month pilot test in four units of the agency. Pilot test participation was on a volunteer basis. Close contact was kept with the units during the course of the pilot test, and comments made in personal contacts and in staff meetings were documented. At pilot test termination, all participating staff completed a detailed questionnaire on the convenience of the forms and on their actual use of the information, and results were used for final revision of the system. Essentially, however, the forms proved to be viable and the information useful to treatment staff, management, or both. The viability and utility of the information system were primarily due, it seems, to the extensive staff input in design and to the role of the evaluator as a stimulus for staff input rather than as sole or even primary source for system design (remembering that this was a fairly simple manual system—in a more complex system the evaluator would of necessity have played a bigger role in design).

Development of an Information System

Experience with information systems and review of the literature demonstrate that time and again certain procedural steps and principles of operation are associated with smoothly running information systems. The concern here is not with the *content* of the system; systematic examination of the purpose(s) of the system and full staff input as suggested in the previous sections should ensure proper content. Nor is the concern with the *format* of the system; insofar as is possible, independent of a specific system, suggestions concerning format are made in the following section. The concern here is with the *process* of operation of the system: with the problems that occur in most systems, regardless of specific design, and with procedures which might help you avoid or minimize those problems. While this discussion by no means includes all potential problems and methods of alleviation (would that it did!), it does include the problem areas that seem to occur frequently, in system after system. They therefore have a high probability of occurring in yours, unless you anticipate them.

There seem to be six general sources of problems during the development of an information system: the time necessary to achieve full system operation, the commitment of management, the process of instituting separate components of the system, the issue of information collected prior to implementation of the new information system, staff preparedness, and quality of the input data.

Time Necessary for Development

The common experience in the development of an information system for a particular setting is that it takes longer than was originally expected and planned for. Elpers and Chapman (1973), St. Clair et al. (1976), and Sletten and Hedlund (1974) all report it to be a time-consuming project which refuses to fit into any objective and preplanned time line. High error rates on input documents, program modifications (as external reporting requirements change) and program debugging, and difficulties in collection of input documents are all mentioned as responsible for increases in planned development time. The most useful messages from this apparently common experience might be first to anticipate needs for a new or revised information system and begin planning as soon as possible; second, double the time necessary for implementation which you obtain from a "no-problem" development; and third, do not make any promises about delivery of information which it would be damaging to break.

Management Commitment

It seems almost too obvious to say that a management information system must have the complete support of management, but it cannot be stressed too much that management commitment is a prerequisite for a viable information system (Elpers and Chapman 1973) and that its all too frequent omission creates our second potential problem area. Smith and Sorensen (1974) point out that top managers will often fail to see the need for their involvement, preferring an uninvolved supportive role instead. This is not sufficient; Lucas (1975) suggests that management has several roles to play, including setting of goals and priorities for information system staff and users, participation in decisions about the information system, provision of needed resources, and influence on users' cooperation and participation (see also Cooper 1973). Ackoff (1971) describes a situation in which a top administrator, on receiving a request for a very costly replacement of the information system equipment, found himself unable to evaluate the request because he knew so little about the system. Assessment of the request by a consultant revealed fairly simple errors in the design of the system which would be relatively inexpensive to eliminate. The errors were of such a nature that the administrator should have been able to find them himself, by asking the right question. Ackoff (1971) concludes that "no MIS should ever be installed unless the managers for whom it is intended are trained to evaluate and hence control it rather than be controlled by it" (p. 268). It seems clear that for a viable information system, management must be knowledgeable about the system and play an integral decisionmaking role in its development and its ongoing implementation; those responsible for system design may have to demand frequent and regular contact with top management to achieve this objective (Rosove 1967).

Implementation of Separate System Components

A third area of potential problems is the implementation of the several components of an information system. In a new organization, with no operational system, there is little choice except to install all components simultaneously.

A decision must be made when a new system has been designed to replace an older one. While it may be very tempting to institute the entire new system at once under the illusion of "starting fresh," experience suggests that components be implemented one at a time and that each component be put into operation only when the previously instituted components are running smoothly and are accepted by users (Lucas 1975). Meanwhile, the original system will be kept running in parallel with the new, as a backup for information while the new system is being debugged. This parallel operation is especially desirable when changing over from a manual to a computerized system.

Cooper (1973) suggests that implementation by "modular increments" has at least three advantages. First, it allows you to assess the adequacy of resources for the information system and to make adjustments prior to installation of the next component if resources appear inadequate. Second, one must assume that the installation of any component will create user problems; fewer problems will occur at the same time when a system is instituted incrementally, and their resolution will be more manageable. Third, there is always the possibility that there is something "fundamentally wrong" with the system. Such flaws are easier to correct if the total system is not yet in operation. The advantages of incremental installation seem to outweigh any advantages of simultaneous installation of all components, although incremental installation is impossible if the new and old systems are too dissimilar (Murdick and Ross 1971). Of course, incremental installation will increase total development time. Furthermore, Cooper stresses that all advantages of incremental installation will be for naught if all users are not aware of this plan from the start. Otherwise, "negative reaction on their part at the time of additions to the system can be disastrous" (Cooper 1973, p. 3).

Inclusion of Previously Collected Information

A fourth source of problems in the developmental process is related to the decision of incremental versus all-at-once installation, that is, what to do with information collected and recorded prior to system implementation. This is especially critical in human service organizations, where treatment decisions and external reporting requirements in particular make necessary the availability of information on the client's admissions variables and previous treatment history at the agency. An agency has essentially two choices. First, at the time of system implementation, staff can be asked to transfer all retrospective information, on currently active clients for example, from the input or output documents of the old system to the input documents of the new system. Although this approach may always be necessary to some extent, it should be avoided as much as possible because it increases the chance for errors in recording and because it may injure the staff's cooperation and morale concerning the new system.

The alternative approach is to have the staff begin to use the new system's input documents as early as possible in the implementation process. If input documents are used several months before the processing capacity of the new system is ready, the worst that can happen is a delay in outputs from the new system; however, if the old system is kept operating in parallel, its outputs can be used. Although some transfer of information will still be necessary, this procedure will keep it to a minimum.

Staff Preparedness

A major problem in the development of a new information system is staff preparedness; lack of staff preparedness can damage the effectiveness of a system more than any other variable. The most obvious means of enhancing staff preparedness is through staff training, but it should not be the sole means: staff preparedness also includes staff input into system design, staff knowledge about a plan for incremental implementation, and staff awareness of the plan for a new system from its inception. Staff preparedness, including staff training, affects system operation in at least two ways. First, the adequacy of training will immediately show up in errors in input documents and in incomprehensible output documents. Murdick and Ross (1971) feel that poor staff training is a chief cause of problems in initial system implementation, and "if the training has been superficial, mass confusion may result" (p. 520). The second result of poor staff preparedness is a drop in morale and a loss of a cooperative atmosphere among staff. If morale drops, resulting carelessness will show up in an increase in errors on input documents. Feedback on the number of errors may cause a further decrease. It's a vicious circle, and it is best to not get into it at all. Prepare and involve the staff throughout the planning and development, and most importantly, provide good staff training.

Several procedures improve staff training. Staff should be trained in small groups, and each group should include only staff from similar units or modalities. Heterogeneous training groups, with different modalities represented in each, appear to impede training. Ideally, staff who have participated in the planning and development of the system should conduct training, as they can best anticipate problems and questions. Examples should be used heavily in training and should include both typical and atypical cases. While *each* staff member should have available a manual with all training information in it, this manual should never, either as a whole or in part, replace actual training sessions. If training is replaced by a manual that staff are asked to read, then they are being asked to train themselves. Training is the responsibility of the planning and development group, not of individual staff members, and it is this group's task to set aside staff time for training, rather than asking staff to do it themselves.

Training does not end with initial training sessions, but continues until errors are at an acceptable level. The two most essential elements of training seem to be the actual experience of using the input documents and follow-up. It is a good idea to schedule a training session after the first cycle of input document use, when staff will be in a position to ask informed and pragmatic questions. [See Cline, Freeman, and Wheeler (1968) for an example of this training procedure in a detached-worker delinquency program.] Until an acceptable error rate is achieved, follow-up on errors should be immediate; this forestalls more errors of the same type by the staff member, and learning is enhanced when feedback follows the error closely. Anticipate a substantial amount of time for such feedback initially, and assign one or more training staff the responsibility and the time for feedback. Feedback is most effective in person or by telephone, followed by a memo; use of a memo alone increases the time between error and feedback and has less impact.

Quality Control of Data Input

A sixth potential cause for problems is the degree to which plans are made to monitor data, or the quality control of data. It seems to be true that no matter how thorough training has been or how cooperative the staff, monitoring is necessary for complete and accurate data. St. Clair et al. (1976, p. 13) reported that only after "a variety of rather fierce meetings and memos from the administration" and "continuous monitoring" of feedback reports by supervisors, did error rates drop substantially. Spitzer and Endicott (1971) report that because of thorough training, they anticipated a need for minimal monitoring. Instead, "because of the 'human condition' a fairly elaborate system of editing [was] necessary" (p. 546). It was mentioned earlier that training must not be a one-shot affair, but must continue as the staff begins to participate in the information system. Monitoring is necessary both to "upgrade" staff skills and to guard against the "human" errors of even experienced staff.

This monitoring should take place continuously, on all input documents, to minimize the delay between initial recording of the error and notice of need for correction. The greater the delay, the greater the difficulty in correcting the error and the greater the possibility of a replacement of the first error by a second. For example, a treatment staff member who neglects to record his activities for 2 hours on his daily log sheet is more apt to reply "I don't know" or to fabricate some activity if asked to fill in the omission several weeks rather than several days later. A maximum allowable delay should be established.

Furthermore, monitoring must be for omissions, inaccuracies, and inconsistencies. The criterion of "logical relationships" among items (see Rosove 1967) might be used to establish standards for inconsistencies. Nealey, Taber, and Nealey (1976) report very poor agreement between patients' self-reports of previous contacts with community agencies (on hospital and clinic records) and the records of the community agencies. Disagreement was due to *omissions* on hospital and clinic records. Bloom (1972) reports a 15 percent rate in logic errors, most of which were due to incomplete reporting (such as discharge of a client with no admission record on that client). Time will have to be spent during the system development in establishing objective standards for each class of errors—omissions, inaccuracies, and inconsistencies—and in setting rejection standards. For example, omission on critical items might automatically mean rejection of the input document, whereas omission on noncritical items might not indicate rejection until there were three such errors.

Monitoring can and should be carried out at more than one level. In a decentralized agency, for example, a clerk in each unit might monitor all input documents before they left the particular unit, and he would place his signature on each errorless document. The documents would again be checked at the central repository before a third monitoring at the time of processing. Whereas some might criticize two stages of monitoring prior to processing as unnecessary, experience indicates otherwise; both Bloom (1972) and St. Clair et al. (1976) report rejection rates at the time of processing despite "front-end" monitoring. It is clear that adequate monitoring will require a substantial allocation of staff time (although this can almost certainly be decreased with time), and management should be required to allocate sufficient staff *and* to designate responsibility for timely and comprehensive monitoring.

Useful Suggestions on Procedural Details

Procedural details of an information system can have a surprising impact on the completeness and accuracy of the input documents and on the utilization of the information. For example, if a program's documents have traditionally been sized 8½ X 11 inches and new documents of a size 8½ X 14 inches are introduced, storage problems may result in inaccessible storage and hence decrease the utilization. Or, if item codes are given in a manual rather than on the back of an input document, inaccuracies may occur because treatment staff do not always have the time to look up the code definitions; another consequence might be overreliance on a few categories. Interestingly, a review of others' experiences in instituting information systems indicates that again and again the same procedural details are found to be important. While many of them seem to be of a "commonsense" variety, this by no means lessens their importance or suggests that anyone developing and instituting a new system will think of them. Therefore, in the interests of helping others avoid learning by trial and error, those procedural details which experience suggests are important are discussed below.

Admissions

Objective criteria will have to be established of persons to be considered clients, and decisions must be made about the information to be recorded on nonintakes.

For those programs participating in the CODAP system, the definition of a client is quite specific in the *CODAP National Management Handbook* (1974). Person (1969, pp. 11-12) suggests that an agency may see several other categories of people as well (categories 1 and 2 are traditional clients):

3. People seen in the course of treating someone else. (These people have been called "collaterals.")
4. People in service programs which are not considered treatment but which are a part of the center program.
5. People who receive consultation as a service to another agency, physician, or professional, or as a self-referred emergency, but who are referred elsewhere and are not entered into the center program.
6. People identified by some part of the center program as individuals but who do not receive direct services.

In considering the information to be recorded on nonclients, the time spent by treatment staff on nonclient activities and the focus of that activity are important factors. For example, if one staff member of a drug abuse treatment program spends a considerable amount of time on consultation with personnel of non-drug abuse programs (Person's category 6) advising them on referrals, and if the individuals to be referred remain the responsibility of the non-drug abuse program personnel, then the focus might be considered to be the personnel of the second program, and not the individuals to be referred. In this case, there would be no need for an input document on those individuals, but the number of individuals discussed per consultation session might be recorded. A second common category consists of individuals who are processed through intake and accepted as clients but who subsequently drop out and thus never receive direct service. Information on these individuals might be retained on the hypothesis that they may show up again, although they should not be considered active clients. A third category of frequent staff-individual contacts consists of requests for information, usually from a front-line secretary; because the concern is not with individuals, a simple count can be kept of the requests (see Lehman, Struening, and Darling 1969). All possible categories should be anticipated, and decisions as to documentation should be made prior to implementation, to avoid staff confusion and different interpretations.

Services Delivered

The methods of recording the nature and extent of services delivered to clients must be developed. Documentation of services delivered can proceed in one of two directions: a focus on staff activities or a focus on individual client treatment. If the focus is on staff activities, staff will usually keep a daily log, on which they will record all work-related activities, identifying any services concerning an individual client by means of that client's identification name or number [see Kurke and Van Houdnos (1974); Person (1969); St. Clair, Silver, and Spivack (1975); and Smith and Sorensen (1974) for examples of such documents and useful discussions of their use]. If the information system is computerized, data on services delivered to individual clients can be easily transferred to a client document, for a history of services received and for billing purposes.

However, the staff activities method can be burdensome for manual systems, and the second approach, a focus on individual client treatment, is recommended for manual systems. In this approach the delivery of service to an individual client is recorded on a separate form for each service delivered; this form can then be placed in the client's medical jacket, for a documentation of service history, and used as a basis for individual client billing. Elpers and Chapman (1973) describe the use of a "services rendered document," with three copies. One is the client's and serves as a record of treatment, an appointment slip (for the next session), and receipt for payment. A second copy stays with the service unit, and a third copy goes to central data processing. A variation is used for group therapy, but since there is one form, the client does not receive a copy. Lehman, Struening, and Darling (1969) report use of a similar "service-rendered" form, which the treatment staff complete even when "anything is done on the client's behalf without the client actually being present" (p. 130). This approach allows multiple copies, as many as are needed to provide information for the different purposes the information system must serve (Cooper 1973).

Staff Activities

Staff activities can, of course, be monitored by means of the first approach outlined under Services Delivered above. Program management needs, however, may require monitoring of staff activities in those programs using an individual client services-rendered form. Staff time sheets on a periodic, rather than continuous, basis may satisfy these needs and will also minimize duplicate recording of activities by the staff (on a services-rendered form and on a time sheet). Smith and Sorensen (1974) describe a "random moment staff activity" study, in which staff were telephoned on a random basis over a 4-week period and questioned about their current activity. Comparison to a continuous self-report system revealed only small differences in results, indicating reporting on a noncontinuous basis yields valid information. Flaherty and Martin (1976) describe use of periodic staff reporting in which staff complete time sheets for one month every 6 months. In a manual information system, in which individual service-rendered forms seem to be most efficient, periodic reporting of staff activities requires minimal staff effort and yields useful information for program management.

Format of Input Documents

The makeup of the input documents themselves has a surprising impact on staff receptivity and on quality of recording. Information should be coded whenever possible; if the relevant categories are unknown, interviewing of treatment staff or a brief pilot test will provide the needed information (Sells 1975). The time necessary to categorize free responses and the loss of data because of inappropriate responses outweigh the advantages of free response flexibility. Code definitions should be on the input document itself, not in a separate manual; if there is insufficient room on the front, definitions can be on the back of the form. Cooper (1973) suggests that important items not have an "unknown" category, because inclusion of such a category sometimes reinforces a tendency on the part of some staff to lessen their effort to obtain the information.

Using different colors for different input documents is a useful means of increasing form recognition (Kaplan and Smith 1974). However, because colored forms do not always reproduce well, consider having color solely on the margin or corner (Kramer and Nemec 1962). Use carbons rather than reproduction for copies, as reproducing will introduce a delay and may result in poor copies. Input documents should be sized for convenient storage in client medical jackets; if sizes vary, an 8½ × 11 inch format is a better choice than 8½ × 14 inches.

Information Utilization

All too often, we come upon the depressing report that information produced by a management information system is not used. Because we should all agree that the purpose of developing a system is *not* to have the most technologically efficient and smoothly running system in existence, but rather to provide useful information, the universality of these findings is indeed depressing. Lucas (1975) suggests why information is not used by its intended users:

According to this research, users do not understand much of the ouput they receive; there is duplication of input and output, and changes are frequently made in systems without consulting users. Because of inaccuracies, users often discount all of the information provided by a system. Many users complain of information overload; massive amounts of data are provided which cannot be digested by the decision-maker. There are also many complaints about the difficulty of obtaining changes in existing systems. A number of users report that they do not actually use the information provided by an information system (pp. 2–3).

Pollack, Windle, and Wurster (1974) and Feldman (1973) each feel that underutilization of information produced by systems is one of the major problems these systems face.

Thus, the critical question for anyone involved in the development of an information system is whether there are any means of increasing utilization, which we can expect to be low under normal circumstances. Or do staff all have personal styles which are negatively associated with information utilization (Lucas 1975)? It is hard to believe that personalities of management and treatment staff are so monolithic!

User's Attitude toward the Information System

A major determinant of information utilization is the user's attitude toward and perception of the information system (Lucas 1975). Findings were reported in a previous section (Staff Attitudes and Input) which suggested that staff input and involvement during the development of a system had a very favorable impact on staff attitudes. This, then, is another cogent reason for representation of all staff components in the planning and development; it can be expected to produce more positive attitudes toward the system and to increase utilization. It seems rather obvious that a system developed by those staff who will be using its output will probably be designed to produce output useful to the staff, but this operating principle has been too often neglected.

Location of Information

A second determinant of utilization is also glaringly apparent and embarassingly simplistic, but we have seen it too often ignored: the location of the information, whether it be recorded input documents or processed outputs. Kramer and Nemec (1962) suggest that location be established by priority of the various purposes of the information system. For example, if a primary purpose was to improve the quality of service delivery, then *each* treatment staff member should have the information he needs; storage in a centralized location, such as a secretary's office, would not be sufficient. A relationship is often found between information availability and information use; staff to whom records are most readily accessible use them the most. The apparently superficial decision of the location of recorded input documents and of processed outputs should not be made lightly, for it will influence utilization.

The Outputs

The third determinant of information utilization is deceivingly simplistic: the processed outputs. It is deceivingly simplistic because the production of well-utilized outputs is a complex process, and not easily achieved. The process has two aspects: the determination of the information to be conveyed on the outputs and the format of the outputs.

The procedure for determining output information begins with the very first stage of system planning, when decisions about the purposes of the system are being made. (The concern here is not with outputs for external utilization, such as external reporting requirements.) For example, two procedures were suggested for determining management needs for information: review of past decisions and anticipation of future decisions. These procedures should yield both particular items to be included on input documents and information (including item relationships) to appear on outputs. Management and staff should, as much as possible, dictate the information needed for decisionmaking, and the system designers (often the program evaluators) should refrain from suggestions, but should only seek to clarify the staff requests for information. Mock-ups of outputs can and should be used to obtain reaction, but only after staff has specified information to be used in the mock-ups. Premature use of mock-ups, with the system designers selecting information, should be avoided; such mock-ups may influence staff thinking too much. The process of eliciting desired information from staff will probably be time-consuming and sometimes frustrating, but it is essential to utilization of system information. The process may be made easier by examination of outputs generated by other similar systems (for examples see Cochran and DuPont 1973; Elpers and Chapman 1973; Smith 1975; and Smith and Sorensen 1974), but this examination should be judicious and limited to avoid undue influence.

Specification of desired output information should be accompanied by timing specifications, or frequency with which the information will be used and thus needed. If outputs are to be released at periodic intervals on an ongoing basis, there should be an agreement to review (at a specific time in the future) the relevance and need for these outputs. Outputs should not be allowed to continue in existence because they were once desired; their utility should be regularly reviewed to avoid information overload for the user.

The second aspect of the outputs is their format; this is primarily the responsibility of the system designers rather than of the users. Weinstein (1975) offers a set of five output dichotomies which will be useful in this design process: periodic versus ad hoc, printed versus machine-readable, statistical tabulation versus listing, numerical versus listing, and tables versus graphs. Each dichotomy has its place, and each output should be designed independently of the others, in order to ascertain the most effective format for the particular output. Raw computer printouts, using computer codes, should be avoided. Kaplan and Smith (1974) suggest that reports should be self-explanatory, so that even the inexperienced user need not use a manual or code book to understand them. The user who must look up table headings in a code book may decide not to bother, and hence will not use that information.

This discussion of utilization should close with Feldman's (1973) caveat that we not assume automatically that information utilization improves decisionmaking:

I may be overly skeptical about the decision making process in mental health (and in other fields as well . . .) but I am not convinced that the availability of more information will improve either the process itself or the quality of the decision . . . In fact, it seems to me that where management information does have a role in decision making, it is most frequently used to justify decisions already made, rather than to help make new ones (p. 41).

The message may be that only if we try, as system designers, to develop systems which will produce utilized information, can we find out if Feldman is right or wrong.

Confidentiality

A discussion of management information systems is not complete without mention of confidentiality, but justice cannot be done to this enormously complex problem in a format such as this. The issues of confidentiality are quite different in computerized and manual systems, and different kinds of precautions must be taken in each type of system. Confidentiality in computerized information systems has received much attention lately; the interested reader can begin with Laska and Bank (1975), Miller (1971), and Noble (1971).

The difficulties in safeguarding the confidentiality of information may be greater in manual systems, because the stored data is in theory meaningful and accessible to anyone, whereas in a computerized system accessibility requires sophisticated knowledge of the particular system. Confidentiality can be protected to an extent by the use of codes instead of individual client names. Care must be taken that cross-reference information between code numbers and names remain in the hands of a very few specified staff members. In the CODAP system for all drug abuse treatment programs that receive federal funds, code numbers are used for individual clients, and the information for cross-referencing remains in the program or clinic (Siguel and Spillane 1976). A "charge-out" system should be used for removal of either completed input documents or outputs with client numbers, in which anyone removing a document must sign his name in a ledger left with someone responsible for the particular documents. Compromises may have to be made in procedures designed to enhance information utilization, in order to safeguard confidentiality. Arrangements should be made for the supervised shredding or burning of outdated documents, and someone should be designated personally responsible for the operation.

Conclusion

A hidden objective in the writing of this chapter was to assist others to avoid those pitfalls in the development of information systems which the author, and so many others, have fallen into. The pattern of common pitfalls encountered by so many and the frequency with which similar suggestions are made for their avoidance suggest that the development of an information system is not a process which is idiosyncratic to each situation. Only when we learn from the experience of others and develop effective information systems can we begin to answer the crucial question raised by Feldman (1973): Does the use of information improve decisionmaking by management and treatment staff?

Note

1. Author's example: a red flag might occur whenever a waiting list was longer than an acceptable criterion or whenever a staff member's no-show rates exceeded a norm.

References

Ackoff, Russell. "Management Misinformation Systems." In *Information Technology in a Democracy*, edited by Alan F. Westin. Cambridge, Mass.: Harvard University Press, 1971.

Alvarez, Rodolfo, and Moore, Wilbert E. "Information-flow within the Professions: Some Selective Comparisons of Law, Medicine and Nursing." In *On Record: Files and Dossiers in American Life*, edited by Stanton Wheeler. New York: Russell Sage Foundation, 1969.

Amos, Edward D.; DuPont, Robert L.; and Lau, John P. "The Management of Large Multimodality, Multiclinic Drug Treatment Programs and Management Information Systems." *Proceedings of Fifth National Conference on Methadone Treatment*, Washington, D.C., March 17–19, 1973.

Astrachan, Boris M. "MSIS Input to Administrative Decision Making." In *Safeguarding Psychiatric Privacy: Computer Systems and Their Users*, edited by Eugene Laska and Rheta Bank. New York: Wiley, 1975.

Bloom, Bernard L. "Human Accountability in a Community Mental Health Center: Report of an Automated System." *Community Mental Health Journal* 8 (4) 251–60, 1972.

Bonstedt, Theodor. "Concrete Goal-setting for Patients in a Day Hospital." *Evaluation*, Special Monograph No. 1, 3–5, 1973.

Client Oriented Data Acquisition Process (CODAP) National Management Handbook. National Institute on Drug Abuse, 11400 Rockville Pike, Rockville, Md. 20852, November 1974.

Cline, Hugh F.; Freeman, Howard E.; and Wheeler, Stanton. "The Analysis and Evaluation of Detached-worker Programs." In *Controlling Delinquents*, edited by Stanton Wheeler. New York: Wiley, 1968.

Cochran, David A., and DuPont, Robert L. "A Statistical History of the Narcotics Treatment Administration," *Proceedings of Fifth National Conference on Methadone Treatment*, Washington, D.C., March 17-19, 1973.

Cooper, E. Myles. *Guidelines for a Minimum Statistical and Accounting System for Community Mental Health Centers*. National Institute of Mental Health, Mental Health Statistics, Series C, No. 7, DHEW Publication No. (ADM) 74-14, 1973.

Crawford, Jeffrey L. "Computer Applications in Mental Health: A Review." In *Progress in Mental Health Information Systems: Computer Application*, edited by Jeffrey L. Crawford, Donald W. Morgan, and Daniel T. Gianturco. Cambridge, Mass.: Ballinger Publishing Co., J. B. Lippincott Company, 1974.

——— · Morgan, Donald W., and Gianturco, Daniel T. *Progress in Mental Health Information Systems: Computer Applications*. Cambridge, Mass.: Ballinger Publishing Co., J. B. Lippincott Comapny, 1974.

Ellis, Richard H. and Wilson, Nancy C. Z. "Evaluating Treatment Effectiveness Using a Goal-oriented Automated Progress Rate." *Evaluation*, Special Monograph No. 1, 6-11, 1973.

Elpers, John R., and Chapman, Robert L. "Management Information for Mental Health Services." *Administration in Mental Health*, Fall 1973, 12-25.

Feldman, Saul. "Editorial Comments." *Administration in Mental Health*, 1973, 39-41.

Flaherty, Eugenie W., and Martin, Frances. "The Utility of a Daily Log Used at Periodic Intervals." *Research and Evaluation Report No. 42*, Hahnemann Community Mental Health/Mental Retardation Center, Philadelphia, Pennsylvania 1976.

Honigfeld, Gilbert, and Klein, Donald F. "The Hillside Hospital Patient Progress Record: Explorations in Clinical Management by Objective and Exception." *Evaluation* Special Monograph No. 1, 19-22, 1973.

Hornstra, Robijn K., and Tritt, Francis L. "Western Missouri Mental Health Center." In *Community Mental Health Center Data Systems*, edited by Carl A. Taube. National Institute of Mental Health, Mental Health Statistics, Series C, No. 2, Public Health Service Publication No. 1990, 1969.

Kaplan, Jeffrey M., and Smith, William G. "An Evaluation Program for a Regional Mental Health Center." In *Progress in Mental Health Information Systems—Computer Applications*, edited by Jeffrey L. Crawford, Donald W. Morgan, and Daniel T. Gianturco. Cambridge, Mass.: Ballinger Publishing Co., J. B. Lippincott Company, 1974.

Kiresuk, Thomas J. "Goal Attainment Scaling at a County Mental Health Service." *Evaluation* Special Monograph No. 1, 12-18, 1973.

Kiresuk, Thomas J. and Sherman, Robert E. "Goal Attainment Scaling: A General Method for Evaluating Comprehensive Community Mental Health Programs." *Community Mental Health Journal* 4 (6): 443-53, 1968.

Klonoff, Harry, and Clark, Campbell. "Measuring Staff Attitudes toward Computerization." *Hospital and Community Psychiatry* 26 (12): 823-25, 1975.

Kramer, Morton, and Nemec, Frances C. *A Guide to Recordkeeping in Mental Hospitals.* National Institute of Mental Health, Biometrics Branch, October 1962.

Kurke, Lewis, and Van Houdnos, Harry. "Staff Activity Reporting From the Bottom up." In *Progress in Mental Health Information Systems: Computer Applications,* edited by Jeffrey L. Crawford, Donald W. Morgan, and Daniel T. Gianturco. Cambridge, Mass.: Ballinger Publishing Co., J. B. Lippincott Company, 1974.

Laska, Eugene M., and Bank, Rheta, eds. *Safeguarding Psychiatric Privacy: Computer Systems and Their Uses.* New York: Wiley, 1975.

Lehman, Stanley; Struening, Elmer L.; and Darling, M. E. "The Development of SARK: An Automated Record System for Neighborhood Service Centers." In *Community Mental Health Center Data Systems,* edited by Carl A. Taube. National Institute of Mental Health, Mental Health Statistics, Series C, No. 2, Public Health Service Publication No. 1990, 1969.

Lucas, Henry C. *Why Information Systems Fail.* New York and London: Columbia University Press, 1975.

Miller, Arthur D. *The Assault on Privacy—Computers, Data Banks, and Dossiers.* Ann Arbor, Mich.: University of Michigan Press, 1971.

Morgan, Donald W., and Crawford, Jeffrey L. "Some Issues in Computer Applications." In *Progress in Mental Health Information Systems: Computer Applications,* edited by Jeffrey L. Crawford, Donald W. Morgan, and Daniel T. Gianturco. Cambridge, Mass.: Ballinger Publishing Co., J. B. Lippincott Co., 1974.

Murdick, Robert G., and Ross, Joel E. *Information Systems for Modern Management.* Englewood Cliffs, N.J.: Prentice-Hall, 1971.

Nealey, Vicki; Taber, Merlin; and Nealey, Stanley M. "How Accurate Are Client Reports?" *Administration in Mental Health,* 3 (2): 186-92, 1976.

Nelson, Carl, and Morgan, Lawrence. "The Information System of a Community Mental Health Center." *Administration in Mental Health,* Fall 1973, 26-38.

Noble, John H. "Protecting the Public's Privacy in Computerized Health and Welfare Information Systems." *Social Work* 16 (1971): 35-41.

Person, Philip H. *A Statistical Information System for Community Mental Health Centers.* National Institute of Mental Health, Mental Health Statistics, Series C., No. 1, U.S. Public Health Service Publication No. 1863, 1973.

Pollack, Earl S.; Windle, Charles D.; and Wurster, Cecil R. "Psychiatric Information Systems: An Historical Perspective." In *Progress in Mental Health Information Systems: Computer Applications*, edited by Jeffrey L. Crawford, Donald W. Morgan, and Daniel T. Gianturco. Cambridge, Mass.: Ballinger Publishing Co., J. B. Lippincott Company, 1974.

Reznikoff, Marvin; Holland, Charles H.; and Stroebel, Charles F. "Attitudes toward Computers among Employees of a Psychiatric Hospital." *Mental Hygiene* 51 (1967): 419-25.

Rosove, Perry E. *Developing Computer-Based Information Systems*. New York: Wiley, 1967.

St. Clair, Catherine H.; Silver, Maurice J.; and Spivack, George. "An Instrument to Assess Staff Time Utilization in a Community Mental Health Center." *Community Mental Health Journal* 11 (4): 371-80, 1975.

St. Clair, Catherine H., et al. "Allocating Time and Manpower to Computerize a CMHC Information System." *Research and Evaluation Report No. 41*, Hahnemann Community Mental Health/Mental Retardation Center, Philadelphia, Pennsylvania 1976.

Seaberg, James R. "Case Recording by Code." *Social Work*, 10 (1965): 92-99.

———. "Systematized Recording: A Follow-up." *Social Work* 15 (1970): 32-41.

Sells, S. B. "Techniques of Outcome Evaluation in Alcohol, Drug Abuse, and Mental Health Programs." In *Program Evaluation—Alcohol, Drug Abuse, and Mental Health Services*, edited by Jack Zusman and Cecil R. Wurster. Lexington, Mass.: Lexington Books, D.C. Heath and Company, 1975.

Siguel, Eduardo N., and Spillane, William H. *The Client-Oriented Data Acquisition Process (CODAP)*. National Institute on Drug Abuse (NIDA), Washington, D.C., July 1976.

Sletten, Ivan W., and Hedlund, James L. "The Missouri Automated Standard System of Psychiatry: Current Status, Special Problems, and Future Plans." In *Progress in Mental Health Information Systems: Computer Applications*, edited by Jeffrey L. Crawford, Donald W. Morgan, and Daniel T. Gianturco. Cambridge, Mass.: Ballinger Publishing Co.; J. B. Lippincott Company, 1974.

Smith, Todd S., and Sorensen, James E. *Integrated Management Information Systems for Community Mental Health Centers*. National Institute of Mental Health, DHEW Publication No. (ADM) 75-165, 1974.

Smith, William G. "The Ideal and the Real: Practical Approaches and Techniques in Evaluation." In *Program Evaluation—Alcohol, Drug Abuse and Mental Health Services*, edited by Jack Zusman and Cecil R. Wurster, Lexington, Mass.: Lexington Books, D.C. Heath and Company, 1975.

Spitzer, Robert L., and Endicott, Jean. "An Integrated Group of Forms for Automated Psychiatric Case Records." *Archives of General Psychiatry* 24(1971): 540–47.

Suchman, E. A. *Evaluative Research*. New York: Russell Sage Foundation, 1967.

Taube, Carl. *Community Mental Health Center Data Systems*. National Institute of Mental Health, Mental Health Statistics, Series C, No. 2, Public Health Service Publication No. 1990, 1969.

Truitt, Ethel I., and Binner, Paul R. "The Fort Logan Mental Health Center." In *Community Mental Health Center Data Systems*, edited by Carl A. Taube. National Institute of Mental Health, Mental Health Statistics, Series C, No. 2, Public Health Service Publication No. 1990, 1969.

Ulett, George A., et al. "Realities and Prospects for the Use of Computers in Psychiatric Hospital Management." *Psychiatric Annals* 3 (1): 27–53, 1973.

Weinstein, Abbott S. "Evaluation through Medical Records and Related Information Systems." In *Handbook of Evaluation Research*. vol. 1. Edited by Elmer L. Struening and Marcia Guttentag. Beverley Hills, Calif.: Sage Publications, 1975.

Wilner, Daniel M. "Evaluation: State of the Technical Art." In *Program Evaluation—Alcohol, Drug Abuse, and Mental Health Services*, edited by Jack Zusman and Cecil R. Wurster. Lexington, Mass.: Lexington Books, D. C. Heath and Company, 1975.

Wolford, Jack A., and Keller, Dorothy S. "Western Psychiatric Institute and Clinic." In *Community Mental Health Center Data Systems*, edited by Carl A. Taube. National Institute of Mental Health, Mental Health Statistics, Series C, No. 2, Public Health Service Publication No. 1990, 1969.

**Evaluating Outcome in Correctional
Drug Abuse Rehabilitation
Programs**
Jonathan A. Morell

Introduction

Drug abuse rehabilitation must be an important element of any program that is seriously interested in correctional rehabilitation. This is so because of the large number of offenders who are also drug abusers and also because of the extent to which the drug abuse culture and the criminal life-style are so inextricably intermeshed. This intermeshing may involve a causal relationship between drug abuse and criminal activity, as in the case of an addicted individual without an adequate source of income; or it may simply reflect an overlap between two life-styles which is brought about by a variety of cultural and sociological factors. In either case, drug abuse is often a large and an important part of the life of many criminals. If a correctional rehabilitation program is to succeed, it must also deal with the problem of drug abuse which either causes, or is an important element in, the life-style of many offenders. This chapter will deal with the evaluation of drug abuse programs. It is predicated on the assumption that valid evaluation of a program's impact on its members is essential to the improvement of rehabilitation services. Without such feedback, intelligent planning for the improvement of services is impossible.

Although the focus of interest of the chapter is on drug abuse rehabilitation programs that occur in the context of the correctional system, the analysis which will be presented will deal with drug abuse rehabilitation programs in general. This is because the issues involved are common to all such programs, and there is little point in needlessly limiting the applicability of the discussion.

The present analysis will look at the problem of outcome evaluation in drug abuse rehabilitation from two different angles. The first will be a general methodological critique of evaluation designs that are currently in use, as well as suggestions for improvement. The theme of this section will be ways to increase knowledge about where a program has succeeded or failed and how to improve our knowledge of such matters. The second section will discuss in detail each of the approaches to outcome evaluation that are actually practiced in the field, and will deal with both the specific types of information that each approach can yield and the disadvantages of each method.

The first section (the methodological critique) will be (almost) equally applicable to each of the approaches that make up the second part of the discussion. By combining the information in each section the reader will be able to obtain an understanding of the elements of good outcome evaluation design, and of how those elements can be applied to the different approaches to outcome evaluation that are actually practiced in the area of drug abuse.

A Critique of Outcome Evaluation Research in
Drug Abuse Rehabilitation

Current outcome research in drug abuse can be classified into three categories.[1]

Follow-up: This type of evaluation attempts to assess a drug rehabilitation program by studying the program's past members (Adams et al. 1971; Langenauer and Bowden 1971; Stephens and Cottrell 1972).

Client-type Comparisons: The major concern of this type of research is a comparison of the effects of treatment on different subpopulations of drug abuse program members and, occasionally, between drug abusers and nonabusers (Gasser et al. 1974; Levine et al. 1972; Paulus and Halliday 1967; Pittel et al. 1972; Price and Jackson 1974; Renault 1973; Schut, Wohlmuth, and File 1973; Sheffet et al. 1973; Toomey 1974).

Treatment Modality Tests: The relative effectiveness of different treatment modalities is compared (De Leon, Skodol, and Rosenthal 1973; Dole, Nyswander, and Warner 1968; Gearing 1971; Rosenberg, Davidson, and Patch 1972; Sugarman 1974).[2]

A survey of the drug abuse literature in each of these categories leaves one with the distinct impression that most outcome evaluation research in the field of drug abuse rehabilitation represents minor variations on a single theme in research design, to wit:

Dependent Variables. The dependent variables used in most drug rehabilitation evaluations are drug use, program attendance, dropout rate, employment/school behavior, illegal activity, and "psychological adjustment" as measured by scales of psychopathology (MMPI, EPI, depression scales, etc.—this class of variable is far less common than the first five on the list.)

Independent Variables. Treatment in toto, or at best, a comparison between two large, complex, and ill-defined treatment modalities.

Control Groups. None. (There are occasional attempts at comparing drug abusing and non-drug-abusing populations.)

Assignment to "Conditions": Anything but random.

Each of these elements will now be discussed with a focus on the practical problem of increasing the efficacy of drug abuse rehabilitation programs.

Dependent Variables

Evaluation in Terms of the Process of Rehabilitation. Clients in drug abuse treatment programs are asked to make fundamental changes in their needs, priorities, and ways of life. In essence, they are asked to undergo profound changes in their behavior and in the psychological structures that underlie their behavior. (In this sense the problem is similar for many types of therapy or rehabilitation.) Drug use, illegal activity, and employment/school behavior are all very fundamental aspects of an individual's existence. Program compliance variables are not quite as fundamental, but they are undoubtedly tied to aspects of behavior that are well rooted. Although hard evaluation of drug abuse treatment is almost entirely lacking, the consensus of opinion of those working in the field is that treatment has little or no effect (Bourne 1974). Given the profundity of the change that treatment is supposed to bring about, this conclusion is by no means surprising. In effect, we are using relatively weak "experimental manipulations" and expecting them to effect outcome variables that are *highly* resistant to change. In the meantime, subtle but potentially important effects go undetected, and all information concerning the *process* of change is lost.

The implicit assumption in the preceding statement is that treatment can ultimately be improved by an understanding of the psychological and sociological process that underlies constructive rehabilitation change. Whether this assumption is true is certainly an unresolved matter that is open to empirical investigation. It may well be that drug abuse rehabilitation as we know it simply cannot do what we want done, just as one cannot expect penicillin to cure a viral infection. The case, however, is far from settled, and part of the uncertainty is due to our poor choice of dependent variables in previous research and evaluation. Because we do not collect information on the psychological and sociological process of rehabilitation, we never know if a rehabilitation effort is moving in the right direction or how it might be improved. We know that we are not effecting profound change in our clients, and we have no feedback as to how to better our efforts. We also know (from advances in other fields) that using information about the process of change does offer hope for the development of improved drug abuse rehabilitation programs. In order to obtain the needed information on the change process, however, we must include in our research dependent variables that reflect subtle and/or small changes in a client's thinking and functioning. But how to choose the "correct" dependent variables? There are, after all, an infinite number of possibilities, and we cannot collect and analyze data on all of them. The solution is to be guided by theory. ("Theory" is used here in its broadest sense, i.e., some idea or explanation of why the rehabilitation process works in a particular manner.) Unless one starts out with a preconceived sense of how the rehabilitation process works, it is impossible to make an intelligent choice as to which dependent variables should be studied. The object, of course, is to start out with that guide (i.e., theory) that one expects will be of greatest help in choosing those variables that best indicate the process of constructive rehabilitation change.

Now consider some examples of theories which suggest dependent variables that might help improve drug abuse rehabilitation. These examples are not intended as a comprehensive list but merely as illustrations of how the use of theory can generate dependent variables which yield information on the rehabilitation change process. They are presented with the following assumptions in mind. First, the treatment context is a typical drug abuse program. Second, the goals of treatment are (1) elimination of illegal activity, (2) elimination of illicit drug use, (3) promoting constructive employment and/or school behavior, (4) promoting good program attendance, and (5) preventing clients from dropping out of the program. Third, there is an underlying process that can be used to understand a person's behavior in terms of meeting or not meeting these goals. Fourth, understanding the process must be attempted by making an intelligent guess as to the nature of the process, and then carrying out systematic attempts at substantiating that guess.

The first example derives from "social learning theory" or, more generally, the modern view of attempting to predict behavior from a knowledge of internal states (Mischel 1973). This view contends that individuals act within an ever-changing social context in which they make specific cognitive and behavioral choices, and that people are active, thinking, information-processing beings. Since in terms of subjective perceptions no two situations are exactly alike, one should not assume consistency of behavior across situations. Further, one's unique learning history dictates how one will perceive and define a situation. The key to understanding how a person will make such choices lies in an understanding of what the situation means to him or her in terms of willingness to exert effort, potential payoffs, personal needs, and perceptions of the situation. With such an orientation one might collect information on the following dependent variables: First, what do people really want from a program? Congruence between personal needs and services rendered may have much to do with keeping people in treatment, affecting their attitudes toward the goals of the program, their willingness to participate, and similar "program attitude" variables. Second, do those who stay in a program change their needs to conform to what the program can give, or do initial needs remain inflexible? Such information would be very useful in differentiating between potentially successful and unsuccessful clients. Third, to what extent do these "need-program" congruence factors affect measures other than attendance and dropout? A person may be satisfied enough to stay in a program but not satisfied enough to work at rehabilitation. Fourth, how well are each of a client's needs being met by the program? Do all needs have to be met very well? Moderately well? What if a person's main concerns are being met moderately well, but his or her secondary concerns are being met very well? It is obvious that a client will stay in a program if his or her needs are being met, but do different patterns of meeting these needs make a difference? Fifth, how difficult does a person perceive the task of meeting his or her rehabilitation goals, and can a program affect those perceptions? Sixth, what is the subjective value of success in treatment? How diffuse or differentiated is the client's perception of that value? Can those perceptions be changed as a result of treatment? Seventh, what are the sources of external pressure that are keeping a person in treatment? Family? Legal? Self-motivation? Quality of street drugs? How strong are these pressures? The greater the number of strong pressures, the greater the probability that a person will stay in treatment. It is not likely that any single source of pressure will stay consistently high for long periods of time. For long-term sustained pressure many different sources are needed.

The second example involves the "social support" theory of community mental health (Caplan 1973). The essence of this theory is that successful treatment in any community mental health context is dependent upon the network of social support that surrounds the client. Thus a program would ask its clients questions such as: How many of your friends use drugs? How many are in treatment? Do your friends and relatives support or oppose your getting treatment? Do you have friends in the program with you? How much time do you spend with straight people, ex-addicts, drug abusers, etc.? Do your children know about your drug use? Do they approve or disapprove? How do you spend your leisure time? What groups do you belong to? Do you like your work?[3] All these issues could be monitored at several times during the course of treatment on the theory that the greater one's social support for success in treatment, the greater the probability of success.

Both of these examples are based on a specific theory of why people can be expected to react to treatment in particular ways. Both postulate a dynamic to explain success in treatment, and both specify dependent variables that can be expected to have a causal connection to drug use, attendance, dropout, work/school adjustment, and illegal activity. A rehabilitation program might well affect the "covert" variables but not affect gross behavior change. If this happens, at least one has a sense of the strength of the rehabilitation efforts, where they need improvement, and hints as to how rehabilitation treatment should be reconceptualized. (At the same time one is testing specific psychological theories. This is one of the areas in which there is a strong link between the needs of social science and the needs of social service.)

Limitations (and Extensions) of the Prescription. A serious problem with the approach just advocated is that social science as manifested by the current state of psychological and sociological theory is inadequate to the task assigned to it. Social science is, at present, not well enough developed to supply a guideline that has any certainty whatsoever of leading to constructive rehabilitation change. In essence, the rehabilitation planner is faced not with a problem of science, but with a problem of technology. One of the main characteristics of

84

technological tasks is that they involve real world problems whose solution often goes beyond the current state of scientific knowledge. In this regard, the following quotation is instructive:

Technologists apply science when they can, and in fact achieve their most elegant solutions when an adequate theoretical basis exists for their work, but normally are not halted by the lack of of a theoretical base. They fill in gaps by drawing on experience, intuition, judgment, and experimentally obtained information (Wiesner 1970, p. 85).

This characterization of technology suggests an important and interesting perspective on how evaluation should actually be carried out. First, theory is important. To the extent that theory in social science can serve as a guide to action, one should use it, since it is the most accurate and powerful guide to action that one can possibly utilize. Second, theory is something that is developed by scientists, and it is not the same thing as "experimentally obtained information." Experiment is important because it can yield accurate, objective information on which action can be based. Such information will be accurate, however, only if the experimentation is carried out in a careful manner and with procedures that ensure the validity of findings. One might well view any evaluation as an experiment which has the potential to guide future action. Thus, even if evaluation is not meant to be "science" or to contribute to theory, it still has potential to help future program planners. Third, a large part of program planning is guided not by theory or experiment, but by the experience, intuition, and judgment of the planners. The major goal of evaluation is to decrease the extent to which planners have to rely on these subjective and personal considerations, but they will always be important sources of guidance and information.

In sum, theory must always be the starting point of outcome evaluation, and dependent variables must always be chosen with an eye toward collecting information on the most probable process of rehabilitation change. Theory alone, however, is inadequate to the task of guiding action in the practical sphere. In the inevitable cases where theory fails, other methods of knowing and understanding must be brought into play. These methods are experiment, experience, intuition, and judgment.

Independent Variables

In evaluation, independent variables are those elements of a program about which one wishes to draw conclusions. (These might include particular ways that a program treats its clients, special characteristics of the clients that are allowed into a program, unique aspects of staffing, or any similar characteristic that defines the relationship between program and client.) This section will deal with the use of independent variables in drug program evaluation, and with the problems that are associated with the current practice. First, the current method of making inferences about the effects of independent variables will be explained. Then two types of improvements will be discussed: those that fit into true experimental designs, and those of a nonexperimental nature.

At present the independent variable in most drug abuse evaluation studies is the rehabilitation program in toto. (There are exceptions, but even these usually test two very complex treatment systems.) Even if "success" is detected there is no information as to the specific program element that caused the observed effect. This lack is a problem for several reasons. First, even if success is detected, it is likely to be very partial. Unless one knows exactly what caused the effect, one cannot improve future efforts. Second, treatment is costly in terms of time, effort, and money. As a matter of economy one would like to allocate resources where they will do the most good. Third, from a scientific and theoretical point of view, one is always curious about why things work as they do, and present research does not help to answer such questions. (For an explanation of how the often diverse needs of social science and social service can be resolved, see Morell, in press.)

The Experimental Design Solution. The solution that will be proposed here aims at maximizing the effectiveness of treatment modalities that are currently in vogue.[4] This is done on the assumption that although radical changes in current methods may be necessary for substantive success, such changes are also politically unfeasible. Further, it is very likely that whatever the future course of drug abuse and correctional rehabilitation, the traditional modalities will always be present, and it is legitimate to try to maximize the efficacy of this type of treatment.

The gist of the proposed technique is the introduction of systematic variations into the existing treatment process and the random allocation of clients to conditions. This is merely advocating the use of experimental design to assess the effects of different specified aspects of treatment. (For an excellent list of examples in which experimental evaluations have been carred out, see Boruch 1974.) There are, of course, numerous variations to make this method even stronger. These involve use of multiple measures, systematic follow-up, and the like. Minimum prerequisites, however, are systematic variation and random assignment—for these are the minimum requirements of any experimental design. The specific treatment variations to be introduced must be determined by one's best guess (i.e., theory) as to what will work.

One should note that problems of independent and dependent variables are related. As an example, say that one is interested in the effects on treatment of training drug abuse counselors in the Truax-Carkhuff counseling method (Truax and Carkhuff 1967). This method is predicated on the theory that accurate empathy, nonpossessive warmth, and genuineness will affect the extent to which a client engages in self-disclosure. A further assumption is that self-disclosure is the key to therapeutic success. Given this system, one must as a minimum measure both a counselor's use of accurate empathy, nonpossessive warmth, and genuineness and the client's self-disclosure in counseling sessions.

The systematic variation idea seems simple enough, and few would fault its strength as a research tool. Yet there are very few studies that employ this method. The lack of such studies in drug abuse can be explained by a consideration of two factors. First, it is very difficult to set up an experimental study in a drug abuse or a correctional program. In order to carry out such research one must do several things. (1) Get program staff to agree to the research in general and to allocate certain types of treatment to particular individuals. (2) Obtain permission from a program to change standard operating procedure and to dictate program policy. Such requests are justifiably resented by those who have to operate within the organizational setting. (3) Make demands on the time of program staff, often without any extra pay. (4) Dictate (or at least influence) the "orientation" of the program, i.e., its treatment philosophy. Such orientation is often viewed by administrators and staff as their exclusive preserve and is of very great importance.

These problems are compounded when a drug program is actually taking place as part of a correctional setting. Such programs include restrictions on the freedom of members, a governing structure that must subordinate many changes to the needs of security, and members who may be interested in a drug rehabilitation program solely as a way to ease their life in the correctional system. Further, problems of budgeting, staffing, and programming in such drug programs are all made more difficult by the need to coordinate with similar problems faced by the host correctional setting.

Because of these factors it is often easier to do a nonexperimental study in which one is limited to interviews, paper and pencil tests, and outside-the-program follow-ups.

The second important factor is that many heavily funded labor-intensive evaluations that exist in drug abuse favor survey techniques involving very large numbers of people in many diverse geographical regions (Adams et al. 1971; Langenauer and Bowden 1971; Sells, 1972). The effort and money that is invested in such evaluation could be put into experimental studies that would involve fewer people from a smaller geographical area, but this does not happen. There are two likely reasons for this. First, much drug abuse evaluation research is run by people with clinical or medical rather than research backgrounds. This biases research in favor of the type of work that is involved in assessing the safety and efficacy of drugs. The bias is further entrenched because drug program evaluation often really does involve programs that use and dispense drugs. Whatever evaluation exists in drug abuse is almost exclusively involved with methadone maintenance programs. There is very little outcome evaluation attempted in polydrug abuse programs. Researchers involved in drug testing are extremely oriented toward wide-ranging studies with very large numbers of people. This is because the Food and Drug Administration will not approve a drug unless its safety has been demonstrated with a large number of people. Another reason for the large study bias is the notorious regional variation in patterns of drug abuse. There is a strong feeling among researchers that only a wide-scale study can yield an accurate picture of the drug abuse situation.

Alternative Approaches to Experimental Evaluation. If as a result of these or similar factors an experimental evaluation is impossible, what choices remain? Should one give up on the assumption that any other alternative will result in an invalid evaluation and in untrustworthy results? The answer, clearly, is no. First, it is clear that many important and interesting topics that do not lend themselves to experimental research are studied in a fruitful manner. (Most of sociology, anthropology, economics, and political science fall into this category.) Second, there is never any magic dividing line between the valid and the invalid. There is no way to guarantee that any study has yielded "valid" results. Any study can (and should) be criticized. The evaluation plan that has been advocated so far is based on the notion that the experimental model contains the highest probability of giving results that will tell planners what effect a program has and how the program should be improved. There are many "second-best" approaches, but they should not be utilized unless the advantages of the best solution are understood and efforts are made to implement that best solution. In the spirit of the famous maxim of scientific methodology "the scientist has no other method than doing his damnedest," we will turn to an investigation of the second-best alternatives that face the evaluator.[5]

Quasi-Experimental Designs. The literature on this topic is extensive and well developed, and it won't be dealt with in detail here (Campbell and Stanley 1963). Suffice it to say that the worth of a research design is measured in large part by the number and type of "plausible rival hypotheses" that it is able to rule out. Various designs that are not true experiments rule out some, but not all, plausible rival hypotheses, and they do this with varying degrees of certainty. The literature on quasi-experimental designs is an attempt to categorize and organize these options so that a researcher can choose the design that best fits the needs of the situation. This literature is the best source available for alternatives to experimental evaluation.

The Adversary Model. Recently a method of evaluation has been proposed that is based on weighing evidence in much the same manner that operates in a court of law (Levine 1974). The basis for proposing this model is that traditional research methods simply cannot deal with complex social programs that are subject to the numerous unforeseen, uncontrollable, and unpredictable forces that are always present in any real life social program. The adversary model contends that program evaluation is far more similar to the problems of decision and determination that occur in legal contexts than it is to the problems that can be dealt with by traditional methods of social science research. Thus, adversary evaluation proposes a system to weigh the opinions of people who can logically be expected to know and understand the effects of a social program. Since the traditional courtroom system has refined these methods over a very long period of time, the proposed method borrows heavily from courtroom procedure.

This method has several very appealing features. First, it does not necessitate the data collection contortions that are common to most social research. (It does not rule out such efforts, since all useful information is acceptable. But it does not necessitate the collection of such data either.) Thus the time, inconvenience, and expense of traditional research are circumvented. Second, it admits the evidence of all parties who can be expected to have knowledge of a program's effects. This includes staff, clients, outside observers, and the like. Third, it proposes a detailed method of weighing and determining the implications of all relevant opinions.

The problem, of course, is that informed opinion has been shown to be wrong many times before. A program may well have effects that cannot be detected without the aid of powerful data collection instruments and rigorous research design. Program effects may not be obvious, or in fact they may even be counterintuitive to commonsense. People may change attitudes and not change behavior, or only behavior, or both in varying proportions. Further, both attitudes and behavior are multifaceted concepts, and the precise locus of change may not be clear to any of the parties involved. It is also true that much evaluation is concerned with how program effects change over time, and this may be very difficult to determine without a traditional, well-executed research design.

The adversary model of evaluation and the traditional evaluation methods are not incompatible. It would be ideal if a traditional evaluation were carried out first and data interpretation was then carried out by use of the adversary system. It is also true, however, that the adversary model can stand alone in places where traditional evaluation is impossible, and that it can yield important information concerning the effects of a drug rehabilitation program.

Process Evaluation. Strictly speaking, this method of evaluation is not outcome evaluation, but is rather an attempt to understand the "internal workings" of an organization, to determine the contextual factors that influence the outcome that an organization is having, and to help administrators make policy decisions that do not necessitate information on "outcome variables."[6] Although it does not supply any hard data on outcome, it does help one form a sense of the effect that a program should be having, given a particular working environment, set of resources, and organization. Also, it can help support the results of outcome evaluation that might not otherwise be trusted. These functions are a legitimate aspect of any research project, be it evaluation or any other type of research.

"Objective" data cannot be understood without an understanding of a whole host of contextual information. Further, contextual information, by its nature, is not subjected to rigorous, empirical testing (Campbell 1974). A researcher's intuitive understanding of a study always plays a large part in interpreting results, discrepant findings, and implications. This type of understanding, which appears in the most rigorous social research, can easily be conceptualized as "process" understanding. Thus, process evaluation is nothing more than development and refinement of this type of data in order to extract the maximum amount of useful information from an evaluation study. If a research context does not allow for a strong outcome evaluation design, the best course might be to forsake such research, and try to infer program effect from a careful process evaluation. Such information *cannot* yield any definitive information on outcome, but it can give one a sense of understanding about a program. It is better to have a well-developed sense of understanding than an outcome evaluation design that may generate incorrect information and then lend an aura of "science" to those incorrect results.

No Evaluation. There are a host of powerful, well-reasoned, and defensible reasons not to carry out any outcome evaluation at all (Zusman and Bissonette 1973). These include issues such as the difficulty of carrying out good research designs, concern with investing scarce treatment resources in evaluation, political arguments concerning which type of programs get evaluated, and the low probability of obtaining any type of positive findings. It may well be that in many situations these arguments are correct, and that the wisest choice is not to carry out any outcome evaluation at all. This choice must, however, be exercised out of knowledge and understanding rather than blind distaste for some aspect of the outcome evaluation process. Resources are scarce (time, workforce, and money), and we do need some guide to their intelligent allocation. Outcome evaluation is the single most powerful tool that can be used to provide such a guide.[7] If, in a given situation, outcome evaluation is contraindicated, the decision not to evaluate must result from a careful, knowledgeable decision that potential advantages are outweighed by potential disadvantages.

Control Groups

The ideal drug abuse evaluation study should contain a "no treatment" control group. Drug abuse is influenced by a host of environmental factors, and one cannot estimate the impact of a program without knowledge of the drug abuse context in which the program is operating. The fact that people begin and stop abusing drugs of their own accord is the most obvious reason why control groups are needed, but the situation is still more complex (Valliant 1970). Patterns of abuse and the substances abused are in a constant flux (Greene and

Du Pont 1973). The demographic characteristics of the abusing population are not constant (Senay et al. 1973). Many individuals take "vacations" from drug abuse, and such people cannot be considered nonabusers. A knowledge of these factors is essential for an accurate estimate of the impact of a rehabilitation program. Unfortunately, obtaining such control groups is an exceedingly difficult task. The primary problem is that most drug abusers commit illegal acts. This is because with most drugs of abuse mere possession is a crime [Public Law No. 91–513 (1970)]. (Alcohol, tobacco, and caffeine are major exceptions.) It is the rare drug abuser who has a legal, legitimate access to the drugs he or she abuses. As a result, many drug abusers (especially those who are not in a rehabilitation program) are loathe to do anything that might decrease their anonymity. This problem is even more serious in the case of a drug rehabilitation program that is tied in to the correctional system. In these cases it is almost a certainty that crimes other than drug possession are involved, and this makes voluntary cooperation on the part of a control group almost impossible. This is especially true in the follow-up phase of any evaluation, when people who were incarcerated are released and (presumably) become involved in the life-style they had before incarceration. A second problem is that drug abusers are not usually among the most socially rooted members of society (Robins, Davis, and Goodwin 1974). They tend to move often and not to belong to organizations (business, school, etc.) or to have telephones or addresses in their own names. Third, they are often members of groups that share a conspiracy of silence vis-à-vis the non-drug-abusing world. Finally, drug abusers do not usually live easy lives (Preble and Casey 1969). A large percentage of their existence is taken up in a difficult and energy-consuming search for drugs or the resources to obtain drugs. Thus it is not likely that a researcher would find too much altruistic volunteer activity among drug abusers.

Even if a researcher succeeded in obtaining nontreatment control subjects, he would have very great difficulty in keeping them, and the control group cell of his analysis would have an exceedingly high dropout rate. Statistically, a large differential dropout between experimental cells poses very difficult problems (Applebaum and Cramer 1974).

From a practical point of view, then, one cannot expect the development of a body of drug abuse literature comparing "treatment" and "no treatment" groups in experimental designs. If we are to have good drug abuse treatment research, we must explore alternate methods of obtaining valid information concerning program impact. The method proposed here involves the judicious use of intraprogram comparisons.

In a previous section the technique of "systematic variation" was suggested as a method of determining what specific elements of treatment work best. The same technique can be used to give hints as to the external validity of outcome research. Assume that a body of literature develops which indicates very little difference in the effects of a large number of treatment variations that have been tested. Given this state of affairs, one can draw one of two conclusions. First, there is a basic effect of the treatment modality, and minor variations on the theme have no effect. Second, the basic modality has no effect, so variations on it are useless. Without external comparison one cannot tell which conclusion is correct. Suppose, however, that the hypothetical body of literature shows marked differences in the effects of different variations. This would indicate that some types of treatment work and some do not; i.e., the basic modality has potential. In other words, if one sees great variations in the effects of different types of rehabilitative programs, one can assume that some types of rehabilitation can indeed help drug abusers. Such a conclusion is not tenable from a strictly logical point of view. It may be, for example, that relative to outside events some variations are regressive and some just hold their own. But science does not progress by logic alone. Concepts such as "plausibility," "probability," and "reasonableness" play an important part in how scientists go about their business (Harré 1970, chap. 4; Kaplan 1964, chap. 7; Popper 1965, chap. 1). Here, too, they can help one decide which alternatives can be most practically pursued.

Summary

This section has been an attempt to propose a general methodological critique of the evaluation of drug abuse rehabilitation programs. It was based on the assumption that knowledge about the effect of a rehabilitation program is crucial to the improvement of services. The types of evaluation that are actually carried out in the field were presented first, so that the reader might start off with a conceptual understanding of what is actually done. Specific problems that are common to each of those types of evaluation were presented, and tentative solutions were advanced. These problems and solutions fell into three categories. First, there is the problem of dependent variables; i.e., what does the evaluator actually choose to measure, and how do such measurements help one to understand the process of rehabilitation change? The discussion argued that current studies concentrate on variables that are highly resistant to change, and that, as a result, information concerning the process of change was lost. Second, the matter of independent variables was presented. The way in which these elements of research design are conceptualized at the beginning of an evaluation is a major factor in determining the types of inferences that can be drawn about a program. Experimental and nonexperimental methods of setting up independent variables for study were presented. Third, the problem of no-treatment control groups in drug program evaluation was discussed. It is extremely difficult to obtain such groups, and one must usually find ways to do without them. The proposed solution centered on the use of multiple comparisons between different treatment alternatives.

Such was the general critique of drug abuse program evaluation. Now that the concept of strong outcome evaluation has been presented, one can turn to an in-depth investigation of three approaches to outcome evaluation that are actually found when one surveys the relevant literature. It will be seen that the differences that exist among these approaches center on the types of questions that each can be used to answer, and not on the inherent worth or validity of each method.

Approaches to Outcome Evaluation in Drug Abuse Rehabilitation

This section will deal with the three approaches to outcome evaluation that are found in the field of drug abuse rehabilitation. These are comparisons of program effects on different types of people, follow-up studies, and tests of specific treatment elements or modalities. It is certainly true that these approaches do not always exist in their pure forms, and it is not hard to find numerous examples of evaluation that combine various elements of each type. It is also true, however, that it is meaningful to try to understand drug program evaluation in terms of these three forms, since it is clear that evaluators do in fact choose one of these forms as a dominant theme in the work that they do.

Client-type Comparison

Uses. Evaluation of this type usually involves a study of the psychological and/or sociological characteristics of program members in an attempt to find out whether some types of people are helped more than other types by the treatment that is provided. This information can be used in three different ways. First, it can give planners a sense of where a program needs improvement. As an example, such an evaluation might show that females tend to be helped less than males, or that the only people who are helped are those who display a constantly high level of motivation and need for achievement. In the first example, planners would be made to realize that the special needs of women members were not being met. In the second example, program changes might be instituted to keep levels of motivation and need for achievement high. A second (and related) use of this type of evaluation is to help clinicians. Knowledge of the characteristics of the successful client might give clinical service providers a sense of the characteristics and problems they should concentrate on during the course of treatment.[8] Finally, client comparison evaluation can be used to help set up an intelligent screening process to determine who should be admitted into a drug abuse rehabilitation program. In practice, the pressure of funding mandates, the need to maintain full enrollment, and a workforce shortage do not usually allow rigorous pretreatment screening. The principle, however, is sound, and client-type comparison evaluation can be an invaluable aid whenever such screening is attempted.

Disadvantages. For all the possible uses of this method of evaluation, it still has a relatively low potential to be of any substantive help in program planning or treatment. In order for such information to be really useful, one would have to be able to predict behavior from a knowledge of psychological characteristics. Without this ability, such evaluation has only limited potential to contribute to the "science" part of the "science-intuition-experience-luck" quartet (see note 8). Unfortunately, the science component is the most powerful component of the four (with the possible exception of luck, which is unpredictable and may work for and against one with equal probability). Most research evidence shows that it is extremely difficult to predict behavior from a knowledge of internal psychological characteristics. The notion of behavior consistency based on psychological traits is most likely incorrect (Mischel 1973). The concept of an "addictive" or a "drug-abusing" personality is also most likely incorrect (Platt and Labate 1976, chap. 8). To whatever extent one can predict behavior from a knowledge of psychological characteristics, the process is extremely difficult to carry out (Bem and Allen 1974). It is not likely that a treatment program under the daily press of business would be able to undertake such a process.

A knowledge of demographic differences between successful and unsuccessful clients might be of greater use to a program than a knowledge of psychological differences. Demographic data are relatively easy to collect and to validate. Here too, though, problems exist in the translation of a knowledge of differences into useful information. What is it about people of different ages, or sexes, or family living situations, that influences the probability of success in a drug rehabilitation program? Unless these questions can be answered, constructive program changes cannot be effected. Here, too, is a case where making such determinations might be a complex task that is beyond the ability of any single rehabilitation program.

Follow-up Evaluation

Uses. It is abundantly (and painfully) clear that the effects of most social rehabilitation programs decline rapidly after a client has left a treatment. This is particularly true in the areas of corrections and drug abuse, where influences to return to prerehabilitation behavior patterns are so strong. It is very unlikely that rehabilitation programs in either of these areas will permanently change a person's life-style. Given this fact, it becomes very important to determine the rate at which people return to their preprogram behavior. It is also important to determine the rates of change for various aspects of the rehabilitation process. The only way this can be done is to carry out careful follow-up studies of program members. At some point, and in some manner, a decision must be made as to whether the advantages of a program warrant the continuation of that program. Although this decision is not the province of the evaluator, the evaluator is in a unique position to provide accurate information on which decisions of this type can be made.

A second use of follow-up evaluation is to check on the occurrence of unintended consequences of rehabilitation action. It is particularly important in the present case because one would like to be able to weigh all the advantages and disadvantages of the effects of a drug abuse rehabilitation program. As an example, one might find that by decreasing the extent of an individual's drug abuse, one has increased the efficiency with which the person engages in criminal behavior. (Although this particular result may be very difficult to document in an actual follow-up evaluation, it does illustrate the point.) A second example might be the case of a person who has become more effective and efficient at obtaining illicit drugs as a result of the education and "professional" contacts that he has made while in a rehabilitation program. It is certainly true that rehabilitation programs might have long-term negative consequences, and follow-up evaluation is probably the best vehicle for detecting such effects.

Disadvantages. There are two serious difficulties with follow-up-type evaluation. First, it does not yield information concerning the process by which a program has affected its members. It may tell one what a program is doing, but not why or how. Although one can ask people to recollect their time in a program and to articulate how it impacted upon them, there is no guarantee that memories will be accurate or that people attend to the crucial elements. A second disadvantage, which is particularly serious in the fields of corrections and drug abuse, is that it is very difficult to locate, contact, and obtain permission to interview a large proportion of past program members. This may introduce a very serious bias into the research, since it is quite likely that people who can be found and interviewed are different from those who could not be brought into the study.

If a follow-up evaluation also collected data while people were still in the rehabilitation program, this difficulty could be ameliorated (but not corrected). One would be able to begin tracking and follow-up immediately, thus increasing the probability of locating people and obtaining interviews. Also, one would have at least some sense of how those who could not be found differed from those who could be found. Unfortunately, many follow-up studies are planned after a program is over or at some well-advanced stage in a program's existence.

Modality Test Evaluation

Uses. Of the three types of evaluation, this method is the only one that focuses directly on the importance and effectiveness of specific elements of a treatment program, rather than on the characteristics of program members. As a result, it has the greatest potential to establish causal links between program activities and constructive change. If a clinician or an administrator wants to know what elements in a program are working, and what elements to include in any new program, this method of evaluation is the method of choice. In fact, there are those who might argue that this method of evaluation is the only legitimate method of outcome evaluation.

The guiding principle in determining the value of any outcome evaluation study is whether the results will have potential to provide an organization with useful feedback. Given this principle, one can indeed justify all three methods of outcome evaluation. It is true, however, that modality test evaluation does have the highest potential to be useful.

Disadvantages. Of all types of outcome evaluation, this method is most likely to necessitate the evaluator's involvement in daily program functioning. This includes both program planning and the daily activities of clinicians. If elements of a program are to be tested, treatment components have to be carefully defined and adhered to. The necessary pretest and ongoing data collection must be carried out. The freedom of clinicians to exercise their own judgment as to appropriate treatment is decreased. The types of clients that can be admitted into a program (or certain parts of it) often have to be restricted, and special methods of allocating clients to treatment conditions must often be instituted. The evaluator's demands on staff time are relatively large. Meetings are usually necessary to keep a research project operating according to schedule. Clinicians often have to fill out forms and supply data. Follow-up and client comparison evaluation do not usually involve the day-to-day participation of agency staff in the research. Modality test evaluation usually does necessitate such involvement. As with other aspects of living, one has to pay for quality, and one has to make a judgment as to whether quality is worth the price.

General Demands of Adequate Methodology

In most discussions of outcome evaluation, the modality test approach is usually associated (either explicitly or implicitly) with the difficult-to-carry-out "experimental method." This is the type of evaluation that demands control groups, extensive intervention in agency functioning, the imposition of the will of the evaluator on administrators and clinicians, and the like. Client comparison and follow-up evaluation, on the other hand, are usually considered "easier" to do. They tend to be correlational, to be conducted for the most part outside of the confines of the treatment program, and to be relatively unobtrusive or bothersome to agency personnel. To an extent, this is true. A well-done modality test evaluation probably is more bothersome to a rehabilitation program than a well-done client comparison or follow-up study. The extent of the difference, however, is considerably smaller than one might realize. All three types can be experimental, quasi-experimental, or correlational. The extent to which an evaluation is difficult, expensive, and demanding of staff time depends, for the most part, on the degree of certainty that one would like to have in one's conclusions. In order to illustrate this point, we will now turn to a consideration of various elements of evaluation design that affect the validity of results, which are common to any outcome evaluation that one might wish to carry out, and which are likely to necessitate special procedures by evaluators and agency staff during the course of rehabilitation treatment.

Are there ways to deal with the inevitable dropout bias? From both a logical and a statistical point of view, dropouts are a serious threat to the validity of conclusions drawn from any evaluation study. Would the results hold true if data had been collected on all, rather than some, of a sample? This is an especially difficult problem if several groups are involved and if the dropout rate is not equal across all groups (Applebaum and Cramer 1974). There are ways to deal with this problem—mostly through the judicious use of control groups and the analysis of "pretest" data. Unfortunately, client comparison and follow-up evaluation designs are often chosen in order to avoid the necessity of obtaining controls and pretest information. Controls and pretests are usually associated with "experimental" modality test evaluation. The logical necessity for such design elements, however, is *not* specific to modality test evaluation. It is true that some types of outcome evaluation cannot be carried out at all in a post hoc fashion, and that some types of outcome evaluation can be carried out poorly in a post hoc fashion. It is not true, however, that *any* outcome evaluation can be carried out well unless thorough planning has been done prior to the start of the program that is being evaluated. Such efforts must include work by program staff in order to carefully collect necessary pre-test and in-treatment evaluation data.

Are the appropriate data being collected? Any researcher must make as intelligent and informed a guess as possible as to the factors that influence the phenomenon to be studied. This guess must be based on a thorough knowledge of previous research, experience, and the informed opinions of experts. It is not always easy to make these decisions since varying opinions almost always exist as to what is important. The decisions must, however, be made. There is a practical limit to the amount of information that respondents will be willing to supply, and there is a practical limit on the time and money that can be spent in data collection. These decisions are no less difficult in one type of evaluation than in another. What are one's questions, and what information must be gathered to answer those questions? This is a fundamental problem in all research, and the care with which it is resolved will inevitably reflect on the value of the conclusions drawn.

Are the data-gathering tests valid and reliable? Is there consistency in how they are administered, in how they are scored, and the like? This, in essence, is a question about the accuracy of the measurement that is carried out during the evaluation, and it is an equally serious matter for any evaluation or research that involves the collection of data. If time and effort are not put into ensuring quality control of measurement, then the evaluation is not worth doing. The greater the effort and time put into such tasks, the more likely the study is to yield worthwhile information. Again, this is true for any type of outcome evaluation.

Do appropriate statistical techniques exist to analyze the data, and have the data been designed to take advantage of the most powerful statistical techniques that are appropriate? Statistical analysis is not an omnipotent method of data analysis. Rather it is a collection of tools that have limited uses and well-defined areas of applicability. It is clear from the close relationship between the development of applied statistics and the development of research design that the two fields are closely related. (In fact, one could quite legitimately argue that the two fields are isomorphic.) It is entirely possible to produce a research design whose data cannot be analyzed, or whose data could have been analyzed in a more powerful fashion, had certain changes been made. These considerations exist whenever data are collected, and they apply equally to all three types of outcome evaluation.

Does the evaluation design admit plausible rival hypotheses? The concept of plausible rival hypothesis derives from the notion that any given study might be biased by an infinite number of factors, but that the investigator need be concerned only with those biases that can reasonably be expected to seriously affect one's findings. As examples, consider the following examples: a combination of follow-up/client-type comparison evaluation shows that better-educated program graduates maintained drug-free lives, while younger graduates did not. Was this because the program worked best with the educated, or because the availability of illicit drugs decreased and older abusers were simply too tired and worn out to continue the difficult life of a drug abuser? A modality test evaluation indicates that program members who volunteer for treatment do better than those who are forced into treatment by court pressure. Is it that initial level of motivation to participate is crucial to rehabilitation success, or is there something fundamentally different about the type of abusers who get caught up in the criminal justice system? In other words, the crucial element may not be motivation at all, and abusers who are forced into treatment by some means other than judicial pressure (family pressure, as an example) might also benefit from treatment. In both these examples, two different explanations of results were proposed. One explanation attributed beneficial results to some action that is under the control of the rehabilitation program, and the other explanation involved matters beyond the program's control. All the explanations, however, are reasonable, and might well be correct. Unless specific control groups were used in each case, the matter cannot be resolved.

Control groups are admitted into research design for the specific purpose of ruling out plausible rival hypotheses. Ideally, these groups should be randomly selected, but nonrandom control groups can also be of immense benefit in this matter, if they are carefully chosen (Speer and Tapp 1976). The crucial point is that plausible rival hypotheses are serious impediments to drawing conclusions from any type of evaluation, and difficult, labor-intensive methods of dealing with such problems must be invoked if a high-quality outcome evaluation is desired.

Are the necessary pretest data available? In any type of outcome evaluation, it is often important to compare the status of program members with their status before entering the program. Sometimes this type of data is available because these data were collected for treatment or administrative purposes, as part of the standard operating procedure of a rehabilitation program. Usually this is not the case, and pretest evaluation data are either missing or in a form that is not useful for the purposes of research or evaluation. In such cases, worthwhile outcome evaluation cannot be had unless a program's staff are willing to modify their standard operating procedure and to devote special effort for the purposes of evaluation. As an example, consider a client comparison evaluation which indicated that married people did better in treatment than single people. This result is not too surprising, since married people are likely to be older, more socially stable, and (perhaps) better adjusted than single people. Before such information can be useful to a program, however, one would like to check on several related issues. Did the married people start out better than the singles, or was there actually a difference in how they interacted with the treatment process? Such information might be gleaned from clinical records of a person's drug abuse history, but the evaluator should not count on being able to do so. Suppose the program in question does not exercise rigorous control over the completeness or the accuracy with which such records are kept? What if there is no special form or agreed-upon format for such records? What if information on drug history is recorded only in broad outline without specifics? In such cases the necessary information is lost to the evaluator. The difficulty might go even a step further. Suppose the evaluator wanted to try to explain the phenomenon of the superior performance of the married group, and he had reason to believe that the answer lay in the initial motivation with which people enter drug abuse rehabilitation programs. This is certainly an important matter, and it is not at all unlikely that an evaluator might wish to explore this hypothesis. But do existing records contain any information on initial motivation? Is that information in the form of specific data that the evaluator has reason to believe (i.e., a theory) are important? In all likelihood, such information does not exist in patient records. Thus we have two pieces of information that are of vital importance to the evaluator, one of which exists in records, but not in usable form, and the other of which does not exist at all. The evaluator is left with the original finding that marrieds fare better than singles in treatment, and has no idea what to make of the finding or how to determine whether the finding has any implications for how the program is doing its work.

The elements of research design that were presented above were put forward to illustrate the point that none of the three basic types of outcome evaluation are easy to carry out. Considerable effort is necessary to ensure the validity of the inferences no matter which type of evaluation is used. Moreover, it is clear that the effort that is called for must fall, at least partially, on program staff who are not normally involved in evaluation. If evaluation is to succeed, clinical staff must make special efforts *during the course of treatment*. With evaluation, as with clinical/therapeutic issues, "help" is not a passive concept for those who wish to receive it. All parties must actively participate if the help is to be successful.

Summary

This section has been an attempt to explain the uses and disadvantages that are found with each of the three types of outcome evaluation which are routinely carried out in the field of drug rehabilitation program evaluation. The distinguishing characteristic of each type of evaluation is the nature of the question that it is best suited to answer, and not the ease with which it can be carried out or the amount of consideration that must be paid to methodological issues.

Although each type was described separately, it should be clear that any given evaluation design can include elements from each type of evaluation, and that the choice is dependent upon the questions that need to be answered. The separation was presented here partly for ease of explanation, and partly because most drug program evaluation clearly shows one of these types as a dominant theme.

Conclusion

The first part of this chapter established the following facts. First, dependent variables must be picked so that the evaluator can obtain information not only on gross elements of behavior change, but also on the process by which constructive change takes place. Without such information, it is difficult to find out whether a program is working in the right direction and where it is failing. Second, independent variables must be laid out so that valid inferences can be made from the data. The best way to do this is with a true experimental design, but numerous alternatives also exist. Third, appropriate control groups are necessary to guard against plausible rival hypotheses.

The second part of this chapter explained the uses of three basic approaches to outcome evaluation: modality tests, follow-ups, and client-type comparisons. The discussion then presented the notion that methodological concerns in each of these methods are highly similar. Thus, the best way to approach outcome evaluation is to decide on a plan based on the questions of major interest, and then to apply the guidelines that were presented for the full use of independent variables, dependent variables, and control groups. This prescription necessitates a lot of careful work on the part of evaluators, clinicians, and administrators. One might well make the intelligent judgment that the work involved in an evaluation is not worth the potential payoff, and if this is the considered judgment, one might be better off not evaluating a program. Such a decision should not be made, however, without the full knowledge that a well-designed outcome evaluation is the single best method of determining how to improve the quality of treatment in drug abuse rehabilitation programs. This chapter has been an attempt to delineate the types of efforts that are made in this direction, and to explain how the usefulness of the information derived from such attempts can be maximized.

Notes

1. These divisions are by no means perfect or mutually exclusive. In fact, the second section of this report will discuss the implications of combining these different types in a single evaluation. These divisions do, however, represent meaningful distinctions for two reasons. First, a review of the literature clearly indicates that present studies do fall roughly into these categories. Second, the distinctions are conceptually meaningful in terms of the types of questions that can be answered with each type of research.

2. One might also include the fourth category of "research critiques." These are papers that do not report a particular evaluation study, but which discuss issues relating to drug program evaluation. As examples, see Brown (1974), Kern (1974), Maddux and Bowden (1972), Sells (1973 a, b), and Sirotnick (1974).

3. The author is indebted to Dr. Faye Goldberg of the University of Chicago, Department of Psychiatry, Drug Abuse Research Unit, for this series of questions.

4. Advocating such a method opens one up to the charge of helping to entrench the status quo, and an ineffective status quo at that. The charge has a good deal of validity and should not be taken lightly. For a discussion of the problems of the consequences of psychologists' attempts at therapeutic action, see Beit-Hallachmi 1974.

5. This remark is made by P. W. Bridgeman in a book entitled *The Logic of Modern Physics* (Bridgeman 1928). It is quoted by Kaplan in a work devoted to the methodology of behavioral sciences (Kaplan 1964).

6. *Process evaluation* is a general term for nonoutcome evaluation, and the precise definition is dependent upon who is doing it. The explanation of it given in this chapter represents the most common elements of this method of evaluation.

7. Outcome evaluation cannot help one choose between different areas of effort, since that is a matter of public policy and not of science (as, for example, a choice between drug rehabilitation and day care). Within a given area, however, outcome evaluation can provide information as to what a program is affecting and how to best improve its performance.

8. In both of these examples, there is no intention to imply that the descriptive characteristics which differentiate successful and unsuccessful clients are in fact the causative variables of rehabilitation change. It does mean that a clinician or administrator might gain worthwhile programmatic or therapeutic insights from this type of information. Rehabilitation is not merely the successful application of social science. It is the application of a clinician's skill as determined by whatever science, intuition, experience, and luck can be brought to bear on the task.

References

Adams, R. G., et al. "Heroin Addicts on Methadone Replacement: A Study of Dropouts." *International Journal of the Addictions* 6 (2): 269-77, 1971.

Applebaum, M. I., and Cramer, E. M. "Some Problems in the Nonorthogonal Analysis of Variance." *Psychological Bulletin* 81 (6): 335-43, 1974.

Beit-Hallachmi, B. "Salvation and Its Vicissitudes: Clinical Psychology and Political Values." *American Psycholgist* 29 (2): 124-29, 1974.

Bem, D. J., and Allen, A. "On Predicting Some of the People Some of the Time: The Search for Cross Situational Consistencies in Behavior." *Psychological Review* 81 (6): 506-20, 1974.

Boruch, R. F. "Bibliography: Illustrative Randomized Field Experiments for Program Planning and Evaluation." *Evaluation* 2 (1): 83-87, 1974.

Bourne, P. G. "Methadone Maintenance: An Evaluation." Duplicated report. Washington: The Drug Abuse Council, 1974.

Bridgeman, P. W. *The Logic of Modern Physics*. New York: Macmillan, 1928.

Brown, B. S. "The Role of Research in a Narcotics Treatment Program." *Drug Forum* 3 (2): 173-82, 1974.

Campbell, D. T. "Qualitative Knowing in Action Research." Kurt Lewin award of The Society for the Psychological Study of Social Issues; meeting with the American Psychological Association, New Orleans, September 1, 1974. Also in press, *The Journal of Social Issues*.

_____ . and Stanley, J. C. *Experimental and Quasi-experimental Designs for Research*. Chicago: Rand McNally College Publishing Co., 1963.

Caplan, G. *Support Systems and Community Mental Health: Lectures on Concept Development*. New York: Behavioral Publications, 1973.

102

De Leon, G.; Skodol, A.; and Rosenthal, M. S. "Phoenix House: Changes in Psychopathological Signs of Resident Drug Addicts." *Archives of General Psychiatry* 28 (1973): 131-35.

Dole, V. P.; Nyswander, M.; and Warner, A. "Successful Treatment of 750 Criminal Addicts." *Journal of the American Medical Association* 206 (12): 2708-11, 1968.

Gasser, E. S., et al. "The Eysenck Personality Inventory with Methadone Maintenance Patients." *British Journal of Addiction* 69 (1974): 85-88.

Gearing, F. R. "Evaluation of Methadone Maintenance Treatment Programs." In *Methadone Maintenance*, edited by Stanley Einstein. New York: Marcel Dekker, 1971.

Greene, M. H., and Du Pont, R. L. "Amphetamines in the District of Columbia: I. Identification and Resolution of an Abuse Epidemic." *Journal of the American Medical Association* 266 (12): 1437-40, 1973.

Harré, R. *The Principles of Scientific Thinking.* Chicago: The University of Chicago Press, 1970.

Kaplan, A. *The Conduct of Inquiry Methodology for the Behavioral Sciences.* Scranton, Pa.: Chandler, 1964.

Kern, J. C. "Evaluating Community Drug Abuse Agencies." *Journal of Drug Education* 4 (2): 129-39, 1974.

Langenauer, B. J., and Bowden, C. L. "A Follow-up Study of Narcot Addicts in the NARA Program." *American Journal of Psychiatry* 128(1): 41-46, 1971.

Levine, D. B., et al. "Personality Correlates of Success in a Methadone Maintenance Program." *American Journal of Psychiatry* 129 (4): 456-60, 1972.

Levine, M. "Scientific Method and the Adversary Model: Some Preliminary Thoughts." *American Psycholgist* 29 (9): 661-77, 1974.

Maddux, J. F., and Bowden, C. L. "Critique of Success with Methadone Maintenance." *The American Journal of Psychiatry* 129 (4): 440-47, 1972.

Mischel, W. "Toward a Cognitive Social Learning Reconceptualization of Personality." *Psychological Review* 80 (1973): 252-83.

Morell, J. A. "The Relationship Between Social Science and the Mental Health Care Delivery System: An Analysis of Conflict and Some Proposals for Peace." *Administration in Mental Health,* in press.

Paulus, I., and Halliday, R. "Rehabilitation of the Narcotic Addict: Results of a Comparative Methadone Withdrawal Program." *Canadian Medical Association Journal* 96 (1967): 655-59.

Pittel, S. M., et al. "Three Studies of the MMPI as a Predictive Instrument in Methadone Maintenance." Fourth National Conference on Methadone Treatment. National Association for the Prevention of Addiction to Narcotics, San Francisco, 1972.

Platt, J. J., and Labate, C. *Heroin Addiction: Theory, Research, and Treatment.* New York: Wiley, 1976.

Popper, K. R. *Conjectures and Refutations: The Growth of Scientific Knowledge*. New York: Harper Torchbooks, 1965.

Preble, E., and Casey, J. J., Jr. "Taking Care of Business—The Heroin User's Life on the Street." *International Journal of the Addictions* 4 (1): 1-24, 1969.

Price, S., and Jackson, K. "Correlates and Extent of Drug Abuse on a Methadone Maintenance Program." *British Journal of Addiction* 69 (1974): 173-179.

Renault, P. "Methadone Maintenance: The Effect of Knowledge of Dosage." International Journal of the Addictions 8 (1): 41-47, 1973.

Robins, L. N.; Davis, D. H.; and Goodwin, D. W. "Drug Use by U.S. Army Enlisted Men in Vietnam: A Follow-up on Their Return Home." *American Journal of Epidemiology* 99 (4): 235-49, 1974.

Rosenberg, C. M.; Davidson, G. E.; and Patch, V. D. "Patterns of Dropouts from a Methadone Program for Narcotic Addicts." *The International Journal of the Addictions* 7 (3): 415-25, 1972.

Schut, J.; Wohlmuth, T.; and File, K. "High Dose Methadone Maintenance: An Evaluation." *The British Journal of Addiction* 68 (2): 145-50, 1973.

Sells, S. B. "Research on Evaluation of Drug Abuse Treatment Outcome with the DARP." Texas Christian University Institute of Behavioral Research, *Speical Report No. 72-17*, 1972.

———. "Evaluation of Treatment for Drug Abuse." Texas Christian University Institute for Behavioral Research, *Special Report No. 73-14*, 1973a.

———. "Evaluation of Treatment for Drug Abuse." *Proceedings of the 5th National Conference on Methadone Treatment*, Washington, D.C., March 1973b, 1362-1368. Sponsored by the National Association for the Prevention of Addiction to Narcotics.

Senay, E. C., et al. "IDAP—Five Year Results." *Proceedings of the 5th Methadone Maintenance Conference*, Washington, D.C., March 1973.

Sheffet, A., et al. "A Model for Drug Abuse Treatment Evaluation." *Preventive Medicine*, 2 (1973): 510-23.

Sirotnick, K. "A Comprehensive Evaluation Model for Multimodality Programs in the Treatment of Drug Abuse." *Journal of Psychedelic Drugs* 6 (2), 1974.

Speer, D. C., and Tapp, J. C. "Evaluation of Mental Health Service Effectiveness: A Start-up Model for Established Programs." *American Journal of Orthopsychiatry* 46 (2): 217-28, 1976.

Stephens, R., and Cottrell, E. "A Follow-up Study of 200 Narcotic Addicts under the Narcotics Rehabilitation Act (NARA)." *British Journal of the Addictions* 67 (1972): 45-53.

Sugarman, B. "Evaluating Drug Treatment Programs: A Review and Critique of Some Studies on Programs of the Concept House Type." *Drug Forum* 3 (2): 149-53, 1974.

Toomey, T. C. "Personality and Demographic Characteristics of Two Sub-types of Drug Abusers." *British Journal of Addiction* 69(1974): 155-58.

Truax, C., and Carkhuff, R. *Toward Effective Counseling and Psychotherapy*. Chicago: Aldine, 1967.

Valliant, G. E. "The Natural History of Narcotic Addiction." *Seminars in Psychiatry* 2(4): 486-98, 1970.

Wiesner, J. B. "The Need for Social Engineering." In *Psychology and the Problems of Society*, edited by F. Korten, S. W. Cook, and J. Lacey. Washington: American Psychological Association, 1970, pp. 85-94.

Zusman, J., and Bissonette, R. "The Case against Evaluation (with Some Suggestions for Improvement)." *International Journal of Mental Health* 2(2): 111-25, 1973.

Predicting Parole Outcome in Correctional Drug Abuse Treatment
Christina Labate

Predicting parole outcome in drug abuse treatment programs has long been a questionable undertaking—especially since little research has been done in this area. Consequently, in being concerned with parole outcome at this point with incarcerated drug abusers, we must look to the research studies done in corrections in general, until more advanced research reports become available in the area of correctional drug abuse per se.

The Concept of Prediction

In a correctional system in which the primary objective is the prevention of recurrent criminal behavior, the crucial decisions involve choice of treatment. More often than not, however, determination of the course of treatment which is most likely to achieve this goal is a complicated and uncertain process. Selection of any particular treatment program is usually guided by a belief that such a program is best suited to the characteristics of the offender. For example, nonimprisonment alternatives such as probation and parole are chosen when the weight of accumulated evidence suggests a favorable outcome. A reliable process for the selection and implementation of such alternatives is obviously crucial to the achievement of correctional system goals. Systematic examination of offender characteristics in relation to treatment outcome provides valuable feedback in improving the decisionmaking process.

The officials of the criminal justice system must make the choice among a variety of available treatment techniques, and they may be guided in their decisions by a substantial body of literature which has accumulated over the past several decades. The attempt to predict recidivism is at the core of these investigations. Utilization of the insights distilled from empirical investigations may significantly contribute to the rehabilitation effort. This chapter will first discuss the nature of and the rationale underlying the attempt to predict recidivism; second, briefly review the major historical methods of prediction; third, review in some detail current research on the prediction problem; and finally, evaluate the use of formal prediction devices in the correctional setting. The chapter will also outline applications to treatment evaluation and areas where additional research is needed.

Assumptions

The use of formal prediction devices in a correctional setting relies on the assumption that individuals possessing a certain pattern of common characteristics will tend to react similarly to similar situations. The prediction problem specifically involves an attempt to predict an individual's future behavior on the basis of what one is led to expect from previous assessments of that individual. Such assessment may be in the form of interviews and casual observation, or it may follow a more structured approach via the administration of psychological tests or other formal test instruments. However, prior to the investment of time and effort in administering test instruments, one should have a substantiated conviction that the results of such an assessment will provide information that is relevant to the decisionmaking process. On the basis of an observed relationship between predictor and criterion categories (outcome measures), an attempt is made to determine the most probable outcome for different subgroups of persons exhibiting similar patterns of characteristics. Predictions, therefore, involve an estimate of expected performance which is based on knowledge of the previous performance of others who exhibit similar characteristics. The process is made more efficient by limiting assessment to those characteristics that show an empirical relationship to the outcome measures.

There are essentially five steps involved in prediction studies as outlined by Gottfredson (1967). First, the criterion categories must be established, and this involves a clear definition of the behavior to be predicted. Second, the characteristics on which prediction is to be based must be selected and defined. Third, a representative sample of the population of interest must be selected, and the relationship between criterion and predictor variables must be determined on this subsample. Fourth, and often overlooked, a cross validation of the observed relationship between predictors and criterion must be made on a new sample. Finally,

... [T]he prediction methods may be applied in situations for which they were developed, provided that the stability of predictions has been supported in the cross-validation step and appropriate samples have been used (Gottfredson 1967, p. 173).

Formal selection instruments assign a score to each individual on the basis of which selection is made (e.g., parole, type of treatment, etc.). The score is independent of the test administrator's judgment. Where prediction instruments are incorporated into the parole selection process, an offender would be evaluated on the prediction instrument items and assigned a score on the basis of that evaluation alone. Knowledge of that score would then, presumably, be utilized in the decision to select or reject for parole. The selection decision, however, involves a number of additional factors beyond mere knowledge of an individual's score. The proportion of successes and failures in the population from which the individual derives must also be considered, as well as the distribution of scores of the successes in that particular population. For instance, if one knows a certain offender possesses characteristics X, Y, and Z and one has empirical evidence that, in the past, other offenders possessing these characteristics were significantly more likely to succeed in treatment program A than those who did not, then using that knowledge in the decision to transfer the offender to treatment program A increases the likelihood of successful outcome in that particular case over a random or intuitive distribution of offenders to treatment programs. The organization of this information in a formal prediction instrument substantially increases the likelihood that the decision made regarding offender disposition will achieve the objectives of the correctional system.

Defining Outcome Criteria

However, the process involved in reaching the stage where a prediction instrument can be used with confidence is a lengthy one. As Gottfredson (1967) has suggested, the first step is defining the criterion categories (i.e., the behavior one wishes to predict). At first glance, it appears to be a simple matter of dichotomous outcome classification into "successes" and "failures." However, outcome criteria stated simply in terms of success and failure are often very crude. Thus, the extent to which such criteria are vague and ambiguous reduces the reliability and validity of the prediction. For instance, is a "failure" one who has committed a new crime or one who has had his parole revoked for a technical violation? Is a "failure" one who fails to make a satisfactory adjustment to society—perhaps in terms of chronic unemployment, repeated failure in school, or constant petty offenses? What about the case where a former offender has successfully completed all the requirements of parole supervision and is released only to commit another offense subsequently? Is this a treatment success or failure?

Clear definition of outcome criteria is obviously not a simple matter. One may certainly use a variety of objective measures in the case of unsuccessful parole outcome which represent varying degrees of "failure," e.g., filing of petition for revocation, issuance of a warrant, revocation of parole, or actual recidivism. A statistically reliable index may be obtained from these criteria for they are readily quantified and are objective, and their presence or absence is easily observed. They may be combined and weighted in a variety of ways to ensure proper representation of degree or seriousness of "failure." However, there is an element of subjectivity insofar as the presence of any of these events may reflect the judgment of the probation officer. The above indices of failure do not necessarily reflect the actual number of violations a paroled offender may have committed. Again, a parole officer's judgment enters into the reporting of certain offenses, and no parole officer can be expected to detect every violation.

It has been suggested that, just as one accepts police estimates of the number of crimes which are committed, perhaps one should accept recidivism rates as most closely approximating a reliable index of failure to achieve the objective of preventing recurrence of criminal behavior. However, Vasoli (1967) notes that

> . . . [T]he weakness inherent in a measure based on recidivism alone becomes all too apparent when it is realized that criminality is not the only form of misbehavior by probationers (p. 26).

Furthermore, the above criteria may not depend solely on the behavior of the offender but on that of the courts, the police, parole agents, etc. ". . . [A]n increase in 'parole violations' may reflect increased offending behavior by parolees, increased surveillance by parole agents, or changes in policy of the paroling authority" (Gottfredson 1967, p. 173). The behavior of the victim may also be a component in reporting parole violations. To the extent that the efficiency of law enforcement, policy changes, and changes in categories of behavior defined as acceptable or not enter into the "objective measures" of parole outcome, the reliability and validity of predictions based on these criteria will be substantially reduced. Gottfredson (1967) points out that there is a need to develop more adequate assessments of criminal behavior that are independent of social agency response.

Similar problems are inherent in using "adjustment" as a criterion of outcome. While it broadens the basis of assessment to include a positive focus, *adjustment* remains a fairly vague term. It does not lend itself to quantification or objectivity. Again, evaluation of adjustment depends, in large measure, on the judgment of parole officers as well as on the actual behavior of the parolee. While some degree of consensus is approached, even greater subjectivity is introduced into indices of successful outcome employing "favorable adjustment" as a criterion. The meanings of "maladjusted" or "adjusted" need to be clarified before they can be used as reliable indices of outcome. Furthermore, as Vasoli (1967) points out, these goals may well be desirable from a long-term societal standpoint, but they may be outside the realm of nonimprisonment effectiveness. As long as parole results in a "law-abiding citizen," Vasoli (1967) suggests that additional behavioral performance may require extensive social services, community support, and counseling personnel.

Perhaps a most useful index of success or failure would combine information from both objective measures and measures of adjustment (e.g., steady employment, return to school, etc.). In any event, the evaluator attempting to develop prediction instruments must be aware of the need to clearly define the outcome criteria. It should be noted that until more reliable and valid criterion indices are available, a certain amount of random variation in the relationship between predictors and criterion must be expected.

Selection of Predictors

The second step outlined by Gottfredson (1967) involves selection of the predictors. These items may be obtained from any source (e.g., tests, observation, records, self-report) as long as they exhibit a significant relationship with the criterion. In other words, a predictor is useful if knowledge of the offender's standing with respect to that item increases the likelihood of a correct classification on the criterion variable. In addition to having a significant relationship with the criterion, useful predictors must be able to discriminate and must be reliable. Discrimination enables one to clearly classify individuals, and reliability ensures stability of repeated observations on that item. Obviously predictors that result in classification of the same individual to different criterion groups on two different occasions (i.e., are unreliable) are not terribly useful. Equally unsatisfactory are predictors that either classify all candidates into the same group or fail to permit clear assignment of a majority of individuals to *any* group.

Generally, predictor items are obtained by examining a representative sample of the population of interest on whom the outcomes are known. In the case of a dichotomous criterion, subjects are separated into their respective outcome groups, and those items which discriminate between the two groups are chosen as "predictor candidates" (Gottfredson 1967, p. 174). The assumption is generally made that the same relationship between predictors and criterion will hold for subgroups of a heterogeneous population. However, recent research suggests that reliable prediction may be better accomplished by construction of prediction instruments on more homogeneous subgroups of the general offender population. This issue will be examined in some detail in a later section of this chapter.

Construction of a Prediction Instrument

Once the initially discriminating items have been isolated, an attempt is made to organize them into some usable fashion. Individual predictors may be combined in two ways: they may be weighted or unweighted. If the items are to be unweighted, they are assigned unit weights—a value of +1 regardless of the strength of their association with the criterion. In a sense such a system merely acknowledges the presence or absence of any given characteristic. The sum of the points then provides the index from which the likelihood of any given outcome is to be evaluated. The unit weight system ignores any intercorrelations among predictor items, but it may be useful when a large number of items are to be used. Gottfredson (1967) explains that in this particular case, "it may be assumed that as the number of positively correlated variables increases, the correlation between any two sets of weighted scores approaches one and the effect of differential weighting of the various items tends to disappear" (p. 177). If, on the other hand, a small number of predictors is desired, a weighting system involving those items having the highest correlation with the criterion is more appropriate.

There are a number of statistical procedures by which differential weighting may be accomplished. Those currently favored are the multivariate methods of regression analysis, multiple linear regression, and linear discriminant function. Theoretically, these provide optimal weighting of each item based on its unique relationship with the criterion. It is also possible with these methods to determine the gain in predictive accuracy offered by each item by observing the reduction in unaccounted-for variance in the criterion.

An interesting study by Simon (1972) suggests that all the multivariate methods of combining variables in prediction instruments work about equally well. However, there are two major disadvantages to the multiple regression and the discriminant function methods. First, both assume that the ". . . criterion magnitudes are linear functions of the predictor variables . . ." (Gottfredson 1967, p. 174). This may, in fact, be an inaccurate representation of the true relationship among the variables. Artificially imposed linearity may reduce the accuracy of prediction when the relationship among the variables actually is better represented by some form of curve. However, the assumption of linearity considerably reduces the complexity of calculation and may be an adequate first approximation of the relationship among the variables. The second disadvantage of the multivariate methods relates to the fact that the weights of the predictor items were originally calculated using the entire population, and therefore they may not reliably predict for more homogeneous subsamples. Finally, the study by Simon (1972) comparing multiple regression and discriminant analysis found serious problems on validation of the predictive equations in that they suffered from "overfitting" to the original sample and were therefore not useful when applied to a new group.

The second procedure by which weighting may be accomplished involves the configural methods (cluster analysis, association analysis, configural analysis). Cluster analysis involves the partitioning of a large heterogeneous sample into smaller homogeneous subgroups. Between subgroups the relevant behavioral patterns are significantly different. This division of the sample may be accomplished on the basis of a single attribute (monothetic), thus providing easily recognizable subgroups. However, with a monothetic partitioning it is possible to wrongly classify individuals if they lack the particular attribute but in all other respects resemble the group into which they would otherwise be placed. Recently Fildes and Gottfredson (1972) used a cluster analysis on a parolee sample of male offenders in which partitioning took place on the basis of six attributes: type of admission, offense, prior prison record, prior sentence, drug use, and alcohol involvement. They obtained a tree diagram with 23 subgroups. Criteria of validity were met as the success rates for each subgroup remained the same when cross validation was attempted on a second sample. However, Fildes and Gottfredson (1972) were unable to replicate the tree diagram with the second sample. They concluded that "before the method is used for prediction purposes . . . it needs to be verified that the subgroups formed do not alter in composition in time with respect to parole performance" (p. 5).

In a second study, Sampson (1974) obtained an increase in predictive accuracy over multiple regression methods by using a visually discriminated cluster analysis on life history information. Within the homogeneous cluster, multiple discriminant analysis was used. However, the study suffers from an absence of cross validation, and it is therefore impossible to say with any degree of confidence that it represents a real advance over the multivariate methods. In fact, a study by Babst, Gottfredson, and Ballard (1968) suggests that both configural and regression methods work equally well in differentiating recidivists and non-recidivists on cross validation. However, the multiple regression techniques provide a continuous distribution of scores. Babst, Gottfredson, and Ballard (1968) note that this is a distinct advantage

. . . in selection applications, wherein both the selection quota and acceptable risk are important determinants of a decision, [as] the cutting score may be shifted with a flexibility not possible in the configural tables (p. 79).

Yet the advantage of a visual configural table which is easily interpreted and accessible to the lay person should not be underestimated. All these considerations must be taken into account in selecting a method of weighting and combining predictor items.

Once the predictors have been selected and weighted, cutting scores must be established such that all cases falling above the cutting score are classified as "successes" and those falling below are classified as "failures." The basis for deciding on the cutting score has been compared to the determination of a "cost-utility" function (Duncan et al. 1953) in which *utility* at a given score is defined as the proportion of failures who are correctly identified and the *cost* as the proportion of successes at that score who are incorrectly identified as failures. The total population can obviously be divided into the following four categories: (1) the number of failures who are rejected or identified as failures, (2) the number of successes who are incorrectly rejected or identified as failures, (3) the number of failures who are incorrectly accepted or identified as successes, and (4) the number of successes who are correctly identified as such.[1] For each cutoff score there will be a specific cost-utility function.

There are several basic rules outlined by Duncan et al. (1953) for selecting the cost-utility function deemed most desirable in a given situation. One could choose the cutting score to maximize efficiency and to minimize the errors of classification. In this case, "efficiency" refers to the fraction by which the number of errors is reduced using any particular cutting score. Implicit in this approach to selecting a cost-utility curve is the assumption that both types of error (acceptance of actual failures and rejection of actual successes) are of equal importance. This is by no means always the case. Where the two types of error are of unequal importance, one might "maximize expense-weighted efficiency" where the "expense" of misclassifying can be defined (Duncan et al. 1953). One could also attempt to equalize the probabilities of occurrence of the two types of errors. In addition, one could decide to accept a group containing a fixed proportion of failures in the situation where it is most important not to overlook a "success." Finally, one could accept a fixed proportion of applicants irrespective of their individual characteristics. In the event that it is simply too time-consuming or expensive to review each candidate, a screening procedure may be used in which a few salient characteristics are examined. Only those candidates exhibiting those characteristics need undergo further evaluation.

One important point to be kept in mind throughout a prediction study, noted by Duncan et al. (1953), is that one often does not know the proportion of successes in a given sample of candidates. The prediction instrument will have been constructed in a population in which this was known, but the population to which the instrument is being applied may vary slightly. It is therefore important to remember that the scores obtained which describe this new population relate more to *estimates* than to actual *known* quantities. As Gottfredson (1967) points out, one cannot say with certainty what an individual's future behavior will be. Predictions must therefore be more wisely phrased in terms of likelihood. Furthermore, while the point seems obvious, it is worth emphasizing that the expected performance relates to the group as a whole, and therefore it may not accurately characterize the behavior of any specific individual within that group. It is precisely this fact which is a focus of controversy in assessing the utility of prediction instruments in correctional settings. In any event, the usefulness of a prediction device is a function of the degree to which it incorporates those factors that are important in making policy decisions.

Evaluating Prediction Instruments

The efficiency of a prediction has been traditionally expressed as the percentage of individuals who have been correctly classified. Validity coefficients such as the coefficient of alienation or the index of forecasting efficiency are commonly used, although one could also express prediction efficiency as simply the increase in efficiency over the random method of selection. Ohlin and Duncan (in Gottfredson 1967) have devised an index of predictive efficiency using the percentage change in error obtained by use of the instrument over base rate predictions. This index allows one to determine the degree to which any prediction instrument improves the accuracy of prediction over one based on knowledge of violation rate alone.

However, while evaluation of predictive efficiency offers a means by which different prediction methods can be compared, there are a number of factors which influence the actual utility of a prediction. Gottfredson (1967) has suggested that the reliability of the predictor items, the "selection ratio," the "base rate," the method of combining predictors, and the representativeness of the sample all affect the utility of prediction. The selection ratio refers to the number of individuals who are "chosen" (e.g., accepted for parole) relative to the total population. Specifically, if only a few individuals are accepted for parole because the cost of incorrectly identifying a failure as a success is high, then fairly low validity coefficients may be acceptable (Gottfredson 1967). The "base rate" refers to the proportion of individuals in the population who fall into the category to be predicted. This base rate affects both the ease with which predictors are isolated and the accuracy of discrimination on cross validation. For instance, in the case of relatively rare occurrences, it will be difficult to isolate predictors because the variation in the criterion is small.

Monachesi (1950) has suggested additional factors related to the efficiency of prediction. Certainly predictive efficiency depends heavily on the accuracy of the information used to derive the predictor items. It also depends on the classification of such information into reliably standardized categories. In all events, however, a prediction instrument must provide more information than is available from knowledge of the base rate of occurrence of the behavior in the population. Sampling considerations are of obvious importance, for the introduction of systematic bias in the original sample will reduce the validity of predictions attempted on a new sample. Furthermore, Monachesi (1950) points out that for the most part researchers do not know whether the predictors they have uncovered remain stable over time. In fact, he suggests that any reliable prediction method must take account of changes in the administration of criminal justice over time.

Historical Overview

The earliest studies in the prediction of recidivism included nearly all the information that could be collected from prison records. As early as 1923 Warner attempted to relate background factors to success or failure on parole, with limited results. Of some 60 items he obtained from preparole records, only two differentiated the success and failure groups, and he erroneously concluded that such information was of little value in decisionmaking. Somewhat later in 1923 Hart, who is credited with originating the parole prediction effort, suggested that perhaps if Warner had combined several of the factors which had individually failed to show significance, the results might be more promising. Furthermore, he suggested that Warner failed to use a measure of the statistical significance of the differences in percentage of parole violators or nonviolators in several item categories.

The first large-scale attempt to determine the relationship between background factors and parole outcome was that of Burgess which received attention somewhat later in the 1920s. The table of expectancy rates of parole violation/ nonviolation which he developed was based on a comparison of violation rates for subgroups of offenders with the violation rate of the overall parolee population. Burgess computed the violation rates for subcategories of offenders exhibiting certain patterns of background factors. When the violation rate for the subgroup exhibiting a specific background factor was lower than the overall violation rate, that factor was deemed a positive one with respect to parole outcome. Each of these positive factors was entered into an experience table with the parolee receiving 1 point for each positive factor in his preparole background. The parole violation rates were then computed for parolees having accumulated different numbers of positive factors. A total of 21 background factors were investigated, and those parolees exhibiting only a total of 2 to 4 points had a 76 percent failure rate while those whose total was 16 to 21 points had only a 1.5 percent failure rate. In attempting to predict parole outcome on the basis of the number of points a parole candidate had accumulated, "it was assumed that future candidates for parole would have the same chance of success as those having the same number of favorable factors in the original population" (Lejins 1962, p. 211). This assumption would hold true only if the conditions of parole remained the same—an unlikely occurrence (Monachesi 1950). Additional problems with the Burgess method revolve around the arbitrary assignment of equal weights to each factor and the potentially substantial intercorrelations among the factors which remained uninvestigated. However, Vold (1935) tested the Burgess method and found it to predict adequately when the changing rates of parole violation for the entire institution were taken into account (Monachesi 1950). Likewise, Sanders (1935) was able to utilize the Burgess method with some degree of success, as was Hakeem in 1948 (Monachesi 1950).

The Gluecks (1930) attempted to remedy the problems inherent in equal weighting of factors by assigning them weights on the basis of their degree of relationship to the criterion. The offenders' scores reflected the percentage of failure within the subgroup of offenders possessing each relevant characteristic. In using only those factors exhibiting a close relationship with the criterion, background factors such as industrial habits, frequency and seriousness of prereformatory crime, arrests, penal experience, economic responsibility, mental status, and frequency of offenses committed within the reformatory were considered. Gottfredson (1967) has criticized the Glueck studies for their failure to use an accurate base rate or to use a representative sample of the population they studied.

These two major prediction efforts were followed by a spate of studies which basically added, deleted, or revised specific variables. The selection of these variables continued to be determined by the content of available prison records. "This common data source led several independent investigators to utilize approximately the same variables which gradually resulted in consensus as to a core of relevant predictor variables" (Dean 1968, p. 214). There was little interest in the development of sophisticated analytical techniques, and there was a general neglect of theory. In 1935 Vold attempted to predict the type of treatment best suited to certain subcategories of offenders by using 29 preincarceration factors organized by the Burgess method in a prediction table. Argow, also in 1935, attempted to develop a criminal liability index indicating the probabilities of reformation and nonrearrest in first offenders. It was not until 1936 that Laune's criticisms of the overwhelming dependence on "static categories" emerged. He argued, to the contrary, that postrelease adjustment must certainly be affected in some fashion by the prison experience, and one should therefore logically incorporate changes undergone by inmates during the course of institutionalization if one hoped to increase the accuracy of predictions. Basically Laune used a peer-rating system originally in an attempt to identify those factors related to successful outcome. However, his method was unfortunately later shown to offer little improvement over that of Burgess.

Later research began to encounter what continues to remain the central problem in prediction research—that of failure on cross validation. Predictions derived from different populations of parolees were often inconsistent. In fact, Ohlin found it necessary to continuously adjust his experience tables. On the whole, the post-World War II prediction attempts were characterized by increasing methodological refinement. The emerging use of computers considerably increased analytic rigor as it then became possible to weight the predictor variables on the basis of multiple regression coefficients. The number of predictor variables employed could thus be considerably reduced with minimal loss of predictive power. However, as late as 1968, Dean continued to note that the majority of prediction studies relied on data collected from prison files involving "static" variables which failed to take into account the parolee's postrelease circumstances. He suggested that perhaps a point of diminishing return had finally been reached wherein mere application of more rigorous analytical techniques to the same type of data would achieve little by way of increase in predictive accuracy. This concern remains central to a number of current investigators and will be discussed further in the review of recent research findings.

Classes of Predictor Variables: Review of Recent Research

Life History Variables

The foregoing review of early investigations reveals that life history or criminal behavior variables enjoyed early popularity in the prediction effort. The Burgess prediction table of parole outcome delineated 21 preparole factors associated with the criterion, including work history, marital status, social type, national and ethnic origins, criminal record, and personal habits. The Gluecks' prediction items overlapped with these to some extent: industrial habits, frequency and seriousness of preincarceration crime, prior arrests, prior incarcerations, economic responsibility, mental status, and frequency of offenses committed while institutionalized. Although many significant correlations with parole outcome have been reported, a majority of these early studies have been criticized on the basis of their methodological techniques (Dean and Duggan 1968). Yet it is easy to understand that the heavy emphasis on attempting to predict outcome from life history variables is derived from their ready availability from existing prison records. However, there currently exists a substantial body of literature confirming or disconfirming the results of these early investigations.

More recently, in an extensive study of 500 federal offenders after a minimum of a five-year postprobation period, England (1955) reported that previous criminal record, age, and unstable lower socioeconomic background were significantly associated with recidivism. Litwack (1961) delineated ten statistically significant differences between recidivists and nonrecidivists among juvenile parolees, including height, mother's age, age at first court appearance, age at time of commitment and at parole, and adjustment to institutional rules. The search for effective discriminating variables also revealed that juvenile history, type of offense, and employment and marital status are significantly related to parole outcome (O'Donnell and Stanley 1974). In fact, a prediction attempt by O'Donnell and Stanley (1974) involving the preceding four variables in a series of multiple regression equations resulted in an 80 to 83 percent range of predictive accuracy. A report by Craig and Glick (1963) on ten years' experience with the Glueck social prediction table suggests a relationship between early family care patterns and subsequent delinquency. They found three factors—supervision by mother, discipline by mother, and cohesiveness—to predict more efficiently than the original five factors proposed by the Gluecks (i.e., discipline by father, supervision by mother, affection of father, affection of mother, and cohesiveness of family).

Payne, McCabe, and Walker (1974) also report confirmation of a significant association between selected background variables and recidivism in a sample of offenders who had been committed to a psychiatric hospital. The single most powerful predictor of reconviction in this study was the presence of a prior conviction record, supporting the preponderance of similarly focused research. Also in agreement with a number of other studies was their finding that the second most powerful predictor was the type of current offense. However, their additive prediction model (including a third variable of psychiatric diagnosis) was more successful in identifying the low- rather than the high-risk groups. The generalizability of their findings is unfortunately limited by two considerations: the absence of cross-validation information and the potential unrepresentativeness of their hospitalized sample.

Similarly Babst, Koval, and Neithercutt (1972) were able to construct an index of past criminal behavior which was found to be significantly related to parole outcome when the effects of length of institutionalization were minimized.

In a sample of 7245 male offenders on whom life history information was obtained from the Uniform Parole Reports, the type of admission to prison (e.g., new court commitment, probation revocation, parole violation, etc.) was found to be most highly related to parole outcome. Not surprisingly, offenders without previous sentences or probation or parole violations were the most likely subgroup to succeed on parole, with an 80 percent success rate. The accuracy of outcome discrimination was further refined by Babst, Koval, and Neithercutt (1972) with the addition of items relating to previous criminal behavior, information on alcohol or drug abuse, and the offender's age at release (with those over 25 years old being more likely to succeed).

Generally, investigations have found some index of past criminal behavior to be one of the best predictors of parole outcome. In fact, the California Youth Authority Base Expectancy Table indices included type of offense, age at first admission and at parole, county and court of commitment, admission status, prior commitments, and delinquency contact record (Cartwright et al. 1972). However, one of the major problems in a significant proportion of studies employing life history and criminal behavior predictors is their failure to be confirmed on cross validation. Such was the case with a study by Fildes and Gottfredson (1972), as reported earlier, in which a cluster analysis was used to relate type of admission, offense, prior prison record, prior sentence, drug use, and alcohol involvement to recidivism. An interesting study by Sampson (1974) may shed some light on this problem of replicability. Sampson's (1974) results indicate that the best prognostic variables change over time, with those variables predictive of successful outcome at a one-year follow-up being different from those variables predicting success at two- or three-years postrelease. Unfortunately, in the absence of cross validation, Sampson's (1974) findings are only suggestive and certainly warrant further investigation.

However, as is true of much of the research on the prediction problem, contradictory results are not uncommon. Cockerill (1975) found occupation, education, race, sex, marital status, age, father's occupation, and number of children to significantly differentiate probation successes and failures. Yet, none of his "antisocial behavior" variables such as offense, number of previous convictions, or interval between most recent and current offense could be shown to differentiate the two groups. But it is possible that this failure was due to some unreliability in his criterion categories as he failed to outline clear definitions of success and failure. Blum and Chagnon (1967), on the other hand, clearly defined recidivism as the commission of an indictable offense with a minimum sentence of one year and attempted to control for the effects of type of offense by investigating only property offenders. Life history variables such as age at incarceration, juvenile convictions, adult conviction prior to release, last school grade completed, age leaving school, emotional stability, and Otis IQ were investigated relative to their predictive power. In using multiple linear regression techniques, only three of the eight variables were found to be of statistical significance: age, presence or absence of juvenile conviction, and adult conviction. Furthermore, the predictive power of these three variables, either individually or in combination, was severely restricted as only 13 percent of the variance in the criterion was accounted for by all three. Results from a study by Barron (1962) using Ohlin's Parole Prediction Report on 347 parolees were similarly uncomfirmatory. Using factors of type of offense, sentence, type of offender, home status, family interest, social type, work record, community type, parole job, number of associates, personality, and psychiatric prognosis, Barron (1962) observed a substantial discrepancy between the expected and the actual parole violation rates. He therefore concluded that a random method of selecting men for parole would be as successful as attempting to predict on the basis of Ohlin's Parole Prediction Report. Similarly, Cartwright et al. (1972) found a composite measure using both social and personal factors to more accurately predict parole outcome than life history variables did.

Despite the apparent early success at predicting recidivism from life history variables, it seems obvious in light of more recent research that the utility of such information should be accepted with caution. A number of investigators have attempted to account for these mixed results by citing the inadequacy of prison record data which have been collected by correctional officials to meet their immediate needs. Such data collection techniques often prove inadequate for research purposes (Dean and Duggan 1968; Buikhuisen and Hoekstra 1974; Dean 1968). "Working with existing records leaves us with questions about the reliability and the validity of the data concerned" (Buikhuisen and Hoekstra 1974, p. 63). Furthermore, many investigators have commented on the fact that the focus has been almost entirely on discovering the empirical relationship between predictor items and the criterion, without reference to the theoretical usefulness of the items (Gottfredson 1967; Buikhuisen and Hoekstra 1974; Rogers 1968). Gottfredson (1967) suggests that "the strictly empirical, atheoretical approach of many prediction studies has . . . led to neglected opportunities for improvement of both prediction and criminological theory" (p. 175). There are also criticisms of the "static" nature of background-life history factors. Little can be done by way of therapeutic intervention regarding age, family history, and previous criminal record. There are those investigators who are not convinced that using such variables is the most fruitful approach to predicting outcome.

Buikhuisen and Hoekstra (1974) attempted to deal with some of these criticisms by interpreting their results within the theoretical framework of Sutherland's differential association hypothesis of criminal behavior. Some 451 offenders were examined with respect to ten items differentiating the recidivists from the nonrecidivists. Those items successfully differentiating the two outcome groups included marital status, broken home, negative atmosphere at home, siblings also delinquent, reared in an institution, many moves, psychiatric reports, many previous convictions, and a history of long periods of detention.

Phi coefficients showed only a weak relationship with the criterion, and partial correlations revealed that only the number of previous convictions and the number of times an offender had moved prior to sentencing significantly contributed to predicting recidivism. Multiple correlations revealed that only 17 percent of the variance in the criterion could be accounted for with these variables. However, the authors then investigated the hypothesis that returning to one's former address upon release would significantly increase the likelihood of recidivism. This hypothesis was derived from Sutherland's emphasis on the importance of criminal contacts to the maintenance of criminal behavior, and presumably returning to one's former residence constitutes a continuation of criminal contacts. Interestingly, Buikhuisen and Hoekstra (1974) obtained a significantly lower percentage of reconvictions among those parolees who did not return to their former address. The authors suggested, therefore, that both internal and external factors were important in predicting recidivism.

. . . [T]he potential positive effect of moving is dependent on the characteristics of the criminogenetic factors operating. In cases of crimes predominately caused by external factors a change of environment may be optimally helpful (Buikhuisen and Hoekstra 1974, p. 67).

A factor analysis of their data revealed three factors accounting for 30 percent of the variance: family stability, criminal history, and asocial milieu. Buikhuisen and Hoekstra (1974) concluded that while moving has a positive effect, the ultimate outcome depends on other factors including family environment and the presence of individual traits likely to result in delinquency.

Supporting results have been obtained by Craig and Budd (1967) regarding the importance of criminal associations to recurrent criminal behavior. In an examination of juvenile offenders, the authors concluded that juveniles most frequently commit property offenses while in the company of others and that 90 percent of the more serious offenses were committed in the presence of companions. Furthermore, in 80 percent of their cases in which the offense was "serious," recidivism occurred. However, while arguing for the existence of a significant relationship between companionship and recidivism, the authors caution that their results are derived from group trends and therefore may not be applicable to individual cases. Yet despite the emergence of several studies employing a theoretical approach and interpretation as well as those which highlight the importance of investigating less "static" factors than background characteristics, much research remains to be done in this area.

Personality Variables

The MMPI. Attempts to predict parole success on the basis of personality variables constitute the second most extensively explored category of predictors.

Generally, personality inventories were believed to offer great potential advantage in predicting from current status rather than from past behavior. Panton (1962b) points out that successful adjustment involves the interaction of many psychosocial forces of which personality is one. ". . . [B]y virtue of its limited flexibility, [personality] serves as a focal point and governs to a great degree the rehabilitative measures taken . . ." (Panton 1962b, p. 484). As in the case of life history characteristics, a variety of personality correlates of parole outcome have been reported. Much of the research in this area has focused on the MMPI, principally because it has been found to be useful in a wide variety of situations (Hathaway and Monachesi 1963; Rempel 1958). Despite early optimism regarding the utility of the MMPI alone in predicting recidivism, more recent research employing cross-validation samples has, at best, offered mixed support, and at worst has failed to confirm the value of the MMPI in prediction. Generally the *Hy* and *Pd* scales appear to be the most discriminating relative to parole success or failure, although Dunham (1954) reports that *D* scale elevations significantly discriminated recidivist adult offenders.

Mixed results were obtained by Panton (1962b) in attempting to use the MMPI as a predictor of successful parole. The mean profiles of 41 male parole violators were compared to the mean profiles of 2198 consecutive admissions to the prison population, with the result that the violators scored lower than the general prison population on the *Mf* scale. When compared with nonviolators, the violators exhibited (1) a greater frequency of two or more scale scores above $T = 70$, and (2) greater frequency of T scores above 70 on the *Hs, D, Hy, Pd,* and *Ma* scales. Panton constructed a 26-item Parole Violator scale from those MMPI items which differentiated the parole violators from the nonviolators. The 26 items represent four clusters: (1) those related to hostility, resistance, and independence; (2) those related to social imperturbability, callousness, frankness, and amorality; (3) those suggesting a lack of responsibility and inadequate personal relations; and (4) those suggesting poor morale, doubt, and premorbid thoughts. However, Panton's (1962b) Parole Violator scale failed to be confirmed on cross validation.

Panton (1962a) also attempted to identify habitual criminalism using the MMPI, although again the results must be interpreted with caution. A comparison of MMPI profiles for 50 first offenders and 50 "habitual criminals" (three or more previous felony sentences) revealed differences on the *Pd, Ma,* and Prison Adjustment scale of the MMPI (Panton 1958). The elevation for the habitual criminals ". . . implies a greater sociopathy and a lower tolerance for stress than is indicated for the nonhabituals" (Panton 1962a, p. 133). The most effective differentiation was obtained with a combination of the *Pd* and Prison Adjustment scales constructed from 77 items which Panton (1962a) subsequently labeled the Habitual Criminal (HC) scale. The HC scale survived initial cross validation but was of somewhat less predictive accuracy in identifying those offenders having only one or two previous sentences. Panton (1962a) cautions against general use of the HC scale until it undergoes further cross validation.

The MMPI has shown some utility as a basis for the construction of prison adjustment prediction scales. Panton (1958) was able to correctly identify 76 percent of an "adjusted" inmate group and 75 percent of a "nonadjusted" inmate group on the first validation sample with a 42-item Prison Adjustment scale (where "adjustment" was indicated by the absence of infractions of prison rules). Panton (1958) attempted to refine the scale by using only 36 items which survived additional cross validation, and this resulted in an 82 percent accuracy of prediction on two separate "adjusted" inmate groups and an 87 percent, an 85 percent, and a 93 percent accuracy of prediction on three "nonadjusted" inmate samples. Panton concluded that his Prison Adjustment scale represented a gain in predictive power over clinical prognoses alone for the "nonadjusted" prisoner groups. Similarly, Wattron (1963) was able to construct a prison maladjustment scale using 72 items derived from the MMPI that correctly identified 83 percent of a maladjusted validation sample. However, this prison maladjustment scale failed to prove useful in identifying potential recidivists, thereby limiting its utility in parole prediction research.

Despite the modest success some investigators have had in predicting recidivism from the MMPI alone, the majority of investigations have failed to confirm its usefulness in prediction. Smith and Lanyon (1968) failed to obtain significant results in their attempt to predict probation violations from MMPI responses. They concluded that the use of a base expectancy table resulted in predictions that were more accurate than those from the MMPI. Freeman and Mason (1952) repeatedly failed to validate several scales differentiating recidivists from nonrecidivists by using the MMPI. Christensen and LeUnes (1974) used a short form of the MMPI and were able to obtain a discriminant function which differentiated murderers and narcotics offenders from other types of offenders. However, they were unable to similarly compute a significant discriminant function for predicting recidivism. Likewise, Mack (1969) concluded from his investigations that ". . . results . . . strongly suggest that the MMPI, considered alone, is not associated with recidivism to any important extent within such homogeneous populations" (p. 614). Mandel and Barron (1966) also failed to cross-validate recidivism scales developed from the MMPI. When they later attempted an alternative prediction based on overall profile configurations, a sorting by five clinical psychologists of 372 MMPI profiles yielded predictions of nonrecidivism that were actually *less* accurate than what would be expected by chance alone. Not surprisingly, Mandel and Barron (1966) concluded:

We are therefore in agreement with Clark (1948) that "blind" inspectional analysis of MMPI profiles alone does not yield significant differences between groups of the type under consideration and that such analysis is of little or no value in predicting future recidivistic and nonrecidivistic behavior in individual cases (p. 36).

Attempts to combine MMPI data with other information have been only moderately successful in predicting outcome. Briggs, Wirt, and Johnson (1961) were able to identify potential delinquents by combining information related to family disruption with information from MMPI profiles associated with delinquency. However, several attempts to actually predict recidivism have failed. When Mandel and Barron (1966) added life history, interview, and observational data to the information provided by the MMPI profiles, they again failed to predict the criterion groups. They suggested by way of explanation that environmental factors such as family influences, vocation, and economic status vary in different groups of offenders and that such factors are likely to play an important role in accounting for recidivism. Similarly, Gough, Wenk, and Rozynko (1965) were unable to surpass the 63 percent accuracy of their predictions from a base expectancy table and the California Psychological Inventory when data from the MMPI were incorporated. On the basis of predictive equations derived from a multiple regression analysis of these three instruments, Gough, Wenk, and Rozynko (1965) concluded that the single most powerful predictor of parole outcome was case history information organized into a base expectancy table (59 percent accuracy rate). Thus it would appear that, despite its usefulness in other clinical contexts, the MMPI is only of modest value in the effort to predict parole outcome.

Other Personality Instruments. The search for effective predictor variables has resulted in a number of theoretically isolated investigations which have employed a variety of additional personality measures. Unfortunately, few of the predictor items reported have been investigated by other researchers. The absence of cross validation and the failure to confirm initially promising predictor candidates in other offender samples characterize the research on other personality instruments. These studies remain isolated findings which are unconfirmed by further investigation.

Taylor (1967), cognizant of the literature on peer-rating techniques, attempted to validate the subjective self-evaluations of delinquent girls of each other's readiness for parole against the independent ratings of the parole board. Interestingly, the girls' predictions of who was most and least likely to succeed on parole agreed very closely with the parole board ratings. Those girls obtaining the lowest rank orders in the peer-rating procedure tended to fail on parole within 6 months of their release. An attempt was made to formalize and objectify the information which was utilized by the girls in making these ratings by examining the relationship between psychometric data and recidivism in the same population of delinquent girls. Unfortunately none of the psychological test instruments, including the MMPI, the 16 Personality Factor Test, the IPAT Humor Test, the Eysenck T.R. scale, Raven's Progressive Matrices, the Criminal Attitude scale, and two behavior rating scales, exhibited any discriminatory power.

The Eysenck Personality Inventory was also used in a study by Eysenck and Eysenck (1974) although the authors suggest that the sample sizes were too small to permit definite conclusions. The recidivists among the small group of borstal boys whom they investigated scored significantly higher on the extraversion scale with trends on the P and neuroticism scales. Significant differences on the neuroticism scale of the Eysenck Personality Inventory between groups of recidivists, nonrecidivists, and normals were also found in a study by Black and Gregson (1973). However, the results of this later study failed to confirm the finding by the Eysencks of any significant differences on the extraversion scale.

Black and Gregson (1973) concurrently investigated time perspective as a potential discriminator between recidivists and nonrecidivists on the hypothesis that:

It seems as though the recidivist has not developed a sense of "becoming" and his behavior suggests that he is likely to have less extensive future and past time perspectives than "normals" and to anticipate fewer "personalized" events (Black and Gregson 1973, p. 50).

Both prisoner groups exhibited a shorter range of future time perspective than normals, but there were no significant differences between the recidivists and the nonrecidivists within the prisoner group. The hypothesis relative to past time perspective was not supported. However, while the findings are interesting, the fact that the investigators were unable to equate for age between the three groups may have resulted in artifactual effects on time perspective and extraversion.

The potential predictive power of empathy and socialization has also been recently investigated by Deardorff et al. (1975). Hogan's empathy scale was administered to 13 first offenders, 17 repeat offenders, and 16 controls (normals), as was the socialization scale of the CPI. The nonprisoners and the first offenders scored significantly higher on both empathy and socialization than the recidivists. Once again, while the results are suggestive, the sample sizes were small and any conclusions must await confirmatory findings.

Self-esteem was examined relative to parole adjustment by Bennett (1974) who suggested that successful parole outcome would be positively related to self-esteem as measured by the Coopersmith Self-Esteem scale during the prerelease period. Results showed a low positive correlation at 6 months and almost none at 1 and at 2 years' follow-up. When Bennett examined the influence of base expectancy scores, time served, age at intake, age at release, educational achievement, and mental status, the relationship between adjustment and prerelease self-esteem decreased further. Bennett (1974) concluded that ". . . factors other than self-esteem are more closely related to adjustment after the initial period of adjustment" (pp. 354–55) and that perhaps inmates failed to shift the basis of their comparisons from their fellow inmates until after their release. If such is the case, Bennett suggests that an inmate's self-esteem immediately following his release tends to be artificially high. In light of what one might be led to expect from criminological theories, it would certainly seem that the role of self-esteem in determining parole outcome is an area of personality assessment deserving considerably more attention.

A number of studies have focused on more global psychiatric ratings and diagnostic categories in the attempt to uncover personality correlates of parole success. However, these investigations have met with mixed success. Stang (1967) reports that forensic psychiatrists' predictions of recidivism following examination of offenders were correct in only 50 percent of the cases investigated. Cloninger and Guze (1973) conducted a psychiatric study of female felons 2 to 3 years following parole with respect to criminal recidivism. Not surprisingly recidivism was found to be significantly related to past criminal record, high school dropouts, and never having been married. In addition, however, recidivism rates were also found to be positively correlated with psychiatric diagnoses in the case of sociopathy, drug dependence, and homosexual behavior. Unfortunately, high intercorrelations between criminal history items, social history items, and diagnostic ratings make it difficult to single out the contribution of any one factor. The only factor which was clearly related to recidivism and whose relationship is supported by numerous other studies was drug abuse.

A study by Satten et al. (1970) uncovered "a meaningful association . . . between level of ego disorganization of . . . 162 delinquent boys . . . and their involvement in criminal activities after release" (p. 277). The proportion of boys who were convicted for felony offenses tended to increase in proportion to the severity of observed ego pathology. This pattern terminated in the most severe cases as the boys were hospitalized. An earlier finding by Payne, McCabe, and Walker (1974) regarding hospitalized offenders suggests parallel results. Psychiatric diagnostic group was found to be a weak predictor of recidivism, with schizophrenics having the lowest probabilities of reconviction and psychopathics the highest. However, statistical significance was lost upon exclusion of those offenders who were readmitted to the hospital without a reconviction. Payne, McCabe, and Walker (1974) note ". . . schizophrenics' probabilities of reconviction are lowest largely because they tend to be readmitted either before committing another offense or without being prosecuted for it" (p. 61). Another study by McWilliams (1975) highlights additional potentially interactive effects between social agency response and outcome which mitigates against conclusion of a direct relationship between psychiatric diagnosis and recidivism. In an examination of sentencing and recidivism by personality type, McWilliams (1975) discovered that probation officers were more likely to recommend probation for introverted neurotics and that, once on probation, this group was least likely to be reconvicted. Based on Eysenck's theory of criminal behavior, McWilliams (1975) suggests that extraverts tend to condition less well and are therefore more likely to be delinquent while neuroticism acts as a drive reinforcing extraversion or introversion tendencies. He further suggests that the decision to recommend probation may, in fact, be related more to the characteristics of the probation officer than to those of the offender. Similarly, Cowden (1966a) found neurotic delinquents to exhibit a significantly more positive postrelease adjustment (based on parole agents' reports) than social delinquents and suggested that the neurotic delinquent is perhaps more susceptible to adult influence. Cowden and Pacht (1967) found that a clinical service global prognosis based on ratings of degree of anxiety, guilt, dependency, and depression were related to outcome as were the ability to relate to adults and degree of religious involvement. Findings by Levi and Tracy (1971) similarly suggest that drug addicts showing high degrees of anxiety, depression, and activity, as measured by the Johnson Temperament Analysis Test, are more successful as outpatients at 3 years' follow-up.

Several recent studies have investigated the possibility of a relationship between institutional adjustment and postrelease outcome in an effort to uncover "intermediate" predictor variables. Cowden (1966b) suggests that for juvenile offenders there may be a more distinct linear relationship between behavior within the institution and behavior in postrelease circumstances which would allow correctional officials to utilize institutional adjustment in prediction. If such a relationship is found to empirically exist, an indirect approach to therapeutic intervention relative to long-term outcome may become possible. Once those factors relevant to fostering a positive institutional adjustment are uncovered for different types of individuals, manipulation of those factors to provide the most beneficial environment for the juvenile offender may certainly prove more feasible within the confines of an institution. However fruitful such an approach may prove to be, empirical investigations of the potential predictive power of institutional adjustment are few. Cowden (1966b) studied 270 first commitment boys over a follow-up period of 5 years. Age and personality prognosis were the variables most significantly related to institutional adjustment, while seriousness of offense and home environment were found to be unrelated. Recidivism was found to be associated with institutional adjustment, personality prognosis, and age. A combination of institutional adjustment and personality prognosis factors resulted in increased predictive efficiency. However, Cowden (1966b) points out that his findings are limited by the restricted range of socioeconomic status and home environments he sampled. His results revealed that the higher socioeconomic status boys had committed the more serious offenses, suggesting that middle-class boys are not institutionalized as delinquent as readily as lower-class boys. While Cowden (1966b) cautions that he was better able to predict institutional adjustment than recidivism, his findings suggest that the presence of continuing behavior problems in the institution are indicative of more intractable problems which result in continued delinquency. A second study by Dunham (1954) also reveals a significant relationship between institutional conduct and recidivism among adult offenders, with the recidivists showing a significantly greater frequency of punishment for institutional rule violations than the nonrecidivists. On the other hand, somewhat confusing results were obtained by Cymbalisty, Schuck, and Dubeck (1975) in their examination of academic achievement level, institutional adjustment, and recidivism among juvenile delinquents. Their hypothesis was that ". . . strong academic motivation, higher academic achievement level as well as better institutional adjustment reflect a greater degree of conformity which may represent a better prognosis for parole outcome" (p. 289). "Institutional adjustment" evaluations consisted of bimonthly ratings by the staff on conduct, attitude, work and study habits, personal habits, cooperation, and initiative. Cymbalisty, Schuck, and Dubeck (1975) found a significant positive relationship between institutional adjustment and parole outcome, but the correlation was low. School grade and behavior were also significantly related to parole outcome in the hypothesized direction. Disappointingly, however, the magnitudes of the correlations were small, and the variables were highly intercorrelated with the multiple correlation between all variables and parole outcome accounting for only 11 percent of the variance. However, Cymbalisty, Schuck, and Dubeck (1975) believed an adequate degree of predictive efficiency was achieved by partitioning subjects into subgroups on the basis of all possible combinations of institutional adjustment (three levels: excellent, average, and poor), academic achievement (three levels), and two levels of IQ (high and low with an IQ of 90 as a cutoff). Those who were intellectually above average or average, who also exhibited high academic achievement and excellent institutional adjustment, achieved 66 percent and 71 percent success rates, respectively, while those who were intellectually average or above average with poor behavior and low academic achievement exhibited only an 18 percent rate of success. An additional effort to relate intellectual and cognitive factors to parole outcome was made by Englehardt (1970). A discriminant function analysis revealed that ten variables related to intellectual functioning effectively discriminated between rehabilitated and nonrehabilitated socially maladjusted boys in a special education program. However, contradictory results had been obtained earlier by Dunham (1954) in an investigation of adult offenders. None of the variables related to educational achievement (high school grade, total education, age on leaving school, Stanford Achievement score, Wide Range Vocabulary Test, Moore's Arithmetic Reasoning Test, or the Spelling Test) and only one of the IQ variables (Digits Span of the Wechsler) which Dunham investigated were significantly related to recidivism.

Combination of Variables

Several studies have attempted to combine both life history and personality variables with varying degrees of success. Wenk and Emrich (1972) collected demographic, intellectual, vocational, and psychological information on over 4000 assaultive youths in California. They found recidivism to significantly relate to three variables: a violent admission offense (over 70 percent favorable outcome), four or more previous admissions (46.5 percent favorable outcome), and moderate to serious opiate involvement (42.4 percent favorable outcome). Recidivism was related to the commission of an additional violent offense and correlated with (1) several life history variables (a history of violence, four or more previous admissions, a violent admission offense, psychiatric referral for evaluation of violence potential, severe alcohol problems, and being of Mexican-American extraction), (2) intelligence (violent recidivists were less intelligent than nonviolent recidivists), and (3) a few personality variables derived from the CPI, the MMPI, and the Interpersonal Personality Inventory. Cartwright et al. (1972) similarly attempted to develop a composite predictive index from social, personal, and life history variables for juvenile probationers. From 18 individual predictor measures Cartwright et al. (1972) determined that the social factors (e.g., family background) were more closely related to the criterion than the personal factors, and a combination of both proved to be more predictive of outcome than the life history variables.

One potentially fertile area has received surprisingly little attention in the search for effective parole predictors. A number of parole prediction studies have implicated the postrelease circumstances of the parolee as having some relationship to parole success, but it appears that no systematic investigation of this relationship has been undertaken in correctional research. As early as 1931 Tibbitts reported on a number of factors that he had discovered to be related to parole outcome, including type of neighborhood to which the offender was paroled, whether he was a resident or a transient, and his first job on parole. However, more recent research has neglected to investigate these predictors further. In an excellent article on interaction and parole prediction, Dean and Duggan (1969) point out that according to Cohen's theory of deviant behavior, an interaction between three important life factors (the situation, group norms and identifications, and value orientations) is necessary to result in any given behavior. An examination of 98 parole failures who had been returned to prison on a new sentence and 55 parole successes (at one-year follow-up) revealed that the three variables most closely related to the criterion in each of the above three categories could be combined to increase predictive efficiency over that of using variables in only one or two categories alone. The three situation variables most closely related to parole outcome involved return to a rural rather than an urban environment (rural = favorable), length of time employed on a prerelease arranged parole job (6 months or more = favorable), and the proportion of time employed during the parole period (75 percent time = favorable). The most favorable identification variables included never expecting to have further legal problems at the time of release, considering oneself to be a "cut above" the average inmate, and having a low score on a scale of identification with criminal others. Value orientation items that were favorable to a successful parole outcome were being a first offender, being 26 or older when released on parole, and having a low score on the scale of orientation to criminal means.

The importance of stable employment on parole for successful parole outcome has been confirmed by the results of several other studies. O'Donnell and Stanley (1974) found that those parolees who could maintain steady employment tended to be more successful on parole than those who were unemployed. Similarly, Platt and Labate (1976) found steady employment and the absence of drug use on parole to be associated with successful parole outcome in 79 youthful heroin offenders. Finally, Gottfredson and Lipstein (1975) found the "consistency" of claimed occupation [i.e., ". . . tasks or environments that provide convergent demands and rewards and are presumed to promote job satisfaction and stability" (p. 645)] to correlate with the absence of recidivism in a sample of 341 parolees and probationers. The positive findings linking parole success and employment status and postrelease circumstances are consistent with theories of criminal behavior and are certainly deserving of further investigation. If future research substantiates the existence of these relationships, important implications relative to programming for parolees should be explored in an effort to reduce recidivism.

Summary of Recent Research Findings

A number of trends are evident from this review of recent research on classes of predictor variables. Among the life history variables, some index of past criminal behavior, e.g., number of previous incarcerations, age at first arrest etc., seems to be most consistently related to the criterion of parole outcome. Type of offense is related in a perhaps unexpected direction with offenders against persons generally constituting a better parole risk than offenders against property. The probability of parole violation generally seems to decline with increasing age. However, opiate and alcohol involvement are consistently negative prognostic factors. Among the personality studies fewer consistent results appear. Generally the *Hy* and *Pd* scales of the MMPI differentiate recidivists from non-recidivists, although there is much contradictory evidence on this point. The socialization scale of the CPI has also been found to be useful in predicting parole outcome, as have the more global psychiatric diagnoses of sociopathy and psychopathy. Institutional adjustment has been implicated in prediction studies of juvenile offenders, but again results remain unconfirmed with adults. Perhaps most fruitful with respect to potential for therapeutic intervention are the few studies strongly relating the postrelease circumstances of the parolee to his parole outcome—specifically the factors of steady employment and breaking of the ties with his original neighborhood. The importance of parole employment has also been confirmed with drug-abusing offenders. However, as is the case with most variables that initially appear to have predictive power, a substantial amount of supportive research remains to be done before the generalizability of these early results is confirmed.

Confounding Issues in Previous Research

Concerns have arisen recently regarding the validity of a substantial proportion of the research on predictor variables primarily centering around parole/probation selection procedures and the criteria by which parole/probation is revoked. Recognition of a subjective bias potentially inherent in these two procedures has affected the confidence with which the reliability and the validity of the criterion measures are viewed. Exploratory research into these problems has resulted in the opinion held by many investigators that the relationships reported in several previous studies are, in fact, artifactual.

Scarpitti and Stephenson (1968) call attention to the fact that often "conclusions regarding the effectiveness of probation are generally based upon the number of probationers who complete their supervision without revocation or the amount of postrelease recidivism occurring among those who complete supervision" (p. 361). The authors suggest that these are actually two different measures of success and should be viewed as such. Many unknown and uncontrollable variables influence the above outcomes, including the philosophy of the probation officer, the intensity of the officer's contact with the probationer, the presence of unknown offenses, and the philosophy of the court on continuing probation in light of known offenses. Scarpitti and Stephenson (1968) question the high rate of probationer success reported in some studies, particularly since their own investigations have led to the conclusion that most probationer supervision is superficial and largely ritualistic. They were curious as to why so few specialized programs involving more intensive contacts with offenders claim so high a success rate, in contrast to expectation. Their results on juvenile offenders suggested that the background characteristics of an offender were significantly associated with differential assignment to institutional treatment centers such that the lower-class, poorly educated black offender was most likely to be sent to a state reformatory. Those offenders who were placed on probation, on the other hand, were more likely to have achieved a higher level of education, to have greater employment experience, to come from higher socioeconomic strata, and to have a greater degree of family organization. The pattern of delinquency history an offender exhibited also appeared to affect his assignment to treatment, with nearly half of the probationers having no history of prior court appearances. "Insofar as previous court history and age of first court appearance are associated with continued delinquency, the probationers appear to be the best risks and [the reformatory] boys the worst" (Scarpitti and Stephenson 1968, p. 364). The probationers were found to be less antisocial, less delinquent, less anxious and hostile, to be better emotionally adjusted, and to have a slightly better attitude toward themselves and toward work than the reformatory boys. "From all indications, it would appear that Probation received the less delinquent and better socially and psychologically adjusted juvenile offender" (Scarpitti and Stephenson 1968, p. 365). Furthermore, within the probationer group itself, the successes were more likely to be white, to be in school, to be better educated, and to have a minor delinquency history. With respect to recidivism, the probationer group also had the lowest rates and the reformatory group the highest, even when an attempt was made to control for the substantial differences in background variables. Scarpitti and Stephenson (1968) concluded:

. . . it would appear that Probation rids itself during the course of treatment of those boys who are most delinquent and hardest to resocialize. . . . The low rate of recidivism of the probationers who complete treatment may partially be accounted for by the high rate of recidivism of in-program failures, on the grounds that Probation rids itself of high recidivism risks" (pp. 368, 369).

Other investigators have also examined the possibility that probationers and parolees constitute a highly selected sample of offenders into which systematic bias has been introduced. Bottomley (1973) found that parole boards were more likely to grant parole on the second review than on the first, with more offenders who were serving sentences for violent offenses (52 percent) than for nonviolent offenses (41 percent) being recommended for parole. Those inmates who were recommended for parole had more stable marriages and better work records in prison, had arranged for jobs on discharge, and were more likely to be "model prisoners." "The most common single factor which was taken into account in making recommendations for parole was evidence of the man's changed attitudes in prison towards a more positive (and law-abiding) way of life" (Bottomley 1973, p. 33). The introduction of systematic bias in the original sample suggests that the correlates of parole outcome that have been uncovered may be artifactual. The generalizability of such results may be limited. Perhaps an entirely different pattern of variables would be discovered if offenders were randomly assigned to treatment groups despite the difficulties such an assignment poses for correctional officials.

Attention has been similarly paid to the potential bias in results which may have been introduced by the nonuniformity of criteria related to the revocation of parole. In attempting to shed some light on the well-known "fact" that type of offense is one of the better predictors of parole outcome, Neithercutt (1972) hypothesized a direct relationship between outcome and a differential standard of parole performance for the more dangerous criminal offenders. He expected that the more "dangerous" parolees (i.e. having committed offenses such as willful homicide, aggravated assault, and rape) would be more likely to be returned to prison on a technical violation. Drawing on the Uniform Parole Reports, a total sample of 83,419 offenders paroled between 1965 and 1968 having a 1-year follow-up was compiled. Detailed examination of records revealed that a lower percentage of "person offenders" were returned to prison on new commitments than were "property offenders." The percentage of "willful homicide" offenders returned to prison on new commitments was the lowest of all categories. Neithercutt (1972) suggested that the practice of returning a parolee to prison as a technical violator may be viewed by the paroling authority as a crime preventive measure relating to the concept of danger.

Finally, from his investigations Neithercutt (1972) concluded:

. . . [R]esults suggest that property offenders are not held to the same standard of parole performance as are person offenders, in that person offenders are much more frequently coded as technical violators though their parole violation rates are consistently far below those of property offenders (p. 87).

Unfortunately, it seems possible that the predictive power of one item (type of offense), consistently shown to be significantly related to parole outcome, may actually be an artifactual result of the differential application of criminal justice. Neithercutt's (1972) study exemplifies precisely the confounding problems outlined by Gottfredson (1967) which result from reliance on social agency reaction in delineating the criteria of outcome.

In a somewhat different approach, Takagi (1969) examined the effects of parole agents' judgments on recidivism rates in two different parole district offices (one characterized by high and the other by low recidivism rates). A total of 14 parole agents were asked to give their recommendations for revocation or continuation of parole in response to nine hypothetical case histories. The two districts differed substantially in their overall likelihood of recommending return to prison despite the fact that the relevant "facts" in each hypothetical case history were identical for the agents drawn from both districts. Even within each parole district the degree of uniformity in decisions was small, with there being greater agreement among parole officers in the high recidivism district. The low recidivism district was described as one in which parole agents expressed a ". . . concern for client needs with emphasis on advocacy" (Takagi 1969, p. 196), while the philosophy of the high recidivism district was ". . . analogous to that of a physician who decides what is best for the client" (Takagi 1969, p. 196). Agents from the low recidivism district reported more job dissatisfaction associated with their personalized approach, while the agents from the high recidivism district reported greater satisfaction associated with their values of professionalism. Takagi (1969) obviously concluded that, with respect to likelihood of being returned to prison, it makes a difference to the parolee which district he is assigned to as well as which parole agent handles his case within each district. Additional information from a study by Adams and Vetter (1971) indicates a significantly lower degree of recidivism in instances where individual parole agent caseload is small. A small caseload allowed the agents they surveyed to devote greater time to each probationer, thereby increasing the intensity of the interpersonal correctional process. This heightened intensity of probation supervision was found to enhance the probability of successful outcome (Adams and Vetter 1971).

It should be clear that until concerns can be disspelled regarding the uniformity of criteria by which parole/probation is revoked, the validity and generalizability of results relating to predictor variables must remain in question. This is not to suggest that the problems inherent in conducting research in a correctional setting and in evaluating outcome are minimal or to be dismissed. Rather, considerable attention should be paid to them, and an acknowledgment of limitations should be included when results are reported.

The Pros and Cons of Prediction: An Overview

The utility of incorporating prediction instruments into the routine evaluation of correctional processes has been a controversial issue almost since its inception. The arguments against their implementation, which are lengthy and varied, are generally expounded by the officials and staff of correctional institutions. On the other side, researchers and evaluators argue the advantages to efficient and consistent dispensation of justice offered by the incorporation of knowledge derived from such empirical investigation. A brief review of the major issues is necessary for an accurate appraisal of the future of predictions in the correctional setting.

Criticisms

Generally criticisms of parole prediction instruments center around several major issues. First, it is often pointed out that predictions are derived from the experiences of *groups* of persons, and therefore they may not be appropriate in predicting any one individual's behavior. Glaser (1962) comments that "the only consistently accurate prediction of probation or parole outcome is not prognosis on individual cases, but prediction of the relative outcome rates for different groups of offenders" (p. 239). Yet it should be obvious to the reader who has come this far that this is an essentially specious argument. Opponents argue that prediction tables are not universally applicable and must be revised periodically. "Factors which are highly predictive at one time may not be at another" (Evjen 1962, p. 218), thus requiring the revision of prediction tables as often as every year. These adjustments must incorporate "changes in parole board policies and in the nature and extent of pre-release preparation and parole supervision, and . . . major social and economic changes" (Evjen 1962, p. 219).

The second major category of objections derives from the limited nature of the information from which the prediction tables are developed. Much of the data contained in both presentencing investigations and parole reports is neither objective and complete nor quantifiable. Furthermore, as extensively discussed earlier, the single criterion of recidivism as an index of parole failure is unreliable. Parole violation warrants may be issued for any number of reasons unrelated to the commission of a new crime. Personal guidelines and philosophy in issuing warrants may certainly vary from individual to individual; thus the presence of subjective bias is undeniable. Furthermore, there are currently no universal criteria for evaluating "good adjustment," as Evjen (1962) points out that ". . . prediction systems based on different measures of success would not predict the same event" (p. 222). However, proponents of an empirical prediction effort would argue that not all the problems noted above are necessarily inherent in the attempt to predict outcome. Rather, they are reflections of an effort to impose systematic analysis on a complexity of processes that currently defy methodologic rigor. As the administrators of justice gradually eliminate arbitrariness and idiosyncracy, as judgments become structured and articulated, and as researchers excise imprecision in an awareness of the need for uniformly clear definitions, such problems will be relegated to the early history of the prediction effort.

The third major issue of criticism relates to the potential for overlooking subjective elements in parole outcome that cannot be easily measured and incorporated into a prediction table. "Predictive tables, in general, do not take into account the dynamic interplay of the many elements of an inmate's circumstances, relationships, and situations" (Evjen 1962, p. 220). It is argued that unexpected stresses in an individual parolee's postrelease environment and differential parole supervision may contribute to a substantial discrepancy between predicted and actual outcomes. Powers (1962) suggests that the absence of perceived individualization limits the usefulness and implementation of prediction instruments. Powers (1962) shares an opinion expressed by many correctional administrators that prediction tables are antithetical to individualized treatment and that their use introduces elements of mechanization and dehumanization into parole decisions. He fears that many of the desirable and commendable considerations that enter into an individually tailored parole decision will be lost because they resist precise measurement. Correctional officials often counter suggestions of formally structuring offender risk categories by arguing that the experienced parole board member is not only highly conscious of potential risks in releasing an inmate on parole but is also perfectly well able to distinguish a "good risk" from a bad one. It has been countersuggested that, in fact, ". . . the statistical findings tend to corroborate the board members' impressions" (Powers 1962, p. 273). Rogers (1968) and Rogers and Hayner (1968) explored this possibility in an investigation of the degree of congruence between items which had been empirically shown to relate to parole outcome and the perception of salience by correctional officials of those items in making parole decisions. "Incumbents in ten correctional occupations" (Rogers and Hayner 1968) were asked to assess the relative value of 20 prediction items in making a parole decision. Results indicated that items perceived to be most favorable to successful outcome were good preincarceration work record, active family interest, first offense, short delinquency record, and length of time served. Items viewed as most unfavorable to a successful outcome were type of offense, lengthy juvenile delinquency record, and a history of frequent intoxication. These results suggest a not insignificant degree of overlap between theory and empirical findings. However, most interestingly, Rogers (1968) and Rogers and Hayner (1968) found the degree of perceptual accuracy to vary directly with the "incumbent's" educational level, income, age, a nonpunitive orientation, progressiveness, distance from offence, and degree of contact with judges and parole officers. Thus the interactions appear to be complex and merit additional exploration.

However, Powers (1962) points out that subjective judgment cannot be avoided even with the use of prediction instruments since the parole board member must still decide how he will evaluate the significance of the fact that an offender derives from a subgroup which has exhibited a low success rate in the past. Powers (1962) argues that viewing an offender in terms of his membership in a particular risk category handicaps the individualization of treatment and results in unproductive stigmatization. Gottfredson (1967) similarly observes that

The application of statistical decision theory methods as a means of minimizing errors in placement or selection decisions will require the assignment of values to the outcomes, i.e., to the consequences, of the decision alternatives; the positive and negative values of outcomes of both correct and incorrect decisions must be considered (p. 182).

A study by Meade (1974) on the impact of a labeling process on recidivism rates presents results which could tend to discount such concerns. However, the study raises several questions which need additional exploration. The delinquency literature identifies certain characteristics which would presumably affect decisions related to offender sentencing, e.g., age, race, socioeconomic status, family structure, and school status. On empirical investigation Meade (1974) found three variables that significantly related to recidivism in a sample of 438 juvenile offenders: age, having a hearing at the time of the first offense, and school status. The seriousness of the offense was found to be negatively related to recidivism. When Meade (1974) controlled for the effects of other variables and assumed no interactions between variables occurred, age accounted for 20 percent of the variance in recidivism; hearing at time of first offense, 18 percent; school status, 15 percent; and type of offense, 12 percent. Altogether the four variables accounted for 64 percent of the variance in recidivism in this population. Meade (1974) concluded that ". . . systematic bias against any racial, sex, or social class group is non-existent . . . At best, these data only suggest the possible negative effects of labeling" (pp. 87–88).

Coming from an entirely different professional orientation, England (1962) has elaborated an extensive list of "dangers in parole prediction," citing as foremost the perpetuation of inadequate parole policies. His arguments deserve quoting at length. "The use of high-quality prediction devices within low-quality parole jurisdictions will make possible the accurate selection of low-risk cases for parole, thus virtually guaranteeing that these areas will eventually boast high success rates" (p. 266). Noting that prediction devices must operate as if parole quality were uniform for all parolees and assume that this quality is adequate for success in the absence of predisposing offender "failure factors," England (1962) criticizes parole prediction devices for not incorporating the actual conditions of parole as a variable in predicting success or failure.

To "take the risk out of parole" by releasing only those estimated to be good bets would reduce parole to a merely technical level for which the limited talents of office clerks and policemen-turned-parole-agents would suffice (England 1962, p. 267).

England (1962) alternatively suggests that, in contrast to present practice, low-risk prisoners should not be imprisoned at all and that high-risk prisoners are the ones on whom rehabilitation efforts should concentrate. Concurrently, England (1962) fears that the conservatism that is characteristic of an administrative agency may lead to the use of prediction devices exclusively at an administrative level.

Its potential for blocking the further improvement of parole, reducing parole to a technical level, increasing the timorousness of parole boards, and obscuring the need for individual treatment may, in fact, result in its becoming good parole's worst enemy (England 1962, p. 269).

It is obvious from the foregoing discussion that the use of prediction instruments is a controversial issue that is unlikely to be resolved until both the officials and staff of the correctional institution and the researchers responsible for evaluating its treatment programs are able to come to a better understanding of each others' positions. As pointed out in the introductory chapters, communication and intelligible feedback are requisites without which the implementation of efficient, appropriate, and valuable evaluation procedures will fail.

The Advantages

Where law ends, discretion begins, and the exercise of discretion may mean either beneficence or tyranny, either justice or injustice, either reasonableness or arbitrariness (Davis 1971, p. 3).

It is undeniable that at present one cannot predict human behavior with any degree of certainty, and therefore misclassifications of offenders as potential parole successes and failures are expected within statistically determinable limits. Parole prediction instruments can offer only guidelines as to the *probability* of a given outcome. Yet, the fact that that outcome can only be stated in terms of likelihood is insufficient reason for abandoning the use of empirically derived guidelines.

Just as in other fields where computation of categoric risks has been found useful . . . so also in parole we cannot afford to forgo the help offered by the summation of experiences with types of offenders similar to the one whose case is under discussion (Lejins 1962, p. 214).

Researchers and evaluation consultants have argued repeatedly that prediction tables are a valuable check on individual judgment and that years of accumulated experience on parole boards is insufficient guarantee of the accuracy of individual judgment (Evjen 1962; Grant 1962; Glaser 1962). ". . . [E]xperience without systematic study and feedback may only mean that the same errors are repeated for many, many years" (Grant cited in Evjen 1962, p. 218). Systematic feedback is essential to increasing the effectiveness of parole decisions and in limiting what K. C. Davis (1971) eloquently argues is the abuse of discretionary power. It is worth quoting Davis (1971) at some length not only because he is a preeminent authority on administrative law but because the issues he has raised speak to concerns occupying much of contemporary thought in the jurisprudential field.

An outstanding example of completely unstructured discretionary power that can and should be at least partially structured is that of the United States Parole Board. In granting or denying parole, the board makes no attempt to structure its discretionary power . . . it does not structure through statements of findings . . . it has no system of precedents. . . . Checking of discretion is minimal. . . . The board has never publicly stated any substantive principles that guide it in determining the probability that a prisoner will commit another crime or whether his release will be compatible with the welfare of society. The board has not publicly listed the criteria that are considered. Nor has it even tried to state the characteristics of cases in which parole will obviously be granted or will obviously be denied. It has not indicated its position with respect to major patterns of cases that are most frequently recurring (Davis, 1971, pp. 126, 127).

In strongly urging the adoption of guidelines for granting or denying parole, Davis argues against the current practice of individual decisions by parole board members that cannot be reviewed. "How could a board member have less incentive to avoid prejudice or undue haste than by a system in which his decision can never be reviewed and in which no one . . . can ever know why he voted as he did?" (Davis 1971, p. 129). However, Davis acknowledges that mere statement of reasons for parole decisions will not guarantee fairness, but at least the institution of structured guidelines will facilitate requisite consistency. Certainly an inmate or parolee has the right to know what standard of performance is expected of him; and as several studies cited in this chapter suggest, differential standards of parole performance for different types of offenders is the rule and not the exception. The incorporation of prediction tables into the standard evaluation procedures of correctional institutions would go a long way toward meeting the request for just limitation of discretionary power. The alternatives, as Glaser (1962) points out, involve retaining vast amounts of information in one's head, thus perpetuating the problems of subjective judgment. The potential for case histories to become unmanageably voluminous rules them out as an efficient and reliable alternative. Prediction tables have the potential for organizing substantial quantities of information in a manageable structure and can provide appropriate weighting of various factors more consistent with empirical findings. Even a cursory review of the prediction literature reveals that common-sense and empirically derived relationships are not always compatible. Finsley (cited in Evjen 1962) notes:

The mechanical predictive tables can sort out and place into categories an abundance of objective data which, if used in conjunction with skilled interviewing, can bring about much better results than either the subjective interview or the prediction table alone (p. 217).

Potential Applications

Perhaps the most valuable and exciting application of prediction instruments is in the evaluation of correctional treatment programs. More efficient allocation of funds and assignment of offenders to correctional programs suitable to their particular needs may be accomplished by the type of evaluative information gathering embodied in construction of a prediction instrument. Prediction methods may also profitably be used as aids in determining probable outcomes of community-based postrelease programs. Certainly substantial sums of money may be wasted annually on assignment of inmates to correctional programs that are not likely to achieve their goals while a proportion of the "good risks" might more readily be assigned immediately to minimal supervision or parole without decreasing the likelihood of successful outcome. The utilization of prediction instruments in the selection decision for early parole or minimal supervision may represent a substantial savings to the correctional institution, which may be rechanneled into treatment programs of known effectiveness. The prediction method provides a measure of the expected performance of a group against which the actual performance may be evaluated. If the prediction is made prior to assignment of inmates to treatment groups, it can later be determined if the outcome is more or less favorable than expected.

If the outcome following treatment can be predicted not only before treatment but *regardless* of treatment, then it is very hard to argue that this treatment makes any difference with respect to the specific outcome studied (Gottfredson 1967, p. 182).

The differences between expected and actual outcomes may be examined relative to treatment (or other) factors influencing such outcome, and the relationship between the program elements and outcome can be presented to decisionmakers. Gottfredson (1967) states:

The most useful role for prediction methods, therefore, will be found when their development and validation is studied continuously as one component of an agencywide information system for assessment of the effectiveness of programs (p. 183).

However, the prediction effort has by no means reached such a state of sophistication. Problems in application are complex and confounded by questions of reliability, validity, and inadequate cross validation.

If such techniques are to be used in the administration of criminal justice, then it must be demonstrated that an accuracy in the prediction of behavior is achieved far beyond that which is now achieved by informal and unsystematized methods (Monachesi 1950, p. 285).

Such a goal may be achieved by

. . . a continuous cycle of development of prediction methods, repeated validation, comparisons of program outcomes, modification of . . . research and practice . . . [requiring] systematic collection of information over the total system and repeated study of relationships to correctional goals (Gottfredson 1967, p. 183).

Note

1. The dichotomous classification is only one case. Outcome may certainly be "graded," and therefore multiple categories would involve modification of the cost-utility scheme.

References

Adams, R., and Vetter, H. J. "Probation Caseload Size and Recidivism Rate." *British Journal of Criminology* 11 (1971): 390-93.

Argow, W. W. "A Criminal-liability Index for Predicting Possibility of Rehabilitation." *Journal of Criminal Law and Criminology* 26(1935): 561–77.

Babst, D. V.; Gottfredson, D. M.; and Ballard, K. B. "Comparison of Multiple Regression and Configural Analysis Techniques for Developing Base Expectancy Tables." *Journal of Research in Crime and Delinquency* 5(1968): 72–80.

_____ ; Koval, M.; and Neithercutt, M. G. "Relationship of Time Served to Parole Outcome for Different Classifications of Burglars Based on Males Paroled in Fifty Jurisdictions in 1968 and 1969." *Journal of Research in Crime and Delinquency* 9(1972): 99–117.

Barron, A. J. "An Experiment with Ohlin's Prediction Report." *Crime and Delinquency* 8(1962): 276–81.

Bennett, L. A. "Self-esteem and Parole Adjustment." *Criminology* 12(1974): 346–60.

Black, W. A. M., and Gregson, R. A. M. "Time Perspective, Purpose in Life, Extraversion and Neuroticism in New Zealand Prisoners." *British Journal of Social and Clinical Psychology* 12(1973): 50–60.

Blum, F. J., and Chagnon, M. "Some Parameters of Persistent Criminal Behavior." *Journal of Clinical Psychology* 23(1967): 168–170.

Bottomley, A. K. "Parole Decisions in a Long-term Closed Prison." *British Journal of Criminology* 13(1973): 26–40.

Briggs, P. F.; Wirt, R. D.; and Johnson, R. "An Application of Prediction Tables to the Study of Delinquency." *Journal of Consulting Psychology* 25(1961): 46–50.

Buikhuisen, W., and Hoekstra, H. A. "Factors Related to Recidivism." *British Journal of Criminology* 14(1974): 63–69.

Burgess, E. W. "Factors Determining Success or Failure on Parole." In *The Workings of the Indeterminate Sentence Law and the Parole System in Illinois*, edited by A. A. Bruce, A. J. Harno, J. Landesco, and E. W. Burgess. Springfield, Ill.: Parole Board, 1928.

Cartwright, D. S., et al. "Measuring and Predicting Juvenile Probation Outcomes: An Exploratory Study." *Criminology* 10(1972): 143–60.

Christensen, L., and LeUnes, A. "Discriminating Criminal Types and Recidivism by Means of the MMPI." *Journal of Clinical Psychology* 30(1974): 192–93.

Cloninger, C. R., and Guze, S. B. "Psychiatric Disorders and Criminal Recidivism." *Archives of General Psychiatry* 29(1973): 266–69.

Cockerill, R. W. "Probation Effectiveness in Alberta." *Canadian Journal of Criminology and Corrections* 17(1975): 284–91.

Cowden, J. E. "Institutional and Post-release Adjustment of Neurotic and Social Delinquents." *Journal of Clinical Psychology* 22(1966a): 477.

Cowden, J. E. "Predicting Institutional Adjustment and Recidivism in Delinquent Boys." *Journal of Criminal Law, Criminology, and Police Science* 57(1966b): 39–44.

———, and Pacht, A. R. "Predicting Institutional and Post-release Adjustment of Delinquent Boys." *Journal of Consulting Psychology* 31(1967): 377–81.

Craig, M. M., and Budd, L. A. "The Juvenile Offender: Recidivism and Companions." *Crime and Delinquency* 13(1967): 344–51.

———, and Glick, S. J. "Ten Years' Experience with the Glueck Social Prediction Table." *Crime and Delinquency* 9(1963): 249–61.

Cymbalisty, B. Y.; Schuck, S. Z.; and Dubeck, J. A. "Achievement Level, Institutional Adjustment and Recidivism among Juvenile Delinquents." *Journal of Community Psychology* 3(1975): 289–94.

Davis, K. C. *Discretionary Justice: A Preliminary Inquiry*. Urbana, Ill.: University of Illinois Press, 1971.

Dean, C. W. "New Directions for Parole Prediction Research." *Journal of Criminal Law, Criminology and Police Science* 59(1968): 214–18.

———, and Duggan, T. J. "Problems of Parole Prediction: A Historical Analysis." *Social Problems* 15(1968): 450–59.

———, and ———. "Interaction and Parole Prediction." *British Journal of Criminology* 9(1969): 345–53.

Deardorff, P. A., et al. "Empathy and Socialization in Repeat Offenders, First Offenders and Normals." *Journal of Counseling Psychology* 22(1975): 453–55.

Duncan, O. D., et al. "Formal Devices for Making Selection Decisions." *American Journal of Sociology* 58(1953): 573–84.

Dunham, R. E. "Factors Related to Recidivism in Adults." *Journal of Social Psychology* 39(1954): 77–91.

England, R. W. "A Study of Post-probation Recidivism among Five-hundred Federal Offenders." *Federal Probation* 19(1955): 10–16.

———. "Some Dangers in Parole Prediction." *Crime and Delinquency* 8(1962): 265–69.

Englehardt, G. M. "Predicting Rehabilitation of Socially Maladjusted Boys." *Journal of Counseling Psychology* 17(1970): 546–49.

Evjen, V. H. "Current Thinking on Parole Prediction Tables." *Crime and Delinquency* 8(1962): 215–38.

Eysenck, S. B. G., and Eysenck, H. J. "Personality and Recidivism in Borstal Boys." *British Journal of Criminology* 14(1974): 385–87.

Fildes, R., and Gottfredson, D. M. "Cluster Analysis in a Parolee Sample." *Journal of Research in Crime and Delinquency* 9(1972): 2–11.

Freeman, R. A., and Mason, H. M. "Construction of a Key to Determine Recidivists from Non-recidivists Using the MMPI." *Journal of Clinical Psychology* 8(1952): 207–8.

Glaser, D. "Prediction Tables as Accounting Devices for Judges and Parole Boards." *Crime and Delinquency* 8(1962): 239–58.

Glueck, S., and Glueck, E. T. *500 Criminal Careers*. New York: Knopf, 1930.

Gottfredson, D. M. "Assessment and Prediction Methods in Crime and Delinquency." *President's Commission on Law Enforcement and Administration of Justice Task Force Report: Juvenile Delinquency and Youth Crime*. Washington: U.S. Government Printing Office, 1967, pp. 171–87.

_____ , and Lipstein, D. J. "Using Personal Characteristics to Predict Parolee and Probationer Employment Stability." *Journal of Applied Psychology* 60(1975): 644–48.

Gough, H. G.; Wenk, E. A.; and Rozynko, V. V. "Parole Outcome as Predicted from the CPI, the MMPI, and a Base Expectancy Table." *Journal of Abnormal Psychology* 70(1965): 432–41.

Grant, J. D. "It's Time to Start Counting." *Crime and Delinquency* 8(1962): 259–64.

Hakeem, M. "The Validity of the Burgess Method of Parole Prediction." *American Journal of Sociology* 53(1948): 376–86.

Hart, H. "Predicting Parole Success." *Journal of Criminal Law and Criminology* 14(1923): 405–13.

Hathaway, S. R., and Monachesi, E. D. *Adolescent Personality and Behavior*. Minneapolis: University of Minnesota Press, 1963.

Laune, F. F. *Predicting Criminality*. Chicago: Northwestern University Studies in Social Science, No. 1, 1936.

Lejins, P. P. "Parole Prediction: An Introductory Statement." *Crime and Delinquency* 8(1962): 209–14.

Levi, M., and Tracy, F. "Prediction of Success of Drug Addicts in Outpatient Release Status Based upon a Personality Inventory." *International Journal of the Addictions* 6(1971): 533–41.

Litwack, L. "An Examination of Ten Significant Differences between Juvenile Recidivists and Nonrecidivists." *Journal of Educational Research* 55(1961): 132–34.

Mack, J. L. "The MMPI and Recidivism." *Journal of Abnormal Psychology* 74(1969): 612–14.

Mandel, N. G., and Barron, A. J. "The MMPI and Criminal Recidivism." *Journal of Criminal Law, Criminology and Police Science* 57(1966): 35–38.

McWilliams, W. "Sentencing and Recidivism: An Analysis by Personality Type." *British Journal of Social Work* 5(1975): 311–24.

Meade, A. C. "The Labeling Approach to Delinquency: State of the Theory as a Function of Method." *Social Forces* 53(1974): 83–91.

Monachesi, E. D. "American Studies in the Prediction of Recidivism." *Journal of Criminal Law and Criminology* 41(1950): 268–89.

Neithercutt, M. G. "Parole Violation Patterns and Commitment Offense." *Journal of Research in Crime and Delinquency* 9(1972): 87-98.

O'Donnell, C. R., and Stanley, K. G. "An Adult Furlough Center: Correlates of Parole Success." *Journal of Community Psychology* 2(1974): 83-85.

Panton, J. H. "Predicting Prison Adjustment with the MMPI." *Journal of Clinical Psychology* 14(1958): 308-12.

_____. "The Identification of Habitual Criminalism with the MMPI." *Journal of Clinical Psychology* 18(1962a): 133-36.

_____. "Use of the MMPI as an Index to Successful Parole." *Journal of Criminal Law, Criminology, and Police Science* 53(1962b): 484-88.

Payne, C.; McCabe, S.; and Walker, N. "Predicting Offender-Patients' Reconvictions." *British Journal of Psychiatry* 125(1974): 60-64.

Platt, J. J., and Labate, C. "Recidivism in Youthful Heroin Offenders and Characteristics of Parole Behavior and Environment." *International Journal of the Addictions* 11(1976):221-236.

Powers, S. B. "Standard Parole Prediction Methods: Views of a Correctional Administrator." *Crime and Delinquency* 8(1962): 270-75.

Rempel, P. P. "The Use of Multivariate Statistical Analysis of Minnesota Multiphasic Personality Inventory Scores in the Classification of Delinquent and Nondelinquent High School Boys." *Journal of Consulting Psychology* 22(1958): 17-23.

Rogers, J. W. "Parole Prediction in Three Dimensions: Theory, Prediction and Perception." *Sociology and Social Research* 52(1968): 377-91.

_____, and Hayner, N. S. "Optimism and Accuracy in the Perception of Selected Parole Prediction Items." *Social Forces* 46(1968): 388-400.

Sampson, A. "Post-prison Success Prediction." *Criminology* 12(1974): 155-73.

Sanders, B. S. "Testing Parole Prediction." *Proceedings of the Sixty-Fifth Annual Congress of the American Prison Association*, 1935, 222-33.

Satten, J., et al. "Ego Disorganization and Recidivism in Delinquent Boys." *Bulletin of the Menninger Clinic* 34(1970): 270-83.

Scarpitti, F. R., and Stephenson, R. M. "A Study of Probation Effectiveness." *Journal of Criminal Law, Criminology, and Police Science* 59(1968): 361-69.

Simon, F. H. "Statistical Methods of Making Prediction Instruments." *Journal of Research in Crime and Delinquency* 9(1972): 46-53.

Smith, J. and Lanyon, R. I. "Prediction of Juvenile Probation Violators." *Journal of Consulting and Clinical Psychology* 32(1968): 54-58.

Stang, H. J. "A Diagnostic and Prognostic Study of a Material Comprising Abnormal Norwegian Delinquents." *Acta Psychiatrica Scandinavica* 43(1967): 111-20.

Takagi, P. T. "The Effect of Parole Agents' Judgments on Recidivism Rates." *Psychiatry* 32(1969): 192-99.

Taylor, A. J. W. "Prediction for Parole: A Pilot Study with Delinquent Girls." *British Journal of Criminology* 7(1967): 418-24.

Vasoli, R. H. "Some Reflections on Measuring Probation Outcome." *Federal Probation* 31(3): 24-32, 1967.

Vold, G. B. "Prediction Methods Applied to Problems of Classification within Institutions." *Journal of Criminal Law and Criminology* 25(1935): 202-209.

Warner, S. B. "Factors Determining Parole from the Massachusetts Reformatory." *Journal of Criminal Law and Criminology* 14(1923): 172-207.

Wattron, J. B. "A Prison Maladjustment Scale for the MMPI." *Journal of Clinical Psychology* 19(1963): 109-110.

Wenk, E. A., and Emrich, R. L. "Assaultive Youth: An Exploratory Study of the Assaultive Experience and Assaultive Potential of California Youth Authority Wards." *Journal of Research in Crime and Delinquency* 9(1972): 171-96.

Part III

Evaluative Research in Correctional Drug Abuse
Treatment: An Illustrative Example

Introduction to Part III

At this point the reader should have a fairly clear idea of both the generally used techniques and the recurrent problems encountered in conducting evaluative research in a correctional setting. The following chapters are presented as an illustration of the practical application of some of the principles discussed in preceding chapters. The treatment program described here reflects an attempt to meet a need for quality research and treatment geared to the specific problems of the narcotic addict offender. The existence of a substantial subpopulation of such offenders in many correctional institutions gives rise to a number of specific problems which must be dealt with if the correctional process is to achieve its objectives. The treatment program described in Chapter 6 represents one attempt to deal with these problems.

The evaluation design which was employed is basically quasi-experimental involving comparisons between (1) the postrelease performances of program participants and that of nonparticipants selected from the same offender population, on the basis of their similarity in essential characteristics to the program participants, and (2) determination of extent of change, if any, on a group of psychological variables. Both experimental and control groups underwent essentially comparable experiences with the exception of treatment program participation. The problems encountered in constructing a purely experimental design, particularly in the case where treatment program effectiveness is being evaluated within the context of a service setting, have been discussed and should be familiar to the reader. Since it is often more feasible to implement a quasi-experimental design in these situations where a rigorous experimental design is impractical, the illustrative model described here should be of particular relevance to evaluative research in a correctional setting.

As previously discussed, the pressure for evaluative research tailored to the needs of the correctional system has often resulted in research of little impact and credibility. The evaluative research effort described in the following chapters has avoided many of the problems inherent in evaluations that are "tacked on" to existing treatment programs, by being an integral component of one such program. It thus illustrates a carefully structured and implemented evaluation process. A periodic review of treatment program effectiveness of this kind allows immediate response to and greater flexibility in molding program elements to the changing needs of the addict offender population.

Part III, then, is divided into chapters describing (1) assessment of need for the treatment program and the evaluation of treatment program effectiveness, (2) a critique of the evaluation design to allow the reader to place it in perspective vis-à-vis the principles presented earlier, and (3) related research on predicting outcome of treatment participants, and on the nature of heroin addiction which was conducted concurrently with the evaluation.

**Evaluation of the Wharton Tract
Narcotics Treatment Program**
Jerome J. Platt, Christina Labate,
and *Robert J. Wicks*

The Institution and the Program

The material presented in this chapter is designed to provide an illustration of evaluative research in drug abuse treatment. It reflects a continuing evaluation of the Wharton Tract Narcotics Treatment Program at the Youth Reception and Correction Center, Yardville, New Jersey, which began in 1970.

Introduction

During the late 1960s and early 1970s, the youthful offender population in New Jersey was characterized by a high incidence of narcotic addiction problems, particularly to heroin. In response to the high rate of heroin addiction histories in those men, the institutional administration made a decision to develop treatment programs. In 1970–71, a former state forestry camp located at the Wharton State Forest was acquired and was designated as a narcotics treatment unit. Support for this program was obtained from the State Law Enforcement Planning Agency under a Criminal Justice Improvement Grant. A decision was made at this time to also implement a program evaluation component, and the institutional consultant for program evaluation, who had already been concerned with evaluating another institutional narcotics treatment program, was assigned to develop and implement a research and evaluation plan for the Wharton Tract.

Description of the Institutional Context

The Youth Reception and Correction Center began operations in January 1968, with a rated capacity of 850 inmates. The reception center serves as the admission point for male offenders committed to the Youth Correctional Institutional Complex. (Since 1974 it has also served this purpose for the New Jersey Prison Complex.) It assesses new admissions medically, educationally, and psychologically, and then assigns them to one of the three institutions comprising the reformatory complex: Bordentown, Annandale, or the 548-bed Yardville Correction Center. Assignment may also be made to one of the four satellite units at Yardville. One of these is the Wharton Tract Narcotics Treatment Program, located in the Wharton Tract State Forest some distance outside the parent

149

institution's grounds. As noted above, the physical plant was originally a state forestry camp and consists of a large open-door dormitory capable of housing 45 residents, with self-contained food preparation and recreational components.

The Program Participants

Admission to the program was open to all admissions to the reformatory reception center who met the following criteria:

1. A confirmed history of from 6 months to 5 years' dependency on heroin.
2. Minimum age of 19.
3. No recent escape history.
4. An initial Institutional Adjustment Committee time goal of from 8 to 20 months.
5. No serious psychiatric disorder.
6. No pending detainers for serious offenses.

Typically, admissions to the Wharton Tract unit consisted of inmates who, while in the reception center, indicated an interest in participating in a narcotics treatment program. They may have done so while being interviewed by the psychologist, chaplain, or other staff members, after which they were interviewed by the program director to confirm their eligibility for the program (in terms of the above criteria) and their continued interest in participating.

Upon admission, the typical Wharton Tract program participant is 22 years of age, with a mean heroin use of some 3.62 years. Typically, their criminal histories included an average of 6.6 prior arrests ($SD = 4.9$), with an average age at first arrest of 16.8 years ($SD = 4.0$). Some 48.2 percent had a prior history of participation in a drug treatment program. Drug treatment programs included drug-free therapeutic communities, out-patient counseling, detoxification, and methadone maintenance programs.

Therapy Program Philosophy

The Wharton Tract program employed a group treatment approach. As Wicks (1974) has noted in summarizing the literature on the subject, this approach is preferred by correctional psychologists because of its high level of success, when contrasted with individual therapy, in dealing with the particular problems of the delinquent adolescent. The fact that this approach also allows more efficient utilization of often limited staff time is an additional reason for its frequent adoption. One of the most widely known approaches specifically designed for youthful offenders, and the one employed at the Wharton Tract program, was the *guided group interaction* (GGI) technique initially developed at Highfields, New Jersey, in 1950. In the Highfields Project (McCorkle, Elias, and Bixby 1958), youthful offenders were involved in intensive group discussions which required them to examine the immediate problems they faced both from their own perspective and from the perspective of others involved, and to move toward a point at which they become responsible for decisionmaking. The Highfields model also generally involves some degree of responsible employment and involvement within the community as well as housing separate from the correctional institution. While it is believed that the GGI approach is at least as effective, if not more so, than other modes of treatment for the youthful offender (President's Commission on Law Enforcement and the Administration of Justice 1967), there do exist several reports of failure to demonstrate this differential effectiveness (Pilnick 1967).

Program Structure

The program is divided into four consecutive phases. During the *first phase* the inmate is evaluated regarding his adjustment to, and further participation in, the program. This phase covers approximately 30 days. During this time the inmate receives orientation by the peer group, program supervisor, and custodial staff, becomes involved in the group therapy program (and individual counseling if necessary and desired), and begins doing routine jobs around the unit. At the end of this period, the inmate's performance is evaluated by his therapy group work supervisor, individual staff members, and himself, and a decision is made regarding promotion to phase 2 of the program.

The *second phase* of the program focuses on the acquisition and development of good work habits and personal responsibility, rather than on particular job skills. A minimum of 60 days is required in phase 2. Inmates participate in a work program conducted in cooperation with the State Department of Environmental Protection. While in phase 2, the resident continues to participate in his therapy group, as he will throughout the entire three phases of the program. He changes groups only when he attains work release status. Time is set aside for the continuation of individual counseling. During the time spent in phase 2, a resident is periodically evaluated by himself, the staff, and other residents. The resident is also given the opportunity to participate in the voluntary school program.

Upon receiving satisfactory evaluations from his therapy group, his work supervisor, the rest of the staff, and himself, the resident is advanced to phase 3 of the program.

During the *third phase*, in addition to continued participation in his group and educational program, the resident is now eligible to earn a job with more responsibility. Weekend trips to the community facilitate transition to responsible community participation upon the resident's release. In addition, those residents who are 90 days short of parole are eligible for weekend home furloughs. There is no designated period of time spent in this phase, for it depends upon the individual's progress within the program. As soon as he feels he is eligible for promotion to the *fourth phase* (work release), the resident can request such promotion. After satisfactory evaluations have been received from the groups listed under phase 2, the resident can be recommended for promotion to phase 4.

Therapy Program Elements

Treatment consisted of three types. (1) *Guided group interactions* (GGI), the primary form of therapy, met 4 days a week for 90-minute sessions. The primary goals of these groups were for the inmate to learn the following: how to adequately resolve interpersonal conflicts; communication skills, including listening; appropriate problemsolving skills; how to give, accept, and utilize feedback; and how individual differences affect daily living. (2) *Couple therapy group*, a voluntary group composed of married residents and their wives also met weekly for 90 minutes. The goals of this group centered around learning to cope with many of the problems faced by residents and their wives, both those directly related to drug addiction and drug abuse and those related to "normal married life." (3) All residents on work release status participated in the *work release therapy group*. This group attempted to deal with the realistic kinds of problems that the resident faces on the job. Additional other forms of therapy which were available included *family counseling*, which was available weekly for all inmates and their families, and *individual counseling*, which was available as needed. Finally, the entire resident population met with the program staff once weekly to have a forum for discussion of problems and decision-making.

In addition to drawing upon the Highfields model (McCorkle, Elias, and Bixby 1958) for the basic philosophical orientation for the group structure of both programs, additional input to staff came from the interpersonal problem-solving therapy program of Platt, Spivack, and Swift (1974). This orientation, which involves specific training in techniques of problemsolving, is empirically based upon findings reported in Platt and Spivack (1973), Platt et al. (1974), and Spivack, Platt, and Shure (1976). This approach operationalizes treatment elements in the GGI process as outlined by Elias (1968).

Development of the Evaluation Plan

The evaluator was an outside consultant, a research psychologist,[1] who was brought into the institution initially for the express purpose of evaluating other institutional treatment programs. He contracted to visit the institution at least twice weekly, during which time he supervised the activities of the research staff which consisted of one B.A. statistician and a statistical clerk. These two staff members carried out the data gathering and analysis tasks during the normal work week.

The program coordinator, who was responsible for all satellite units, including the Wharton Tract, was always available for consultation with the research consultant during the time that the latter was in the institution, and a close liaison was maintained. In an initial series of meetings arranged and chaired by the program coordinator, the consultant met with the program director and staff at the Wharton Tract unit and explained that he would be working closely with them to determine the effectiveness of the program. It was expressly stated that he was not going to be concerned with evaluation of individual staff members, but rather with the rehabilitation aspects of the program. Thereafter, the consultant visited the unit every third week to informally answer questions posed by the staff members (as well as by the program participants).

In addition, every 6 months the research consultant attended a staff meeting and provided feedback on the results of the evaluation. During these meetings, feedback was solicited from staff as to concerns they had regarding evaluation-related issues, such as scheduling data collection sessions so as to minimally interfere with other program activities.

Every 3 to 6 months, the consultant met with the superintendent of the institution, to review progress up to that point and to discuss the evaluator's plans for the next several months, so that the necessary institutional personnel could be contacted so as to facilitate the evaluation. It is perhaps significant to note that the evaluation continued under three consecutive superintendents and under as many program directors. This fact, in part, reflected the ongoing institutional commitment to program evaluation.

The evaluation plan was developed over the initial months during which the consultant was assigned to the program. A broad outline of the plan was first prepared by the consultant, who then met some four times with a committee appointed by the superintendent; this committee consisted of the institutional drug treatment program directors, the director of professional services, the chief psychologist, and staff psychologists. During these meetings the consultant solicited the views of committee members regarding the kinds of changes which participation in the program might effect in participants. Appropriate measurement devices were selected by the consultant to measure these variables, and then they were presented to the committee for approval. The committee was very cooperative, due perhaps to the fact that the consultant worked directly for the superintendent's office. Surprisingly, the committee members expressed no real interest in participating in the conduct of the evaluation themselves. The reasons for this were always difficult to define, but included the following: (1) they perceived that evaluation was not an area of expertise for them, and thus they should not attempt it, and (2) they were concerned about adding to their present workloads.

As developed, the plan for initiating a research and evaluation procedure had several general objectives:

1. To institute a system for monitoring the incidence of substance abuse among new admissions to the institution. This system would provide administration with necessary information for programming.
2. Determining the program's effectiveness in meeting its goal of changing participants along important dimensions of personality, cognition, and attitudes so as to reduce the likelihood of future drug use and related criminal behavior. Such determination would include systematic testing of program participants, to establish if change had taken place, as well as monitoring of parole performance.
3. The determination of those factors related to parole success of heroin-addicted offenders at Yardville, as well as the development of a systematic, statistically based method for predicting outcome both in the program and upon release from the institution.

All procedures developed to implement objectives 1 and 2 were piloted in one of the other institutional drug programs before being implemented at the Wharton Tract.

Evaluation Procedures and Results

Objective 1: Monitoring of Drug Abuse Trends in the Institutional Population

On an ongoing basis, the records of all new admissions to the reception center were examined twice yearly, in January and July, to assess the incidence of drug abuse. Since the men entering this reception center represented a substantial proportion (83 percent) of all males in the state falling in their age group (15 to 30) who were remanded to state correctional institutions, the figures obtained gave a reasonable estimate of drug abuse incidence in this population. Each sample consisted of the first 100 admissions after January 1 and July 1 of each year. The actual number sampled ($N = 1600$ for the years 1968 to 1975 inclusive) represented 9.1 percent of all new admissions for this period. Parole violators were excluded with the result that for 98 percent of this sample this was their first incarceration.

Using a procedure developed by Platt, Scura, and Hoffman (1973), the files of these admissions were examined for drug use history, and each new admission was classified as one of the following: (1) a heroin user, (2) a user of marijuana or other illegal drugs (e.g., LSD, methedrine, barbiturates, etc.), or (3) a nonuser of drugs. Identification and classification as a heroin addict was determined on the basis of medical evidence (e.g., scars), arrests for drug-related offenses, and statements given by the inmate to officers and various officials who had interviewed him which were included in the inmate's permanent record (e.g., examining physician, identification officer, psychologist, etc.). In addition to the above, for an inmate to be classified as a heroin addict, unambiguous documentation of a history of addiction for 6 months or longer at the time of admission was required. Subjects (Ss) were classified as heroin addicts only when there was no disagreement in the information obtained from the several sources used. It was found, however, that in the overwhelming majority of cases where heroin use indicators appeared, there was substantial agreement among information obtained from each of these sources (i.e., interviews, medical examinations, and police records). This method of identification of drug use probably, if anything, resulted in a conservative estimate owing to a possible tendency on the part of inmates not to admit to, or to deemphasize, a drug use history.

General Incidence of Drug Abuse

An analysis of the data for the period 1968 to 1972, reported in detail elsewhere (Platt, Scura, and Hoffman 1973), indicated a clear pattern in the incidence of heroin addiction in youthful offenders in New Jersey. During this time, the incidence of heroin addiction increased from 25 percent to a high of 73 percent of all new admissions in July 1971, and was shown to be independent of incarceration rates for drug offenses. Data for 1973 to 1975 [reported in Platt, Hoffman, and Ebert (1976)] showed this high of 73 percent to have decreased gradually to 41 percent in the final group examined in June 1975, reflecting a shift to use of other drugs besides heroin, but not a decrease in overall drug use.

Table 6-1 summarizes by year the frequency distribution of heroin and non-heroin users in the admissions samples studied. Analysis of this frequency distribution revealed significant differences between the observed and expected cell frequencies resulting from the consistently increasing proportion of heroin users relative to other subjects across the 1968-1972 time period, and the consistent decrease in recorded heroin users from 1972 to 1975.

Availability of these data regarding heroin addiction incidence among new admissions to the reformatory reception center was reported by administration to be valuable in that it allowed them to approach the problem of fiscal planning with some clear estimates as to the size of the need for a response by the institution to drug abuse problems among inmates.

Table 6–1

Frequencies and Percentages of Heroin Addicts and Nonaddicts in Each of Eight Successive Years Covered by the Survey

Drug Status	Sample							
	1968	1969	1970	1971	1972	1973	1974	1975
Heroin Addicts	58 (29.0%)	74 (37.0%)	92 (46.0%)	143 (71.5%)	139 (69.5%)	115 (57.5%)	102 (51%)	97 (48.5%)
Nonaddicts	142 (71.0%)	126 (63.0%)	108 (54.0%)	57 (28.5%)	61 (30.5%)	85 (42.5%)	98 (49%)	103 (51.5%)

Chi square = 15.41, $df = 4$, $p < 0.005$.

Demographic Characteristics of Drug Abusers

When the drug abuse incidence monitoring system was instituted, it was also decided to collect additional information regarding the demographic character-istics associated with drug abuse in this population. The data of primary interest were race, age, formal education, educational achievement, and intelligence. The findings are presented below.

Race. During the 8-year period from 1968 to 1975, the overall racial composi-tion of the heroin addict group, *relative* to the general sample racial composition, remained constant. Concurrently, the percentage of blacks in *both* the addict and nonaddict groups significantly increased ($p < 0.01$ for the addict group, and $p < 0.02$ for the nonaddict group) over this period of time, reflecting the in-creasingly black composition of the reception center population. In the 3-year period following this, these trends were modified. In the group of heroin addicts, the total proportion of blacks declined from 73 percent in 1973 to 63 percent in 1975, while whites represented a growing proportion from a low of 15 percent in 1973 to 32 percent in 1975. Puerto Ricans, taken as a separate group, made up a small and declining portion of both the addict and nonaddict groups. In the group of nonaddicts the proportion of blacks and whites remained relatively constant (Black: 1973, 64 percent; 1974, 64 percent; 1975, 67 percent. White: 1973, 29 percent; 1974, 20 percent; 1975; 28 percent). At the same time, the racial composition of the group of nonheroin drug users showed another ap-parently significant pattern. From 1973 to 1975 whites made up a large portion of this group, going from 62 percent in 1973 to 59 percent in 1974 to 43 per-cent in 1975. Blacks made up a growing part of this group, though always lower than their representation among heroin addicts: 34 percent in 1973, 43 percent in 1974, and 49 percent in 1975.

Age upon Admission. Trends in average age upon admission for different groups reflected the general pattern in the first 5-year period: heroin addicts were consistently older than nonaddicts. Nonheroin drug users, on the other hand, did not show a consistent pattern; in 1973 and 1975 their average age was much lower than either of the other two groups (20 years 2 months for heroin addicts, 20 years 1 month for nonaddicts), but in 1974 it was almost as high as the addict group (21 years 9 months). These results may reflect a fluctuation in that group as a whole.

Formal Education. The analysis of the number of years of formal education achieved by the sample members indicates that in general, in each year of the 8-year period, heroin users attained more formal education than nonusers. In the first 5 years the absolute level of educational attainment moved steadily higher in all groups. In the next three years, the absolute level declined slightly for all groups, and the level achieved became more comparable among groups. The group of nonheroin drug users showed a similar comparable decline in grade level attained, starting from a high of 11th grade in 1973 and moving to the same average of 9.5 years as the addict group in 1975.

Educational Achievement. Examination of educational achievement as measured by Stanford Achievement Test (SAT) scores of heroin addicts versus nonaddicts reveals a basic pattern in which addicts have a higher average achievement level throughout the 8 years studied. However, in neither group was there a consistent rise or fall in absolute scores over time. [Nonheroin drug users, examined as a separate group in the 1973-1975 period, shared an average SAT score higher than the other two groups in 1973-1974 (7.25, 6.4), which declined to a lower point than the addict group (6.0 versus 6.5) in the final year studied.]

Analysis of the simple effects relevant to the race X year interaction indicated that across the 1968-1972 time period, SAT scores for white subjects differed significantly from those of blacks ($p < 0.01$), with a general trend of increasing scores. No significant trends were observed among blacks during this time span. Within each year, whites consistently demonstrated higher SAT scores than blacks ($p < 0.005$).

Mental Level (IQ). Heroin users demonstrated higher main mental level (ML) scores than non-drug users. For the first four years, from 1972 to 1975, the scores of the two groups appeared to grow closer, while rising slightly toward the 100 mark (addicts: 98.8 in 1974). Concurrently, the group of nonheroin drug users exhibited a pattern similar to that in the area of SAT scores: a score far higher than the other two groups in 1973 (108.8), decreasing to about their level by 1975 (95.7).

Summary of Demographic Findings

The above data describe demographic characteristics associated with heroin addiction in the young offender population admitted to the Youth Reception

Center during the 8-year period ending in the second half of 1975. First, some definite differences between heroin addicts and nonaddicts are indicated (sometimes, but not always, in conjunction with race). Second, some surprising trends have been manifested. These two issues will be considered separately.

Incidence. As was indicated in an earlier report on this population (Platt, Scura, and Hoffman 1973), the incidence of heroin addiction increased steadily between January 1968 and July 1971. In January 1972 a slight decline in the incidence of heroin addiction began which continued to July 1975.

Overall Addict-Nonaddict Differences.

Race. With respect to racial composition, no overall significant difference was found in the proportions of whites and blacks in the addict and nonaddict groups between 1968 and 1975. The largest gap occurred in 1973, with whites comprising 29.2 percent of the nonaddict group as opposed to only 14.7 percent of the addict group. In the separate group of nonheroin drug users, the percentage of whites was consistently higher (1973, 61.9 percent; 1974, 59.3 percent; 1975, 42.4 percent) than in the groups of heroin and non-drug users, though it decreased steadily from 1973 to 1975.

Age. With respect to age, heroin addicts were older than nonaddicts in all years except 1972, and whites were significantly older upon admission than blacks during all years.

Formal Education. During the first five years of this study, heroin addicts had completed a greater number of years of formal education than nonaddicts. However, during the last three, the different groups came much closer, with non-drug users surpassing addicts in the final year (grade 10 versus grade 9.5).

Scholastic Achievement. With respect to scholastic achievement, heroin addicts demonstrated significantly higher scores than non-drug users in all years except 1970 (this was true also for white, in contrast to black, addicts across all years). However, from 1973 to 1975 users of other drugs besides heroin demonstrated either higher or comparable achievement to the addict group.

Mental Level (IQ). The heroin addict group also demonstrated significantly higher intelligence levels than non-drug users. (Whites, in general, demonstrated significantly higher mental level scores than blacks.)

Trends over Time.

Race. Overall, the heroin addict group became increasingly black in composition until, in 1973, some 73.9 percent of the sample was black. After that it decreased slightly to 62.9 percent of the addict sample. Among non-drug users the percentage of blacks gained steadily from 63.8 percent in 1973 to 67.2 percent in 1975.

Age. Two trends seem to characterize this variable. Age of the addict group remained steady until 1972, then rose sharply to an average of 22 years 1 month in 1975. Concurrently, age of non-drug users rose steadily until 1972, when it began to drop, reaching 20 years 6 months in 1975.

Formal Education. The entire sample, addicts, nonaddicts, whites and blacks, all showed an increase in number of years of education completed from 1968 through 1972.

Scholastic Achievement. Over the years, a consistent increase was found in the white subgroup SAT scores but not in the scores for blacks.

Mental Level (IQ). For both addicts and non-drug users, no significant trends in mental level took place over the period of time studied. Nonheroin drug users, however, exhibited a high tested IQ (108) in 1973 followed by a sharp decline to the level of the other two groups by 1975 (95.2).

Relationship of the Present Findings to Those of Previous Studies

Platt, Hoffman, and Ebert (1976) reported that these results are generally consistent with those obtained by Ball and Chambers (1970) and Lukoff (1972). Paralleling these earlier studies, they suggest that heroin addicts are older and better educated, have achieved more as a result of formal education, and have a higher intelligence level than non-drug users in the same young offender population.

Since these findings are primarily based on information obtained from official records, they differ from those which Lukoff obtained from personal interviews in the community. Taken together, his findings and those of this study suggest that divergent sources of information lead to the same conclusions regarding the heroin addict's background.

Two trends seem to require comment. First, the number of black addicts in 1975 is greater than it is in 1968, this may be ascribed to an overall increasing percentage of blacks in the New Jersey correctional system during the course of this study. At the same time, however, heroin addiction among the white young offender population has increased at the same pace as in the black young offender population.

Second, a substantial new group of nonheroin drug users, large enough by 1973 to warrant separate evaluation, has appeared. This group exhibits meaningful patterns independent of the other two groups—that is, in racial composition (a higher percentage of whites than the others), in years of formal education, in scholastic achievement, and in mental level (all appearing in 1973 at considerably higher levels than heroin users and non-drug users, and dropping steadily to about the same levels as the latter groups).

The Implications of These Findings

Platt, Hoffman, and Ebert (1976) note that these findings suggest that "the addict possesses, in contrast to his non-drug user peer in the correctional setting, background factors which have, until recently, not been those usually associated with heroin addiction. Secondly, they suggest that the model which views heroin addicts as coming from the most deprived segments of the community must be reconsidered" (p. 234). They go on to discuss the implications for treatment:

Accordingly, those being committed to institutions are increasingly . . . poor risks for . . . less restrictive alternatives. . . . The end result is an institutional population that has been found to be in many cases, unsuitable for placement in the community. With particular respect to the addict population this means a high percentage of addicts who either failed in, or were uninterested in, community drug treatment programs. At the same time, as documented in the present study, this population has become increasingly sophisticated, and thus poses greater difficulties for correctional administrators. For example, addicts often do not perceive themselves as being criminals in the traditional sense, but rather as individuals in need of treatment. Paradoxically, however, because those addicts presently being committed have more personal resources in terms of education and academic accomplishment, they may well be better equipped to deal with their problems if properly motivated" (p. 235).

Objective 2: Determination of Program Effectiveness

The determination of program effectiveness was based upon two separate sets of indices. One was change in the participants along variables judged by the evaluator, in consultation with clinical staff, to be reflecting therapeutic aims of the program. The second was based upon the parole performance of the group under study. In both cases, control group comparison was obtained and used for the development of baselines against which the treatment program group performance could be compared. Since examination of parole performance is perhaps the more important of the two methods used to determine effectiveness of the program, it will be presented first.

Relative Parole Performance of Program Graduates and Controls. The basic information examined was parole behavior for a 2-year period following release from the institution, during which behavior was "nonobtrusively" monitored.

Selection of Controls. A group of control *S*s was selected so as to provide a matched control for each program participant. The criteria used for selection of control *S*s included:

1. Being the next consecutive admission to the correction center after an inmate who had completed the program.
2. Meeting all criteria for admission to the Wharton Tract program, including those for age, drug use, escape history, time goal set by classification committee, absence of psychiatric disturbance, and no pending detainers.

Control *S*s did not differ from those in the program with respect to relevant demographic characteristics, including age and education. They did tend to have a slightly shorter length of history of heroin use, 2.9 versus 3.62 years for the Wharton Tract group. Mean lengths of incarceration for the treatment and control groups were 8.6 months and 9.9 months respectively. All *S*s in both the treatment and control groups had a period of *at least* 2 years' parole to complete following release from the institution, and on this basis a 2-year follow-up period was decided upon. All control *S*s participated in the normal institutional program, including educational and work release programs, and some, but not all, became involved in individual and group therapy.

Behavior while on parole was determined by examining parole reports, which were submitted by parole officers every 6 months. These relatively detailed reports were examined after they had been sent to the institution and placed in the parolee's file, and at no point was contact ever made with parole officers regarding these reports. Thus, the experimental *S*s, as well as the controls, were never singled out as being of special interest. Finally, to ensure the accuracy of the parole data, independent verification of arrests was obtained from state police arrest records. The information obtained from this source was almost 100 percent in agreement with that obtained from the parole reports.

While data on parole status were tabulated twice yearly and reported to the institutional administration, only the results pertaining to the final status of all program graduates at the end of a 2-year period of parole follow-up will be reported here. The parole follow-up data collected on the program graduates and addict controls represent information on a variety of parole outcomes, including recommitment status, mortality, adjustment on parole, and drug use. These data are presented in Table 6–2, and they represent the status of subjects at the point in time of the 2-year follow-up.

A number of differences between the two groups are apparent from these findings, and they will be discussed.

Recommitment. Wharton Tract graduates had a significantly lower ($p < 0.05$) recommitment rate (18 percent) than controls (30 percent). Both groups had a very low rate of recommitment for drug offenses (3 percent), and program graduates were thus much lower in recommitment for nondrug offenses (15

Table 6-2

Final Follow-up, June 1975: Comparison of Wharton Tract Graduates—Controls on Parole Report Ratings

	Wharton Tract (N=163)	Addict Controls (N=163)
Recommitted	29 (18%)	48 (30%)*
Drug user	5 (3%)	4 (3%)
Non-drug user	24 (15%)	44 (27%)**
Suspended sentences	5 (3%)	10 (6%)
Awaiting trial	22 (13%)	26 (16%)
Good adjustment	7 (4%)	8 (5%)
Poor adjustment	10 (6%)	12 (7%)
County jail	5 (3%)	6 (4%)
Missing	6 (4%)	6 (4%)
Deceased	1 (1%)	5 (3%)
Discharged	25 (15%)	25 (15%)
Maximum terminated	10 (6%)	8 (5%)
Good adjustment	33 (20%)	19 (12%)*
Poor adjustment	5 (3%)	3 (2%)
Assigned good	27 (17%)	13 (8%)*
Using heroin	37 (23%)	45 (28%)
Participating in drug program	29 (18%)	35 (22%)

Indicates a significant difference at .05 level (*) or .01 level (**).
Categories are *not* mutually exclusive.

percent) than controls (27 percent). This difference was significant at the .01 level.

Good Adjustment; Assigned Good. At the end of the 2-year follow-up period, there were a significantly higher number of Wharton Tract graduates than controls in both the good adjustment while on parole category (33 versus 19, $p < 0.05$) and in the "assigned good" category (27 versus 13, $p < 0.05$). The "assigned good" category represents those men for whom detailed parole reports had not been filed for the fourth 6-month follow-up, but on whom no arrests, parole violations, or recommitments had been reported.

Used Heroin on Parole. While the differences are not large, it was found that fewer program graduates (37, or 23 percent) than controls (45, or 28 percent) were reported using heroin on parole. Of all outcome categories, this is probably the least reliable one, since it would be difficult for a parole officer to determine use with a high degree of certainty unless it were blatant. Also, these data were not reported for some of the recommitments. For both reasons, it may represent an underestimate of drug use behavior.

Participation in Drug Program. Another small difference occurred on this rating. More controls (22 percent) than graduates (18 percent) were participating in drug programs while on parole, perhaps indicating a greater need for supervision in this area.

Other Measures from Parole Report. On other measures derived from the parole report (awaiting trial status, missing, deceased, discharged, maximum terminated, and poor adjustment) the differences between the two groups were not significant.

First Arrest Status

Table 6-3 provides information related to the arrest status of treatment and control *S*s. Most important would seem to be the fact that significantly more Wharton Tract graduates remained arrest-free (51 percent versus 34 percent), and that if and when they were arrested, this event occurred later during parole (at 238 days versus 168 days). Finally, it is of interest to note that there were significantly fewer arrests in the experimental group for nonindictable, nondrug offenses than in the control group. Of even more interest, perhaps, is the finding that the two groups did not differ with respect to the number of both indictable and nonindictable drug offenses.

Table 6–3
Final Follow-up, June 1975: Comparison of Wharton Tract Graduates—Controls on Arrest Status

	Wharton Tract	*Controls*
Number arrested	79 (49%)	108 (66%)**
Number remaining arrest-free	84 (51%)	55 (34%)***
Totals	163	163
Number of days to first arrest	238 days	168 days***
Number arrested on indictable drug offense	14 (9%)	16 (10%)
Number arrested on indictable non-drug offense	46 (28%)	59 (36%)
Number arrested on indictable offense (Total)	60 (37%)	75 (46%)
Number arrested on nonindictable drug offense	6 (4%)	5 (3%)
Number arrested on nonindictable nondrug offense	13 (8%)	29 (18%)**
Number arrested on nonindictable offense (Total)	19 (27%	34 (21%)*

Indicates a significant difference at .05 level (*), .01 level (**), or .001 level (***).

The above data pertaining to parole status and arrest history while on parole strongly suggest a differential effect of the Wharton Tract program upon postrelease behavior.

Relationship between Program Participation and Parole Success

During the course of the program there were a number of inmates admitted to the program who did not complete it. Relatively few of these "dropouts" were for disciplinary or adjustment problems, with most reflecting administrative transfer for early release, or attendance at special educational, medical, or other treatment programs at the parent institution. During the course of the evaluation, some 29 percent of entrants did not complete the program. Arrest rates for this group of men were also examined, and 30.4 percent were found to be arrest-free after 2 years of parole. This figure differs significantly from the 51 percent arrest-free rate for men completing the program ($p < 0.01$), but not from the 34 percent arrest-free rate for control Ss.

Prior Treatment History and Parole Outcome

As there is evidence to suggest that prognosis of successful outcome improves with increased drug program experience (cf. Platt and Labate 1976), and since approximately half (48.2 percent) of men completing the Wharton Tract program had histories of prior treatment for drug problems, parole outcome status at the end of 2 years was examined as a function of treatment prior to entry into the current program. When parole status for the two groups was examined at the end of 2 years, it was found that some 63.3 percent of those with prior drug treatment demonstrated *clearly* good parole adjustment, as defined by discharge from parole, maximum termination of sentences, or being designated as having good parole adjustment. In contrast, some 51.7 percent of graduates without prior drug treatment histories fell into these categories. This difference between the two groups approached, but did not reach, significance.

Summary. Thus, the evidence relative to parole performance suggests that (1) program graduates have significantly better parole performance than controls (2) program graduates are significantly more successful on parole than non-graduates, and (3) there is a tendency for prior drug program experience to be related to parole outcome.

Personality, Motivational, and Cognitive Changes in Program Participants. In addition to parole performance, another set of data examined to determine change in program participants was the group of measurement instruments intended to tap those traits and other characteristics which the treatment staff felt the program was directed toward affecting. In order to have such data available for pre-post comparisons, all program participants, within a week of entry into the Wharton Tract program, were administered a test battery consisting of the following instruments:

Self-Evaluation Questionnaire (Cutick 1962; Farnham-Diggory 1964). This psychological variable reflects the extent to which an individual believes that he is, and can be, successful in certain situations. This dimension of personality has been shown to be related to overt behavior in many situations. An example here would be resistance to group pressures to conform (Diggory 1966), an attitude of very great importance in the former addict who is trying to stay off drugs. The importance of the self-evaluation dimension as measured by the Self-Evaluation Questionnaire is that this aspect of personality is seen as being a part of the self-system that regulates the extent to which this system is maintained under conditions of stress. For example, during the processing of new information concerning the self, new evaluations of either a positive or negative nature do not evoke immediate, corresponding action by the individual with high self-esteem. On the other hand, for the individual with low self-esteem, new information (of a threatening nature) concerning the self may evoke immediate escape (e.g., drug use) or other behavior aimed at bolstering faltering self-esteem.

Anomie. This term was first introduced by Emile Durkheim (1951) who used it to refer to the breakdown of norms or standards that guide the aspirations and behavior of individuals. Other writers have defined anomie as having no control over one's life or surroundings, as having feelings of isolation and alienation (Hunter 1964), or as the "breakdown of an individual's sense of attachment to society" (McIver 1950, p. 18).

Locus of Control. This variable is a general expectancy operating across a large variety of situations, and it relates to whether the individual believes that he possesses or lacks the power to affect what happens to him. The role of such expectancies has implications regarding the efforts expended in affecting the events in one's life. Among the behavioral dimensions which are correlates of these generalized expectancies for reinforcement, one is particularly relevant to the present evaluation in that it is concerned with an individual's setting and attaining goals for the future. Seeman (1963) found a significant relationship for a sample of reformatory inmates between locus of control and the recall of facts which might affect "chances" for success after being released.

Sensation Seeking. The Sensation Seeking Scale (Zuckerman et al. 1964) represents, according to its authors, an attempt to quantify the construct of "optimal level of stimulation." This scale represents preferences for extremes of sensation, the new and unfamiliar, irregularity as opposed to regularity and routine, enjoyment of danger and thrills, social stimulation, adventure, and general excitement, all factors which have been described as being characteristic of the drug user. The four subscales and the dimensions they measure are as follows:

1. *Thrill and adventure seeking.* A high score reflects a desire to engage in activities involving elements of speed or danger.
2. *Experience seeking.* This factor can be defined as "experience for its own sake." And it reflects, among other things, wanderlust, exhibitionism, the use of marijuana and hallucinatory drugs, associating with unusual and unconventional persons, and the flouting of authority.
3. *Disinhibition.* This factor reflects a hedonistic outlook in life, including heavy drinking, wild parties, and gambling.
4. *Boredom susceptibility.* This scale contains items reflecting a dislike of routine work; predictable, dull, or boring people; a preference for exciting people; and a restlessness when things are unchanging.

Death Concern. This dimension reflects concern over conscious awareness of one's own mortality (Dickstein and Blatt 1966). It may be important in the personality structure of the addict in that the addict who shows little concern with the risks involved in his drug use will be more likely to fail on parole.

Within several days of the treatment program Ss being administered this battery, an identical battery was administered to the addict control group who were spread throughout the general institutional population.

Identical procedures were followed for retesting of members of both groups. Close scrutiny was kept of release dates for all Ss, and when a Wharton Tract program participant was scheduled for release, he was retested some 2 weeks before this point was reached. At the time of posttesting, Wharton Tract Ss were still engaged in routine program activities. Special problems arose, however, in obtaining posttest data from Ss in the control group. Some control group Ss left Yardville (through transfers to other institutions, early release, etc.) so far in advance of the 8.6 months that the average experimental S stayed in the program that their length of exposure to the institution could not be considered equivalent to those of the Wharton Tract Ss; others were transferred to other units of the reformatory complex or were involved in programs that made access to them difficult; some just presented such scheduling difficulties that it was impossible, with the limited staff available, to test them before they left; and finally, a small number, alert to the fact that they would soon be leaving the institution, refused to participate in the retest or did not validly respond to the test procedure.

In all, complete pre-post test batteries were collected on 48 Wharton Tract program participants and 18 heroin addict controls. The 48 Wharton Tract Ss

on whom test data were available represent the first 50 men completing the program. After this point, other evaluation-related requests, which had been deferred for almost 2 years while the present evaluation was initiated, became pressing, and the testing part of the evaluation had to be terminated due to diversion of workforce.

Results. The results of the pre-post measurement of the three groups tested are presented in Table 6-4. They indicate that program participants, but not controls, changed significantly on three points: (1) the *Diggory self-evaluation* measure, suggesting possession of greater resistance to conformity pressures; (2) *Locus of Control scale*, suggesting an increased belief in personal fate control; and (3) on the Sensation Seeking scale, suggesting a decreased preference for high levels of stimulation and excitement (as reflected by a significant decrease on the General Sensation-Seeking scale), a decreased desire to engage in activities involving speed or danger (Thrill and Adventure-Seeking scale), a decreased desire to seek out experience for its own sake, to experiment with new drugs, and to flout authority (Experience-Seeking scale), and decreased hedonism in one's philosophy of life (Disinhibition scale).

Conclusions

The data presented above *suggest* the existence of a significant relationship between graduation from narcotics treatment programs such as those described above and successful parole performance. The results further suggest that it is not only participation in, but *successful* completion of, the program that is related to success on parole.

It would seem reasonable that such a relationship would exist if the same skills necessary for successfully completing the treatment program were also required for successful parole performance. Prior research (Platt, Scura, and Hannon 1973) has suggested that heroin addicts show deficiencies in the ability to conceptualize means of reaching stated goals in real life problem situations. The training focus in the treatment program emphasized, in part, development of cognitive skills related to successful attainment of personal goals. To the extent that these skills are required in coping with the problems a former inmate faces on parole, successful completion of the treatment program would be expected to be related to parole success.

The data obtained from the pre-post administration of the nine personality scales are consistent with and underline the relative success of a treatment approach such as that utilized here in producing positive change with respect to a number of personality traits. At the completion of the program, participants showed movement in the direction of probable decreased susceptibility to drug use on a number of personality traits.

Table 6–4
Preprogram to Postprogram Personality Changes along Nine Traits of Personality for 48 Wharton Tract Program Participants and 18 Heroin Addict Controls

Variable	Group	Mean Preprogram Scores	Mean Postprogram Scores	t Value	Significance of change in scores
Self-evaluation	Program graduates	75.85	83.98	3.73	$p < 0.001$
	Addict controls	75.08	74.04	-0.15	
Anomie	Program graduates	15.37	14.54	1.30	
	Addict controls	13.54	13.92	-0.30	
Locus of control	Program graduates	10.89	8.44	3.12	$p < 0.001$
	Addict controls	9.62	9.23	0.38	
Sensation seeking Thrill and adventure seeking	Program graduates	10.74	9.68	2.57	$p < 0.01$
	Addict controls	7.69	6.92	0.62	
General sensation seeking	Program graduates	11.12	9.97	2.18	$p < 0.02$
	Addict controls	8.08	7.38	0.58	
Experience seeking	Program graduates	10.64	8.77	3.34	$p < 0.001$
	Addict controls	8.03	8.31	-0.19	
Disinhibition	Program graduates	8.73	7.43	2.88	$p < 0.01$
	Addict controls	6.08	6.38	-0.25	
Boredom susceptibility	Program graduates	7.84	6.97	1.30	
	Addict controls	5.54	6.54	-0.89	
Death concern	Program graduates	20.08	19.82	0.34	
	Addict controls	17.15	17.85	-0.48	

The significance of these positive findings is underscored by the fact that no changes of significance occurred in the control group. Thus, incarceration without treatment of the kind described in this program seems to have had no impact with respect to personality change in this population.

Regretfully, a major problem in the design of the study prevents unequivocal interpretation of the above findings as demonstrating the effectiveness of the treatment programs. The problem centers around the lack of random assignment of Ss to treatment and to control groups. An even clearer statement of the effectiveness of this type of program would have been made if random assignment of Ss to control and treatment conditions had been made. Given the realities of individual client need and institution organizational structure, it was not, however, possible to attain this goal in the present study. Thus, treatment effects resulting from differential motivation for treatment on the part of the volunteers for the programs *may* have been a salient factor in the greater success of the treatment groups. This issue is not addressed in the present evaluation. It would be hoped that further replications of evaluation studies of this form of treatment would be undertaken, with available resources to allow for randomization of assignment to treatment and control groups.

Note

1. The senior editor of this book.

References

Ball, J. C., and Chambers, C. D., eds. *The Epidemiology of Opiate Addiction in the United States.* Springfield, Ill.: Thomas, 1970.

Cutick, R. A. "Self-evaluation of Capacities as a Function of Self-esteem and the Characteristics of a Model." Unpublished doctoral dissertation, University of Pennsylvania, 1962.

Dickstein, L. S., and Blatt, S. J. "Death Concern, Futurity, and Anticipation." *Journal of Consulting Psychology* 30(1966) 11-17.

Diggory, J. C. *Self-evaluation: Concepts and Studies.* New York: Wiley, 1966.

Durkheim, E. *Suicide.* New York: Free Press, 1951.

Elias, A. "Group Treatment Program for Juvenile Delinquents." *Child Welfare* 47(1968): 281-90.

Farnham-Diggory, S. "Self-evaluation and Subjective Life Expectancy among Suicidal and Nonsuicidal Psychotic Males." *Journal of Abnormal and Social Psychology* 69(1964): 628-34.

Hunter, D. A. *The Slums: Challenge and Response*. New York: Free Press, 1964.

Lukoff, I. F. "Social and Ethnic Patterns of Reported Heroin Use and Contiguity with Drug Users." In *Some Aspects of the Epidemiology of Heroin Use in a Ghetto Community: A Preliminary Report*, edited by I. F. Lukoff, D. Quadrone, and A. Sardell. Report to National Institute of Law Enforcement and Criminal Justice, 1972.

McCorkle, L.; Elias, A.; and Bixby, L. *The Highfields Story*. New York: Holt, Rinehart and Winston, 1958.

McIver, R. *The Ramparts We Guard*. New York: Macmillan, 1950.

Pilnick, S., and Associates. *Collegefields: From Delinquency to Freedom*. Newark, N.J.: Newark State College, 1967.

Platt, J. J.; Hoffman, A. R.; and Ebert, R. K. "Recent Trends in the Demography of Heroin Addiction among Youthful Offenders." *International Journal of the Addictions* 11(1976): 221-36.

———, and Labate, C. *Heroin Addiction: Theory, Research, and Treatment*. New York: Wiley-Interscience, 1976.

———; Scura, W. C.; and Hannon, J. R. "Problem-solving Thinking of Youthful Incarcerated Heroin Addicts." *Journal of Community Psychology* 1(1973): 278-81.

———; ———; and Hoffman, A. R. "Heroin Incidence among Youthful Offenders: 1968-1972." *Journal of Community Psychology* 1(1973): 408-11.

———, and Spivack, G. "Studies in Problem-solving Thinking of Psychiatric Patients: (I) Patient-control Differences; (II) Factorial Structure of Problem-solving Thinking." *Proceedings of the 81st Annual Convention of the American Psychological Association*, 8(1973): 463-64.

Platt, J. J., et al. "Adolescent Problem-solving Thinking." *Journal of Consulting and Clinical Psychology* 42(1974): 787-93.

Platt, J. J.; Spivack, G.; and Swift, M. "Interpersonal Problem-solving Group Therapy." *Research and Evaluation Report #31* Hahnemann Medical College and Hospital, 1974.

President's Commission on Law Enforcement and the Administration of Justice. *Task Force Report: Corrections*, Washington: U.S. Government Printing Office, 1967.

Seeman, M. "Alienation and Social Learning in a Reformatory." *American Journal of Sociology*, 69(1963): 270-84.

Spivack, G.; Platt, J. J.; and Shure, M. B. *The Problem-solving Approach to Adjustment*. San Francisco: Jossey-Bass, 1976.

Wicks, R. J. *Correctional Psychology*. San Francisco: Canfield Press, 1974.

Zuckerman, M., et al. "Development of a Sensation-seeking Scale." *Journal of Consulting Psychology* 28(1964): 477-82.

**Evaluation of the Wharton Tract
Narcotic Treatment Program: A
Methodological Analysis**
Jonathan A. Morell

Description of the Study

Prerequisite to a methodological critique of any research study is a clear and precise understanding of the research design. This will be the starting point for the evaluation of the Wharton Tract program. (Figure 7-1 contains a schematic diagram of the research.) In essence, the study had the following defining characteristics:

Treatment

The treatment consisted of a "life skills" training program which was designed to rehabilitate incarcerated heroin abusers. The program is based on the guided group interaction (GGI) method of offender rehabilitation. (See pages 150–152 for details.)

Treatment Group

The group was made up of 163 male offenders who met rigid criteria concerning criminal history, conditions of incarceration, and the like. (See page 150 for details.)

Control Group

The primary control group consisted of 163 male heroin abusing offenders from the same prison. A second control group was made up of men who were dropped from the rehabilitation program for one reason or another, and thus did not complete the treatment.

Subject Selection and Allocation to Conditions

Participants were selected on a space-available basis. If the program was full, no members were recruited. If space was available, members were recruited as they entered the prison. Participation was voluntary. Each time the program

172

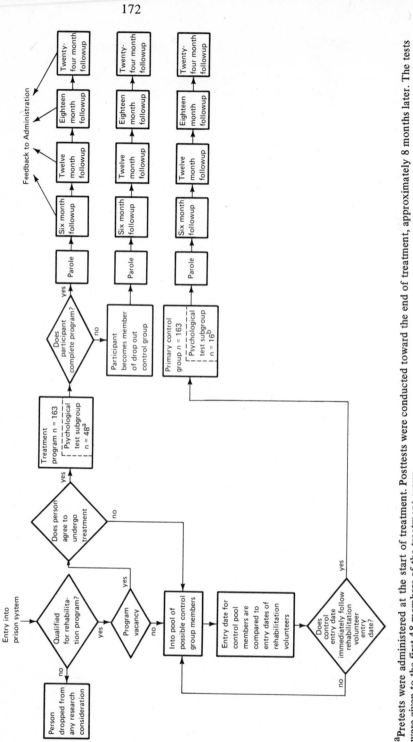

Figure 7-1. Schematic Diagram of Wharton Tract Study.

[a]Pretests were administered at the start of treatment. Posttests were conducted toward the end of treatment, approximately 8 months later. The tests were given to the first 48 members of the treatment group.

[b]Pretests and posttests were administered at approximately 8-month intervals in order to facilitate comparison with the treatment group. Tests were given to the first 18 members of the control group.

was filled, a control group member was recruited from the next group of admissions to the prison who met all program acceptance criteria, but who could not be admitted because the program was full. (In some cases this resulted in some control group members who originally declined membership in the experimental group.)

Dependent Variables

Behavioral measures relating to adjustment to noncriminal life-styles were collected on all study participants after they went on parole and left the program. (See pages 161–163 for details.) In addition, psychological tests were administered to the first 48 recruits into the experimental group and to the first 18 members of the drug-abusing control group.

Data Collection

Psychological tests were administered approximately 8 months apart. The initial administration was at the time when participants first entered the study. Both administrations took place while participants were incarcerated. Postrelease behavioral data were obtained from the twice yearly reports that parole officers prepared for each member of their case load. Parole officers did not know that some of their charges were involved in a research study.

Time Span of Research

The evaluation of the project ran for a 4-year period, with follow-up data being collected for an additional 2 years. Data collection included a 2-year follow-up for each participant.

Framework for Critique

The most basic question that one can ask about any research study is whether the results are internally valid; i.e., can one trust the conclusions that the researcher has drawn concerning the groups that were studied during the course of the research? Cast in another form, this question can be understood in the language of "plausible rival hypotheses" (Campbell 1969). Are there any explanations which compete with those put forward by the researcher to explain the results obtained, and are those explanations as powerful and as likely to be true as those advanced by the researcher? If there is such an explanation, and if there is no test (commonsense or otherwise) by which one of the two explanations can be ruled out, the meaning (and hence the worth) of the research disappears. The search for plausible rival hypotheses must proceed on two fronts. First, one must determine whether there are methodological or analytical errors in the conduct of the study, and whether these errors could have resulted in misleading results. Second, one must determine whether the conclusions which are drawn by the researcher extend beyond the limits that can be supported by the data that have been obtained. If such overextension has taken place, one would probably be able to advance any number of competing explanations.

Still another question that one must ask about a research study is whether the results can be trusted to hold true in contexts other than the immediate boundaries of the research, i.e., the problem of external validity.[1] If this question is answered completely in the negative, a research study becomes useless as a guide to future action or research.

Thus the analysis presented here will address itself to three questions. First, what is the methodological status of the study? Second, do the conclusions of the researcher extend beyond the limits that can be supported by the data?[2] (In essence, are the conclusions which are drawn too grandiose?) Third, does the study have any external validity?

Methodological Status of Study

The most glaring shortcoming in this research is the lack of random assignment of participants to the control and treatment conditions. This is because randomization is the single most powerful tool that can be employed in any outcome evaluation study. Randomization holds this position because of its power to ensure the equality of groups before the application of some treatment. From a strictly logical point of view, randomization is the only way to rule out the possibility that observed posttreatment differences are not merely artifacts of pretreatment differences. There are, however, methods of putting nonrandomized designs to good use (Campbell and Stanley 1963; Speer and Tapp 1976; Weiss 1972). These methods are based on two principles. First, one can set up a situation where it is reasonable and plausible to assume that pretreatment differences do not exist, or at least do not affect the interpretation of research results. Second, one can inspect the data and attempt to determine whether observed pretreatment differences cast doubt on the conclusions that have been drawn.

In the present situation there are reasons to believe that the nonrandom method employed by the researchers did, indeed, produce groups that were equivalent with respect to important behavioral variables. This is because all study participants met the same requirements with respect to age, criminal behavior, sentence, time of processing through the criminal justice system, and the like. The "next consecutive admission" standard was applied for the length of the 4-year study, and it is hard to see how any consistent bias could have resulted from this method. One might postulate biases in this procedure that operate over short periods of time, but it is hard to imagine any factor that would operate consistently over 4 years.

Data analysis does reveal pretreatment differences with respect to the subgroups on which psychological test data were collected. Can one assume that these differences hold true for both groups in their entirety, and if so, what are the implications for the study? These differences indicate that the prognosis for the treatment group was *worse* than the prognosis for the control group. Although we do not know what the situation would have been had data been collected on all participants, it is safe to assume that the pattern would not have reversed itself. In other words, we can proceed on the assumption that the prognosis for the treatment group was either worse than, or equal to, that of the control group. Had the situation been otherwise, we would be hard pressed to attribute positive effects to the treatment program. We would merely attribute any positive findings to the fact that those in treatment started off in a more healthy psychological state than did those in the control group. This is, of course, speculation, and the true state of affairs might be otherwise. It is not, however, likely.

An element of dissatisfaction that remains is the lack of some explanation for the pretreatment differences between the groups on these psychological variables. If such an explanation existed, we could rest content that the entire treatment group was, on the average, less likely to succeed than was the control group. Without such a convincing explanation, a nagging doubt lingers.

In sum, there are several reasons to believe that, despite the lack of random assignment, the results in this study were due to the rehabilitation program and were not artifacts of the method of subject assignment. First, all participants were probably equal on behavioral variables that relate to life-style, criminal behavior, and relationships with the criminal justice system. (Although the authors assure us that this is true, they do not present data to back up their contention. One must admit that such data would greatly increase confidence in the validity of their results.) Second, although the groups were unequal on an array of psychological variables, the direction of difference was such that all tests of treatment effects were conservative.

In addition to the above considerations, there are several other factors that support the validity of the research results. The most notable of these is the convergence between psychological and behavioral change. It is clear from the results reported (Table 6-4) that constructive psychological change did indeed take place as a result of the treatment. The pattern for the control groups is far different and far more stable than that for the treatment group. Further, the changes that took place in the treatment group were both dramatic and constructive. It is also clear that the postparole behavior of the treatment group was far more favorable than postparole behavior of the control group.

If a divergence between psychological and behavioral measures had been found, it would have been extremely difficult to interpret the research results. On the one hand, we might conclude that the psychological-behavior divergence was merely another manifestation of the all too-well-known discrepancy between behavior and internal psychological states (Bem and Allen 1974; Liska 1975; Mischel 1973). On the other hand, we would also have good reason to be suspicious of the research results—suspicious not in the sense that the research was not carried out properly (although this might be true), but suspicious that some factor was operating which the researcher had not dealt with, and which might affect the validity of his conclusions. The point is that, whatever explanation might be correct, a behavioral-psychological inconsistency would have led us into a morass of speculation and would not have strengthened the contention that the Wharton Tract research results were to be trusted. Fortunately such a divergence did not occur. The trust inspired by the convergence between the psychological and behavioral variables is further strengthened by other research, which found that the psychological variables used in the evaluation have been shown (see Chapter 8, study 1) to *predict* success on parole. Thus we can (fairly) safely say that the psychological variables used by the researchers were appropriate, and that the convergence of behavioral and psychological change is more than accidental.

Another factor that speaks for the validity of the conclusions in this research is that they are consistent over the entire 4-year span of the study. If at different times different patterns of results had been found, one would have good reason to believe that the basic system of the research was not to be trusted. This is because the treatment methods remained stable and the characteristics of participants remained stable. Under such conditions it is most reasonable to expect a consistent effect of treatment. This type of consistency is, however, merely a suggestion in support of the validity of the research. It is by no means a guarantee. It may be that fluctuations in the program's effect really did exist and that the research design was in error when it did not detect such changes. Also, if the research results had indicated an oscillating pattern of success, we could not have dismissed the validity of the research out of hand. It is, after all, completely possible that such oscillations were indeed the true state of affairs. The consistency of the research results over a 4-year period is considered to be a positive indication of the worth of the study only because such consistency would be the most expected result if the program were actually successful in helping to rehabilitate its participants.

The final point to consider is what happened to the people who initially entered the program and were then dropped from treatment for one reason or another. (See page 164 for an explanation of the reasons for such dropouts.) Data show that these people did not show any substantive improvement in any of the rehabilitation measures. It is true, of course, that this group is likely to be a highly biased sample. It is also true, however, that they represent a group of people who were qualified for the program, who did not receive the experimental treatment, and who did not improve on the rehabilitation measures that were employed. Had this group shown the same improvement as those who completed the program, the conclusions of the researchers would have been very suspect. The fact that such improvement did not take place is certainly an encouraging sign, although it is not, in and of itself, convincing.

These factors are strong indications that the results obtained by the researchers are not merely accidents of poor research design or a fluke of chance factors. We are justified in believing that the program did indeed induce constructive rehabilitation change in its participants. We cannot be sure of this conclusion, and other research designs have the potential to make us far more confident than we can be with the present study. The present study does, however, lie on the "more valid" end of the continuum, and it is likely that results of the Wharton Tract evaluation can be attributed to the effects of the rehabilitation program rather than to the action of chance events.

We will now turn to a consideration of the second question that must be dealt with in the critique of any research study: Are the conclusions that are drawn by the investigator supported by the data obtained? This is not a matter of the accuracy of the data but of the interpretation that one makes of the significance of that data.

Do the Data Support the Conclusions?

The basic claim made by the authors is that heroin abusers in a correctional setting can be helped by the application of a specific type of rehabilitation training which is based on teaching people various "life function" skills. This claim goes beyond the argument that it was the rehabilitation program per se that caused this change. One could argue that the events that befell the participants in this research were a complex conglomeration of stimuli, not all of which can be considered as integral parts of the rehabilitation program that was being tested. Participants, for example, received special attention and unique living conditions. The purpose of the research and its aims were clear. Various helping professionals undoubtedly interacted with participants in many ways that were not, strictly speaking, part of the rehabilitation program that was being tested. Is it possible that some of these factors were really the causal agents involved? Or more likely, is it possible that some of these factors interacted with the training program in unique ways so that one cannot safely attribute program success to the rehabilitation efforts involved? The best way to answer this question is to replicate the study with a design that specifically addresses itself to these matters. Short of such an effort, one must look for evidence in the existing literature and in the present research that will allow an educated guess on this matter.

It is safe to assume that the special living arrangements and the special care did help to facilitate the constructive change that was noted. The difficulty and impersonality of prison life are well known, and it has been documented that such conditions are almost certainly *not* conducive to constructive rehabilitation change (Wicks 1974). It is also reasonable to assume that the special conditions, in and of themselves, could not have brought about the changes that were observed. The resistance of institutionalized offenders to attempts at rehabilitation is well documented, as is the similar resistance of heroin abusers (Lipton, Martinson, and Wilks 1975; Platt and Labate 1976). A population made up of people who have both of these attributes represents a particularly difficult rehabilitation challenge, and the literature is replete with reports of programs that have failed in such rehabilitation attempts. The success of this program stands in such sharp contrast to other attempts that it would be difficult to ignore the possibility that this program is indeed special. The claims of the researchers are further bolstered by the fact that they can present a cogent theory and relevant supporting research to explain why their program should succeed where others have failed. The present study does not represent an untested or entirely new approach. Rather, it was primarily an implementation of the guided group interaction method of offender rehabilitation used in conjunction with techniques adapted from interpersonal problem-solving therapy (McCorkle, Elias, and Bixby 1958; Platt, Spivack, and Swift 1974; Spivack, Platt, and Shure 1976). These methods do have both a history of success and fairly well-developed supporting theories to explain how they work.

This section started out with the question, Do the data support the conclusions? It should be clear by now that a judgment on this matter rests not only on the research in question but also on contextual background and theoretical information that emanates from outside sources. In the present situation the outside information tells us that the population in question is extremely difficult to treat, that many other attempts were (probably) not successful, and that the present attempt is a member of that class of rehabilitation programs that does have a record of success. It is reasonable, therefore, to assume that the researcher's claims are likely to be correct, i.e., that the change observed in members of the program can be attributed to the specific type of rehabilitation methods that were employed.

So far we have investigated two out of three questions concerning the validity of the present research. First we looked at whether the data can be trusted, i.e., did the numbers obtained result from the rehabilitation treatment or were they manifestations of accidental occurrences? We then considered the problem of whether the data really meant what the researcher interpreted them to mean. Both these questions are concerned with the meaning of the research for the individuals who participated in the study. Neither deals with the problem of whether the results are generalizable to other situations, contexts, and problems. We will now turn to a consideration of these matters.

Generalizability

Can we assume that if this rehabilitation program were carried out a second time, the same results would ensue? In any situation this is an exceedingly difficult question since from a strictly logical point of view one can never generalize beyond the immediate limits of one's research (Popper 1965, chap. 1). Under certain circumstances, though, one might be able to make a relatively safe guess concerning the generalizability of one's findings. As a first step, one would need to know the defining characteristics of one's experimental population. This is a matter of deciding what factors caused the experimental population to interact as it did with the experimental treatment. Age, sex, social class, particular attitudes or experiences, elements of personality, education, membership in the human race, the culture one is socialized into, interaction with the research setting—these are but a sample of the infinite number of possible factors that determine what types of people will be affected by a particular experimental treatment. Some of these factors are very general and are applicable to very large numbers of people. Others are extremely restricted. If one has a sense of what factors were operative, a guess could be made concerning the limits of generalizability. Thus the first step in determining generalizability of research findings is to attempt to develop a sense of those characteristics which determine the type of people that can be expected to react to the experimental treatment in the same way as did the original study participants.

The second step toward generalizability is to conduct the original research in a manner that chooses participants randomly from a well-defined group of people. The advantage of random selection is that the researcher can be sure that, on the average, no factors *other than the ones specifically chosen by the researcher* are impacting on the effect of the treatment being tested. Without random selection from a well-defined population the problem of determining the characteristics of the populations that are susceptible to the experimental treatment becomes an impossibly complex task. It is one thing to randomly sample and to worry only about whether one picked the right population from which to sample. It is quite something else to have no definitive notion of what group of people is really represented by the participants in one's study.

The third element in ensuring generalizability is to employ a research design that can test for the effects of interaction between the participant in a research study and the fact of participation (Campbell and Stanley 1963). Such problems may involve learning due to repeatedly being tested, special treatment one receives, and the like.[3]

In the absence of further research to check on generalizability, one cannot make any definitive statement concerning the external validity of any given research project. One can, however, clearly evaluate a design according to criteria for external validity and leave it to the reader to decide how much "external validity potential" the research actually does have. Such a decision must be made on the basis of how well the research meets the criteria for external validity and on the basis of the reader's knowledge of the behavior of the phenomenon being investigated. The following sections are an attempt to clearly lay out the questions that must be answered by anyone who wishes to estimate the generalizability of the Wharton Tract evaluation.

Defining Characteristics of the Population

The age, criminal history, sentence characteristics, and drug abuse records of all participants were held relatively constant throughout the entire study. All participants came through the criminal justice system in the state of New Jersey. In light of these facts, how reasonable is it that similar people in different criminal justice systems would be different enough from the participants in the present study to react differently to the rehabilitation treatment? Are the size of the sample, the diversity of the sample, and the magnitude of treatment effect large enough to "wash out" any idiosyncratic factors that might limit the generalizability of research findings? Are the defining characteristics of the sample inclusive enough to pick other groups that will benefit from treatment, or did the researchers allow some very important factor to vary widely in their sample?

The guided group interaction technique has proved to be a successful rehabilitation tool with a variety of offender populations (President's Commission on Law Enforcement and Administration of Justice 1967). Thus we know that the Wharton Tract project is not an isolated occurrence. How much weight does this fact have in convincing one that the present study is indeed generalizable?

Random Assignment

Clearly, this study did not employ a method of random allocation of participants to conditions; and we cannot, strictly speaking, claim that the participants in the study were representative of any known population. Without such a claim, of course, it is extremely difficult to make any predictions concerning generalizability. It is also true, however, that the researchers recruited participants on a "next available opening" basis over a period of years. It may be reasonable to assume that this process is sufficiently random to yield a representative sample. There is, after all, no obvious reason to assume that people who happen to be brought into a prison on one day of the week differ in any systematic way from those who are brought in on another day. Further, the "induction day" of program participants was not, on the average, systematically different from that of nonparticipants. On the other hand, there is no guarantee of randomness, and there is good reason to always be suspicious that subtle biases are involved in selection processes that appear to be random. An excellent example of this problem was the 1970 draft lottery, which, despite all attempts and outward appearances, was not truly random (Fienberg 1971). We are left with the question of whether the "next available opening" system resulted in a properly representative sample, and if it did not, whether the bias is serious enough to be of concern.

The final problem in deciding the question of generalizability concerns the matter of whether the fact of conducting research on a particular group of people has for some reason made them so unique that one can say nothing about how others would react to a similar treatment that was not conducted in a research context. As examples, consider the possible sensitizing effects of pretesting, of multiple testing or multiple treatments, and the like. We must attempt to assess how well the present study fares in its built-in checks on these types of problems. It is certainly true that during the course of treatment the 163 people in the treatment group received much more special attention, testing, and the like than did the control group. Further, there was no group that received special attention which was devoid of the meaningful content of the rehabilitation program. It is also true, however, that a check on the reactivity of the psychological tests was carried out. Had there been an effect of testing per se, it would have probably shown up in comparisons between the subsets of the control and experimental groups that received these tests.[4] In fact, no test-retest effect was evident.

Another factor to consider is that over the 2-year follow-up period none of the program participants (experimental or control) were reminded of the project in any way, and the parole officers who collected follow-up data had no idea that any research was in progress. One might argue that if interaction with the "fact of research" is important at all, it would be most likely to show up if people knew that special attention was being paid to them once they were free and on the streets rather than during the time that they were incarcerated.

Are these arguments plausible or convincing? Is it likely that the procedures involved in this research and the population on whom it was performed interacted in some such unique way? Is it reasonable to assume that if this treatment were repeated without the accoutrements of a research design, the effect would be the same? Do the facts presented above concerning control groups and follow-up shed any light on these matters? These are the questions that must be answered if an intelligent judgment is to be made concerning the generalizability of the results of the Wharton Tract evaluation.

Summary

This chapter set out to evaluate the validity of the evaluation of the Wharton Tract program. The critique centered on three elements: the methodological adequacy of the design as it relates to internal validity; the extent to which the conclusions of the researchers are supported by the data obtained; and the matter of external validity, or generalizability of the findings. The "tools" used to carry out the analysis were: first, a knowledge of research design; second, a knowledge of research, theory, and the situational variables which relate to offender rehabilitation; third, a sense of the plausibility and the reasonability of various arguments concerning threats to validity. The general conclusion was that the present study probably does have a good deal of internal validity. It should be added that there are formidable problems in conducting rigorous research in correctional settings, and that the researcher did extremely well considering the problems inherent in the situation. Although no judgment was made concerning external validity, this report did attempt to set up a framework with which such a judgment could be made.

It is clear from the critique that was presented that the concepts of "plausibility" and "reasonability" were essential in determining the validity of the study. This is true for two reasons. First, science cannot prove anything; it can only offer hints as to the state of nature. It is up to the researcher to judge the quality of those hints. This is demonstrated by the concept of "plausible rival hypotheses," and by other writings in the philosophy of science concerning these matters (Harre 1970; Kaplan 1964; Popper 1965).

The second reason for the importance of "plausibility" and "reasonability" is that the research design was quasi-experimental rather than a true experiment. As a result, it is possible to raise a very large number of objections to the validity of the study, all of which are more or less reasonable. In that sense the Wharton Tract study is an excellent example of the problems inherent in conducting non-experimental research. The researcher certainly did a diligent job of carrying out the best possible design in a difficult field situation. Even with such efforts, however, there remain a large number of threats to validity which must be inspected, and for every one of them we have only our sense of the plausible and the reasonable as a guide to their cogency. Each time such a decision is made, the probabuity of error increases. On the other hand, one cannot allow such problems to stop the investigation of important and interesting social problems. No study can be *proved* valid, and all research exists somewhere on an ill-defined "validity continuum." Further, there is no way to know exactly where any study lies precisely on this continuum. One can only use one's best judgment to make an approximate guess. This chapter was an attempt to demonstrate how such a guess might be made.

Notes

1. The critique put forward here greatly simplifies the notion of "validity" by breaking it into only two categories (internal and external). Although finer distinctions between types of validity do exist, the typology used here does serve as a useful framework to discuss the worth of the present study. For those who are interested in an overview of the types of validity, see Chapter 2. For a detailed account of types of validity, the following works are recommended: Campbell and Stanley (1963), Cook and Campbell (1976).

2. From a strictly logical point of view, one must admit the existence of the opposite possibility: Has the researcher drawn conclusions and implications which are too modest, given the results of the research? In practice, however, this is almost never a problem.

3. This is not the place to go into details of what such designs might look like. Excellent information can be found on this topic in the Campbell and Stanley volume.

4. Strictly speaking, this may not be the case. As the reader will remember, the control and experimental groups did show initial differences on these tests. One might argue that different types of reactions to the second testing resulted from the differences in the initial state. In other words, those factors which cause retest sensitivity might act differently depending on the original psychological states of the people who are being tested. If this should be the case, one could *not* use the control-experimental comparison as a check on the test sensitivity problem. It might be hard to make a strong case for the plausibility of this argument, but it is a possibility that cannot be ruled out.

References

Bem, D. J., and Allen, A. "On Predicting Some of the People Some of the Time: The Search for Cross-Situational Consistencies in Behavior." *Psychological Review* 81(6): 506–20, 1974.

Campbell, D. T. "Reforms as Experiments." *American Psychologist* 24(4), 409–29, 1969.

――――, and Stanley, J. C. *Experimental and Quasi-experimental Designs.* Chicago: Rand McNally, 1963.

Cook, T., and Campbell, D. T. "Design and Conduct of Quasi-experiments and True Experiments in Field Settings." In *Handbook of Industrial and Organizational Psychology*, edited by M. B. Dunnette. Chicago: Rand McNally, 1976, chap. 7.

Fienberg, S. E. "Randomization and Social Affairs, the 1970 Draft Lottery." *Science* 171(1971): 255–61.

Harre, R. *The Principles of Scientific Thinking*. Chicago: University of Chicago Press, 1970.

Kaplan, A. *The Conduct of Inquiry: Methodology for Behavioral Science*. Scranton, Pa.: Chandler, 1964.

Lipton, D.; Martinson, R.; and Wilks, J. *The Effectiveness of Correctional Treatment*. New York: Praeger, 1975.

Liska, A. E. *The Consistency Controversy*. Cambridge, Mass.: Schenkman, 1975.

McCorkle, L.; Elias, A.; and Bixby, L. *The Highfield Story*. New York: Holt, Rinehart and Winston, 1958.

Mischel, W. "Toward a Cognitive Social Learning Reconceptualization of Personality." *Psychological Review* 80(1973): 252–83.

Platt, J. J., and Labate, C. *Heroin Addiction: Theory, Research and Treatment*. New York: Wiley-Interscience, 1976.

——— ; Spivack, G.; and Swift, M. S. "Interpersonal Problem-solving Group Therapy. Research and Evaluation Report #31." Philadelphia: Hahnemann Medical College and Hospital, 1974.

Popper, K. R. *Conjectures and Refutations*. New York: Harper & Row, 1965.

President's Commission on Law Enforcement and Administration of Justice. *Task Force Report: Corrections*. Washington: U.S. Government Printing Office, 1967.

Speer, D. C., and Tapp, J. C. "Evaluation of Mental Health Service Effectiveness: A "Start up" Model for Establishing Programs." *American Journal of Orthopsychiatry* 46(2): 217–28, April 1976.

Spivack, G.; Platt, J. J.; and Shure, M. *The Problem-solving Approach to Adjustment: A Guide to Research and Intervention*. San Francisco: Jossey-Bass, 1976.

Weiss, C. *Evaluative Research*. Englewood Cliffs, N.J.: Prentice-Hall, 1972.

Wicks, R. J. *Correctional Psychology*. San Francisco: Canfield Press, 1974.

8

Wharton Tract Narcotics Treatment
Program: Parole Outcome and
Related Studies
Jerome J. Platt and
Christina Labate

Introduction

The preceding two chapters have been concerned primarily with those aspects of the Wharton Tract research component which focused on (1) the assessment of the Youth Reception and Corrections Center's need for narcotics programming, and (2) the evaluation of the Wharton Tract Narcotics Treatment Program. This chapter focuses on evaluation-related research which, while part of the original plan for a research and evaluation procedure, was not concerned with assessing a need or with measuring program effectiveness per se.

The third objective of the original plan was concerned with two issues: (1) the determination of those factors related to parole success of heroin-addicted offenders, and (2) the development of a systematic, statistically based method for predicting outcome both in the program and upon release from the institution.

To meet this objective, four studies concerning the relation of different variables to parole outcome were undertaken. The first reported here concerns an attempt to relate a number of personality variables to parole outcome. The second is a line of research examining the relationship between demographic background characteristics of inmates and parole performance. The third study relates parole success or failure to characteristics of parole behavior and parole environment. The fourth study examines the validity of peer nominations in predicting parole success.

Study 1: Personality Factors Underlying Treatment Program and Parole Success in Youthful Heroin Offenders

The purpose of this study was to examine the relationship between personality factors and program success and parole recidivism in youthful heroin offenders in treatment. Numerous attempts have been made to delineate effective predictors of parole success, as reviewed in Chapter 5.

While the preponderence of research data appears to favor the use of life history information over that from personality instruments, the attempts to delineate underlying personality dimensions associated with parole success should not be abandoned because of the great potential advantage in being able to predict from personality inventories which reflect *current* status as well as in providing a focus for rehabilitation efforts.

Variables related to intellectual and cognitive functioning would appear to offer the most promise. A study by Platt, Scura, and Hannon (1973) has shown youthful offenders to be deficient in the ability to plan logically consecutive means to reach a stated goal. However, few attempts seem to have been made to relate intellectual dimensions to parole outcome or to predict parole success from such variables. One such attempt was made by Englehardt (1970) in an investigation into the feasibility of predicting rehabilitation of socially maladjusted boys in a special education program on the basis of ten variables related to intellectual functioning. A discriminant function analysis revealed that intellectual dimensions effectively discriminated between rehabilitated and non-rehabilitated boys. This study was considerably strengthened by a crossvalidation in which a 75 percent accuracy rate of dichotomous rehabilitation-non-rehabilitation classification was obtained. Such initially encouraging results suggest that further research in this area could yield valuable information.

One important issue which might significantly affect the power of predictive variables has received somewhat less attention—specifically, the relationship between participation in a "treatment" program and parole outcome. This relationship was only peripherally treated in a study by Levi and Tracy (1971) which attempted to enhance the predictive power of a case history-derived base expectancy table by the incorporation of data from the Johnson Temperament Analysis (JTA) test. Success in out-patient release status of drug addicts (tested at 3-year follow-up) was to be predicted on a group of volunteers in a personality improvement course. On the basis of correlation coefficients the authors concluded that the JTA could be used to predict long-term rather than immediate success as an out-patient. The high correlation of three subscales—anxiety, depression, and activity—suggested a personality pattern exhibiting these as characteristic of the drug addict who was successful in the community. However, the effect of participating in the improvement course was not explored beyond noting the existence of a selection factor resulting in Ss who were motivated to change and who possessed the above three characteristics to a greater degree than the general institutional addict population. It would seem that the investigation of a possible interaction between participation in a treatment program and parole success might constitute an extremely worthwhile extension of predictive power. Such an investigation would clearly have implications for design and focus of rehabilitation programs if a relationship to parole success were found to exist. Thus, one object of the present study was to explore the possibility and the nature of such interaction. Carrying out such an investigation in a population of heroin offenders would seem to be valuable for at least two reasons. First, the incidence of heroin addiction among youthful offenders is unexpectedly high and accounts for a significant proportion of the population studied. In addition, the paucity of studies specifically related to a population of heroin offenders suggests this to be a largely unexamined subgroup of recidivists. Furthermore, previous research (Platt and Scura 1974) has shown the validity of one measure—peer judgments of parole success—in predicting parole behavior in this population. Delineation of the personality correlates of these peer judgments in the study by Platt and Scura (1974) suggests that the attempt to define underlying personality factors associated with parole outcome might be undertaken with some hope of success. A first step undertaken in an attempt to predict treatment program and parole outcome would be to identify factors underlying personality characteristics of heroin addict offenders, and then to relate these factors to actual treatment and parole outcome. With the identification of these factors, it may then be possible to attempt development of predictive equations for these outcomes.

In Chapter 6 the observation of a significant relationship between program completion and parole success raises the issue of possible underlying personality correlates of program and parole success or failure. While previous research has suggested that possession of certain personality traits might affect postrelease adjustment (cf. Cowden and Pacht 1967; Levi and Tracy 1971), the delineation of these dimensions in a heroin offender population could result in the expectation of success in developing a predictive equation for parole success.

Subjects consisted of 91 Wharton Tract Narcotics Treatment Program participants. Scores on 33 personality variables were factor-analyzed using a principle components factor analysis after individual scores had been normalized.

These scales were the following on which data had been collected for use in the evaluation: (1) *Self-Evaluation Questionnaire*, a modification of the Cutick (1962) instrument by Farnham-Diggory (1964); (2) the *anomie test*, a modification by Spivack and Levine (1963) of the Srole (1956) scale; (3) the *Locus of Control Scale* (Rotter 1966); (4) the *Sensation Seeking scale* (Zuckerman et al. 1964) (scores were obtained on the Thrill and Adventure Seeking, Experience-Seeking, Disinhibition, and Boredom Susceptibility subscales); and (5) *Death Concern scale* (Dickstein and Blatt 1966).

In addition, the Adjective Check List (ACL) (Gough and Heilbrun 1965) was used. This instrument yields scores on the following scales:

1. *Defensiveness*. A high score here reflects a tendency to try to obtain a more favorable self-description.
2. *Positive Self-concept*. The high scoring individual here appears to be motivated by a strong desire to do well and to impress others, but always by virtue of hard work and conventional endeavor.
3. *Negative Self-concept*. A high score here tends to reflect impulsiveness and a lack of control over the hostile and more unattractive aspects of personality.
4. *Self-confidence*. This scale reflects traits such as poise, self-confidence, and self-assurance. In general, the higher scorer is a more "effective" person in dealing with the world.
5. *Self-control*. High scorers here tend to be serious, sober individuals, interested in and responsive to their obligations.

6. *Lability*. The high scorer here can be seen as possessing an inner restlessness and an inability to tolerate consistency and routine.

7. *Personal Adjustment*. A high score here is associated with a postive attitude toward life, as opposed to being at odds with others, moody, and dissatisfied.

8. *Achievement*. A high scorer can be seen as one who is striving to be outstanding in pursuits of socially recognized significance.

9. *Dominance*. An individual scoring high here is seeking to sustain leadership roles in groups or to be influential and controlling in individual relationships.

10. *Endurance*. A tendency to persist in any task undertaken is associated with a high score here.

11. *Order*. A high score reflects the need to place special emphasis on neatness, organization, and planning in one's activities.

12. *Intraception*. A high score reflects a need to engage in attempts to understand one's own behavior or the behavior of others.

13. *Nurturance*. A higher score has a need to engage in behaviors which extend material or emotional benefits to others.

14. *Affiliation*. A higher score here needs to seek and sustain numerous personal friendships.

15. *Heterosexuality*. A higher score seeks the company of and derives emotional satisfaction from interactions with opposite-sexed peers.

16. *Exhibition*. A high scorer here needs to behave in such a way as to elicit the immediate attention of others.

17. *Autonomy*. A high scorer here acts independently of others or of social values and expectations.

18. *Aggression*. A high scorer here has need to engage in behaviors which attack or hurt others.

19. *Change*. A higher score here is defined as a need to seek novelty of experience and to avoid routine.

20. *Succorance*. A higher score here is defined as a need to solicit sympathy, affection, or emotional support from others.

21. *Abasement*. A higher score here reflects a need to express feelings of inferiority through self-criticism, guilt, or social importance.

22. *Deference*. A higher score here is defined as a need to seek and sustain subordinate roles in relationships with others.

23. *Counseling Readiness*. This dimension is based on items selected on the basis of their endorsement by persons showing a positive response to counseling. Generally, the high scorer here is worried about himself, and not certain of his status.

The factor analysis resulted in a four-factor orthogonal solution representing all 33 variables. (Factors were derived on the basis of the Eigenvalues exceeding

1.0.) The cumulative proportion of the total variance accounted for by the four factors was 68.37 percent.

Factor 1, accounting for 24.49 percent of the variance, was related to both program graduation and parole success. This factor consisted of positive loadings on the following variables: deference (0.78), nurturance (0.88), favorable (0.88), personal adjustment (0.77), endurance (0.56), and self-control (0.75). Negative loadings on the autonomy (-0.87) and the aggression (-0.77) subscales of the ACL also contributed to factor 1.

Factor 2, accounting for 17.38 percent of the variance, was related to neither program graduation or parole success. This factor consisted primarily of loadings on the Sensation-Seeking scale: experience seeking (0.83), disinhibition (0.85), thrill and adventure seeking (0.81) and sensation seeking (0.78), with a positive loading on the death concern measure (0.87) and a negative loading on self-control (-0.37).

Factor 3, accounting for 19.62 percent of the variance, was related to program graduation. The variables loading most strongly on this factor were dominance (0.91), deference (-0.39), counseling readiness (-0.78), favorable (0.49), self-confidence (0.81), abasement (-0.81), and order (0.58).

Factor 4, accounting for 6.97 percent of the variance, was related to parole success and consisted of positive loadings on the deference (0.20), endurance (0.21), self-control (0.23) variables and of negative loadings on the favorable (-0.21), affiliation (-0.52), lability (-0.67), aggression (-0.35), nurturance (-0.20), and heterosexuality (-0.52) variables.

Interpretation of the pattern of loadings on the above factors suggests the existence of coherent groupings of personality traits associated with program and/or parole success. Individuals successful both in the program and on parole seem to be highly conforming, conventional, and passive—often assuming subordinate roles in individual relationships. Those persons scoring high on factor 3, which is related only to program success, seem to be much more forceful, dynamic, self-confident, and independent individuals. Finally, those characteristics related to success on parole but not in the program seem to be the ability to conform in a socially acceptable manner, to adapt nonaggressively, to not seek out others or stimulation. In general, this is a person who appears to be maintaining a low profile in his daily life.

The above findings suggest that successful performance in the program or on parole seems to require very different sets of behaviors. Success in the program appears to reflect those qualities which therapeutic intervention ideally seeks to produce while success on the street is more related to reality for the ex-institutional addict offender. Essentially, being forceful and dynamic has much less payoff for this individual who is under greater scrutiny by law enforcement authorities than does maintaining a low profile. Interestingly, the person who is likely to be successful in both the program *and* on the street seems to be able to conform to a wider variety of environmental demands particularly in light of the apparently contradictory sets of traits underlying success in the treatment program *or* success on parole.

The second part of this study involved an attempt to develop regression equations which could be used to predict parole status in the sample described in the first part. In the case of 89 of the participants, factor scores (on those factors shown in the first part of this study to be related to either program or parole success or to both) were used to derive the regression equations. In the original sample, 73 percent of actual parole successes were correctly predicted from the regression equations. Also, 65 actual parole failures were correctly predicted, revealing an overall rate of 68.5 percent accuracy of prediction. Cross validation in a second sample of Wharton Tract graduates indicated that 70 percent of actual parole successes and 75 percent of parole failures were correctly predicted. This cross validation had an N of only 18, however, so these latter figures must be viewed with caution.

What is the significance of these findings in the context of previous research on the prediction of parole success? First, an attempt was made to determine whether there were underlying personality factors associated with the obtained relationship between program and parole success or failure, and then to delineate these factors. The results indicate that perhaps there are distinct personality patterns, as identified by the factors, associated with program and/or parole success.

Second, previous research has indicated that the use of personality variables in the prediction of recidivism does not approach the level of accuracy obtained from predictions on the basis of life history variables. Perhaps this lack of success has been due, in part, to the use of a narrow selection of personality instruments in a somewhat "arbitrary" fashion for the following reasons: (1) they are routinely administered to inmate populations and are thus currently available, or (2) they are efficiently administered and scored, or (3) they have proved clinically useful in a wide variety of situations (e.g., MMPI, CPI).

Study 2: Relationship of Selected Demographic Variables to Parole Success[1]

To determine the relationship between background factors and parole success, 19 background variables were examined in an initial sample of 48 Wharton Tract program graduates at a point in time 6 months following entrance onto parole (Platt and Labate, 1976a). This sample of 48 included 34 parole successes and 14 parole failures. The variables examined included: (1) *identity*: age, race, religion, marital status; (2) *employment history*: number of months of work experience; (3) *military experience*; (4) *criminal history*: number of New Jersey incarcerations, number of out-of-state incarcerations, age at first arrest, number of arrests, commitment status; and (5) *psychological and medical status:* physical condition, psychological condition, IQ. Only the following variables differentiated the two groups: *age*—parole successes were significantly older (average age = 23.1 versus 21.2); *number of prior arrests*—parole successes had significantly fewer prior arrests than parole failures (6.0 versus 9.2); *race*—there were fewer parole failures in the white (versus the black) group; *religion*—there were fewer Catholics and Protestants proportionally in the parole failure groups than in the parole success groups, but equal proportions of those groups reported as Jewish or "other religion."

The above findings suggested little relationship in this sample between background variables and parole success or failure. Before interpreting these findings, it was decided to undertake a replication of this study in another sample. The major reason for doing so was that the results were inconsistent with the original expectation of a relationship existing between demography and parole success. The population used for this replication was the pool of graduates of another narcotics treatment program at the Youth Correction Center. This population consisted of 88 parole successes and 87 parole failures. The findings in this sample indicated that, using the same variables, only a relatively small number related to parole status.

What are the implications of these findings? As interpreted by Platt and Labate (1976a), they suggest first of all that, in general, the preinstitutionalization background of a man successfully completing the narcotics treatment program at the Youth Correction Center has little relationship to the likelihood of parole success or failure. This is a finding which is inconsistent with those of other studies reviewed by the authors (cf. Platt and Labate 1976a). These findings may also reflect (1) some uniqueness of the present samples, although this seems to be unlikely due to both the selection procedure employed as well as the similar absence of such relationships in both samples, or (2) differences between addict and nonaddict inmates.

Study 3: Recidivism in Youthful Heroin Offenders and Characteristics of Parole Behavior and Environment

In order to investigate the relationship between parole outcome and the characteristics of the environment to which the parolee returns, Platt and Labate (1976b) followed 79 consecutive Wharton Tract program "graduates" until they either failed on parole or were discharged. Using the same methods reported in Chapter 6, data were collected from parole reports on five variables:

1. Return to preincarceration residential locale.
2. Level of crime in residential locale as determined from the New Jersey Uniform Crime Reports.

3. Employment status: steadily employed, intermittently employed, or unemployed.
4. Living situation: parental, marital, or other (alone, with same-sex peers) residence.
5. Drug use on parole.

The findings indicated that both employment status and drug use on parole were significantly related to parole success. While only 4.8 percent of those steadily employed failed on parole, some 75 percent either who had fluctuating employment or who were unemployed were parole failures ($p < 0.001$). Not surprisingly, drug use on parole and parole success or failure were related in that 51.9 percent of those using drugs failed on parole, while only 4.2 percent of parolees who did not use drugs failed ($p < 0.001$). When employment and drug use were examined, drug use, while only present in 29.4 percent of steadily employed parolees, was present in 60.7 percent of those cases where the man was unable to maintain steady employment. No relationship was found to exist between returning to the original geographic locale, returning to an area of high, moderate, or low crime rate, or returning to live with parents, spouse, friends, versus living alone, and parole success.

In interpreting these findings, Platt and Labate (1976b) note that the available data do not answer the question of causality among these variables. For instance, whether drug use or obtaining steady employment is the antecedent variable is not clear, nor is the influence of a third variable—the effects of

. . . frustration in meeting many of the interpersonal and job-related demands of a conventional nondrug using environment (p. 616).

Study 4: Peer Judgments of Parole Success in Institutionalized Heroin Addicts

This study (Platt and Scura, 1974) was undertaken to examine the validity of peer judgments as predictors of parole success in heroin addicts. Since peer judgments have been shown to be valid predictors of behavior in other instances, this seemed to be a reasonable undertaking. [A review of research on peer judgments is presented in Platt and Scura (1974).]

The study examined two questions. One was concerned with determining the validity of peer judgments in the prediction of parole success among youthful incarcerated heroin addicts. The other dealt with determining the personality characteristics associated with being selected as a parole success or failure by one's peers. It was predicted that peer judgments of parole success would be related to actual parole behavior. The expectations were that subjects receiving high and low numbers of peer nominations of parole success would differ significantly along 33 personality dimensions, with subjects nominated as successes having scores in the healthier direction on each of the dimensions.

The sample consisted of 89 men participating in narcotics treatment programs separate from the Wharton Tract. At the time of the peer nomination procedure, all subjects had been in the program at least 4 weeks. Mean length of heroin use for this sample was 3.9 years $(SD = 2.31)$, with a range of 1 to 12 years. Using lists of men housed in units comprising 18 to 24 men each, subjects were asked to provide, anonymously, the names of the four men whom they felt were most likely to make it on the street after parole. On a second list, the subject was asked to check the names of the four men who were, in his opinion, least likely to make it. "Making it on the street" was further defined as staying off drugs and avoiding contact with the law due to illegal activity of any kind including the use of drugs.

Mean composite peer nomination scores were developed for all subjects in both the parole success and failure groups, and these were compared. In order to determine those personality characteristics associated with being judged likely to succeed or fail, two extreme groups were developed with composite peer nomination scores one standard deviation below or above the mean, and then they were compared on the personality variables.

Prediction of Parole Performance: Six-Month Follow-up

At the end of the 6-month parole follow-up period, 53 subjects were parole successes and 36 were failures. The mean nomination scores for the two groups were significantly different at the .01 level. Thus, a significant relationship existed between the judgments of the men by their peers while in the program and actual parole performance.

The data were examined further by dividing the total group of subjects in half at the median on the basis of their composite peer nomination scores. The parole performance of each of the two groups thus formed was then examined. In the high-rated group were 33 parole successes and 15 parole failures, representing an accuracy rate of 68.8 percent $(p < 0.007)$. The low group had 20 successes and 21 failures, representing an accuracy rate of 48.8 percent. Thus, these ratings clearly discriminated among subjects at the upper end of the continuum of scores but failed to discriminate among subjects at the lower end.

Fifteen-Month Follow-up

Parole performance was again examined after 15 months following release from the institution. Parole status data at this time were available for 39 of the 48 subjects in the high rating group and 27 of the 41 subjects in the low rating

rating group. Of the 39 high rating group subjects, 24, or 61.5 percent, were still doing well, a similar finding to the 68.8 percent of this group doing well 6 months following parole, when normal parole attrition over time is taken into consideration ($p < 0.10$). Of the 27 subjects in the low rating group, however, only one had *not* been rearrested. Thus, in the peer-rated failure group, there was a 96.2 percent accuracy rate ($p < 0.001$).

Personality Correlates of Peer Nominations

The second part of the study focused on personality characteristics associated with receiving extreme numbers of peer nominations. Confirmation of directional hypotheses occurred in 17 of 33 comparisons, resulting in a picture of the subject most frequently nominated as a "success" as having the following characteristics: (1) a greater belief in his own likelihood of success in many situations ($p < 0.05$); (2) less anomie ($p < 0.01$); (3) an internal locus of control ($p < 0.025$); (4) a greater concern with giving a favorable self-description ($p < 0.005$); (5) the desire to do well and impress others ($p < 0.025$); (6) the possession of traits such as poise, self-confidence, and self-assurance ($p < 0.025$); (7) an interest in and responsiveness to one's interpersonal obligations ($p < 0.005$); (8) a positive attitude toward life ($p < 0.05$); (9) a higher need for achievement ($p < 0.01$); (10) likely to sustain interpersonal leadership; (11) likely to persist in completing tasks ($p < 0.01$); (12) seeing oneself as having needs for organization and planning ($p < 0.01$); (13) extending material or emotional benefits to others ($p < 0.025$); and (14) seeking and sustaining personal relationships ($p < 0.01$).

In contrast, subjects judged as "failures" by their peers had (1) greater anomie ($p < 0.01$), (2) an external locus of control ($p < 0.025$), (3) tended to be impulsive individuals who exhibit a lack of control over the more unattractive aspects of their personalities ($p < 0.025$), (4) tried to solicit sympathy or emotional support from others ($p < 0.005$), and (5) expressed feelings of inferiority ($p < 0.005$).

The authors concluded that this study indicated the following. First, peer nominations of parole success were significantly related to actual future parole performance in a sample of institutionalized youthful heroin addicts. Second, groups of subjects nominated as potential successes or failures by their peers were also clearly differentiated on the basis of a number of personality measures. These findings were interpreted as supporting those of other studies suggesting the validity of peer judgments as predictors of actual behavior. In this case the behavior being predicted—that of return to drug use on the street after release—was a complex behavior separated by space and time from the situation in which the nominating procedure was conducted.

Discussing the value of these findings, the authors suggest that the client can:

contribute to future planning for his peers and that such planning might be most profitably undertaken cooperatively. For instance, the peer group could aid in identifying specific areas in which problems relating to postrelease success might arise for an individual. Specific planning to deal with such problems might then be initiated (Platt and Scura 1974, p. 514).

Conclusions

Taken together, the results of these studies indicate that there exist a number of variables, personal and behavioral, which are associated with program and parole success among incarcerated youthful offenders in the population studied. Different clusters of personality characteristics can be related to likelihood of succeeding within a drug program, as opposed to subsequent success or failure on parole; and a person possessing both sets of characteristics, or capable of exhibiting both at appropriate times, is most likely to succeed throughout. It also seems reasonable to conclude that personality factors related to parole success are clearly identifiable by peers. In the area of behavioral variables, whether the parolee is employed and whether he is using drugs are factors significantly related to parole success.

Various other variables, however, such as where the subject is from and where he returns upon parole, do not have a significant bearing on the parolee's chances for success. These findings are highly useful in that they provide specific leads to anyone planning a rehabilitation program as to which areas to focus on in supporting the parolee.

Note

1. This study, as well as subsequent studies in this chapter are available in the literature, and thus, will be presented briefly with the emphasis placed on reporting of findings.

References

Cowden, J. E., and Pacht, A. R. "Predicting Institutional and Post-release Adjustment of Delinquent Boys." *Journal of Consulting Psychology* 31(1967): 377-81.

Cuttick, R. A. "Self-evaluation of Capacities as a Function of Self-esteem and the Characteristics of a Model." Unpublished doctoral dissertation, University of Pennsylvania, 1962.

Dickstein, L. S., and Blatt, S. J. "Death Concern, Futurity, and Anticipation." *Journal of Consulting Psychology* 30(1966): 11-17.

Englehardt, G. M. "Predicting Rehabilitation of Socially Maladjusted Boys." *Journal of Counseling Psychology* 17(1970): 546-49.

Farnham-Diggory, S. "Self-evaluation and Subjected Life Expectancy among Suicidal and Non-suicidal Psychotic Males." *Journal of Abnormal and Social Psychology* 69(1964): 628-34.

Gough, H. G., and Heilbrun, A. B. *The Adjective Check List Manual*. Palo Alto, Calif.: Consulting Psychologists Press, 1965.

Levi, M., and Tracy, F. "Prediction of Success of Drug Addicts in Outpatient Release Status Based upon a Personality Inventory." *International Journal of the Addictions* 6(1971): 533-41.

Platt, J. J.; Hoffman, A. R.; and Ebert, R. K. "Recent Trends in the Demography of Heroin Addiction among Youthful Offenders." *International Journal of the Addictions* 11(1976):221-236.

――――, and Labate, C. "Recidivism in Youthful Heroin Offenders and Pre-incarceration Demographic Characteristics." Unpublished manuscript, 1976a.

――――, and ――――. "Recidivism in Youthful Heroin Offenders and Characteristics of Parole Behavior and Environment." *International Journal of the Addictions* 11(1976b):651-657.

――――, and Scura, W. C. "Peer Judgments of Parole Success in Institutionalized Heroin Addicts: Personality Correlates and Validity." *Journal of Counseling Psychology* 21(1974): 511-15.

――――; Scura, W. C.; and Hannon, J. "Problem-solving Thinking of Youthful Incarcerated Heroin Addicts." *Journal of Community Psychology* 1(1973): 278-81.

Rotter, J. B. "Generalized Expectancies for Internal *vs.* External Control of Reinforcement." *Psychological Monographs* 80(1966), 1-28.

Spivack, G., and Levine, M. "Self-regulation in Acting out and Normal Adolescents." (Research grant M-4531 Report) Washington: National Institute of Mental Health, 1963.

Srole, L. "Social Integration and Certain Corollaries: An Exploratory Study." *American Sociological Review* 21(1956): 709-16.

Zuckerman, M., et al. "Development of a Sensation-seeking Scale." *Journal of Consulting Psychology* 28(1964): 477-82.

Author Index

Subject Index

About the Contributors

Eugenie Flaherty received the Ph.D. in psychology from the New School of Social Research in 1973. She has since been engaged in research and evaluation involving service delivery programs. Dr. Flaherty has helped develop management information systems, including a multistate information system for drug-abuse treatment programs. She assisted in the direction of a pilot test of the multistate system, including supervision of field training and an evaluation of utility of the information system.

Jerome M. Siegel is a senior research evaluator at the Hahnemann Community Mental Health/Mental Retardation Center in Philadelphia. He has worked in the areas of human service program evaluation, and mental health records systems. He was trained as a clinical psychologist, and received the Ph.D. from the University of Waterloo (Canada) in 1971.

Jonathan A. Morell's chief interests are in the methodology of evaluation and in the relationship between evaluation research and the conduct of social service. He has served as Chief of Evaluation for the National Training Center on Drug Abuse Region 5, and as a research associate at the Drug Addiction Research Unit of the Department of Psychiatry at the University of Chicago. He is currently Assistant Professor at the Hahnemann Medical College and Hospital.

About the Editors

Jerome J. Platt is professor of mental health sciences, and associate director of research and evaluation at Hahnemann Medical College and Hospital, Philadelphia. In addition to having served as a consultant to a number of education, business, and governmental organizations, Dr. Platt is program evaluation and research consultant to the New Jersey Youth Reception and Correction Center and also serves in an advisory capacity to the Special Offender Treatment Project, New Jersey Division of Narcotics and Drug Abuse Control. He has published extensively in the areas of psychology and drug abuse. Among his most recent books are two on drug abuse: *Heroin Addiction: Theory, Research, and Treatment*, and *Drug Abuse: A Criminal Justice Primer*.

Christina Labate is at the University of Chicago and has coauthored *Heroin Addiction: Theory, Research, and Treatment* with Dr. Platt. She is currently doing research in predicting parole behavior of violent offenders.

Robert J. Wicks is clinical senior instructor, College of Allied Health Professions, Hahnemann Medical College. He has directed mental health treatment programs in the United States and in the Far East. Professor Wicks has published ten books and numerous papers in psychology and criminal justice. In addition, Professor Wicks has served as a consultant and lecturer for federal, state and municipal criminal justice agencies in New York, North Carolina, and overseas.